The Ultimate Collection of

Classic
Quilt Blocks™

Edited by Jeanne Stauffer & Sandra L. Hatch

HOUSE of
WHITE
BIRCHES

PUBLISHERS
SINCE 1947

The Ultimate Collection of Classic Quilt Blocks

Editors: Jeanne Stauffer, Sandra L. Hatch
Associate Editor: Dianne Schmidt
Design Associate: Vicki Blizzard
Copy Editors: Mary Martin, Sue Harvey, Nicki Lehman
Publication Coordinator: Tanya Turner

Photography: Tammy Christian, Jeff Chilcote, Kelly Heydinger, Nancy Sharp
Photography Assistant: Linda Quinlan

Production Coordinator: Brenda Gallmeyer
Book and Cover Design: Jessi Butler
Technical Artist: Connie Rand
Production Artist: Amy S. Lin
Production Assistants: Janet Bowers, Marj Morgan
Traffic Coordinator: Sandra Beres

Publishers: Carl H. Muselman, Arthur K. Muselman
Chief Executive Officer: John Robinson
Publishing Marketing Director: David McKee
Book Marketing Manager: Craig Scott
Product Development Director: Vivian Rothe
Publishing Services Manager: Brenda Wendling

Printed in the United States of America
First Printing: 2002
Library of Congress Number: 2001089865
ISBN: 1-882138-88-0

Quilt Note

Some quilt block designs are so well-known that even someone who doesn't quilt recognizes them by name. These are the same block designs that our grandmothers and great-grandmothers used in their quilts. Everyone loves these classic designs. They make great bed quilts!

We took these same block designs and asked our designers to go to the next level. We wanted to use those traditional block designs that everyone loves, but we wanted projects that had a touch of fancy or a special zing. Or we asked them to use a combination of blocks in a unique way to create a block design that is new and old at the same time!

We selected eight classic designs that are easily recognized as quilt blocks as the themes of our chapters: Wedding Ring, Log Cabin, Sunbonnet Sue, Stars, Nine-Patch, Four-Patch, Baskets and Trees & Houses.

In case you do not have patterns for these old favorites, we included one antique quilt in a classic style in each chapter. Of course, these are large bed quilts because that is what the quilter of yesteryear made.

Today we use quilted items in every room of our homes. That opens up a whole new world for designing and displaying our handiwork. And our designers had fun doing just that, creating a tree skirt, pillows, pot holders, table runners, purse, place mat, chair pad, jacket and more.

They also created lap quilts, wall quilts, kids' quilts, picnic quilts, twin-size quilts and quilts of every size imaginable. Of course, most were designed to take advantage of the new tools and faster techniques we have at our fingertips in today's quilting world.

So whether you prefer to make bed-size quilts or faster and smaller quilted treasures, we know you will be pleased with our selection of projects. There is something for everyone in this book.

Contents

Four-Patch Quilts

*Four-Patch, draw the latch,
Sit by the fire and quilt!*

Four-Patch Pinwheel

❖

Mama's Teacups

❖

Arctic Star

❖

**Four-Patch Posy
Lap Quilt**

❖

**Angel Table Runner
& Stocking**

❖

Four-Patch Link

Four-Patch Pinwheel

From the collection of Sandra L. Hatch

A simple pinwheel design creates an unusual illusion when combined with unpieced blocks.

Project Notes

Although this quilt is made from fabrics popular in the latter part of the 19th century, you may reproduce it using similar fabrics. Reproduction prints in similar patterns are available in most quilt shops. Although the quilt is made with Pinwheel blocks, a Four-Patch design and unpieced fill-in blocks, this simple design is confused on the quilt. The drawing doesn't give this illusion, but the quilt does. What you first see when viewing the quilt is a different block altogether, as shown in Figure 1. Whether you choose to make a quilt with an antique or modern look, you will enjoy the simplicity of the construction process.

Figure 1
The block appears to be pieced as shown, but that is an illusion.

The original quilt has a row of half blocks on one end made with entirely different fabrics, which indicates the quilter ran out of the original fabrics. We have given instructions to complete the quilt with whole blocks with fabrics enough to finish it that way.

Project Specifications

Skill Level: Beginner

Quilt Size: 68 1/4" x 79 5/8"

Block Size: 8" x 8"

Number of Blocks: 42

Materials

- 1 yard each tan and navy prints
- 1 3/4 yards white shirting print
- 3 yards pink-on-pink print
- Backing 72" x 84"
- Batting 72" x 84"
- 8 3/4 yards self-made or purchased binding
- All-purpose thread to match fabrics
- Basic sewing tools and supplies

Four-Patch Pinwheel
Placement Diagram
68 1/4" x 79 5/8"

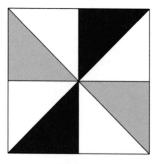

Pinwheel
8" x 8" Block

Instructions

Step 1. Cut six strips each 4 7/8" by fabric width tan and navy prints; subcut each strip into 4 7/8" square segments. You will need 42 squares of each fabric.

Step 2. Cut each square in half on one diagonal to make triangles; you will need 84 triangles of each color.

Step 3. Repeat Steps 1 and 2 with 11 strips white shirting print to make 168 triangles.

Step 4. Sew a white shirting print triangle to each tan and navy print triangle to make triangle/square units as shown in Figure 2; repeat for 84 of each color combination.

Figure 2
Sew a white shirting print triangle to each tan and navy print triangle to make triangle/square units.

Step 5. Sew a navy/white unit to a tan/white unit as shown in Figure 3; repeat for 84 units.

Figure 3
Sew a navy/white unit to a tan/white unit.

Step 6. Join two pieced units to complete one Pinwheel block as shown in Figure 4; repeat for 42 blocks.

Figure 4
Join 2 pieced units to complete 1 Pinwheel block.

Step 7. Cut eight strips 8 1/2" by fabric width pink-on-pink print; subcut strips into 8 1/2" A squares. You will need 30 A squares.

Step 8. Cut two strips 12 5/8" by fabric width pink-on-pink print; subcut strips into 12 5/8" squares. Cut each square on both diagonals to make B fill-in triangles; you will need 22 B triangles.

Step 9. Cut two 6 5/8" x 6 5/8" squares pink-on-pink print. Cut each square on one diagonal to make C corner triangles.

Step 10. Arrange pieced blocks with A squares, B fill-in triangles and C corner triangles in diagonal rows as shown in Figure 5; join in rows. Press seams in one direction.

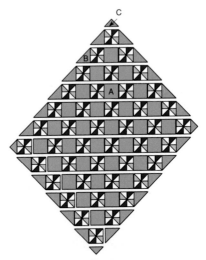

Figure 5
Arrange pieced blocks with A squares, B fill-in triangles and C corner triangles in diagonal rows.

Step 11. Join the diagonal rows; press seams in one direction.

Step 12. Prepare quilt top for quilting and finish referring to the General Instructions. ❖

The photo shows what appears to be the block, but is really the A squares with the corners of four blocks.

Mama's Teacups

By Sandra L. Hatch

The teacup print used in this Four-Patch quilt reminds me of my mother and her morning cup of tea.

Project Notes

The blue teacup print used in this quilt has a one-way design. It may not have made much difference if the teacups were all in an upright position, but I wanted them to be that way; this made the planning of the quilt a bit more complicated. The top and bottom borders have to be cut across the width of the fabric and pieced to fit, while the side borders are cut along the length of the fabric. The large C triangles are all positioned so that the teacups are upright. This is really not difficult as each square cut on both diagonals yields triangles in the right positions. This was a fun quilt to make even with the extra work needed in the planning.

Project Specifications

Skill Level: Beginner
Quilt Size: 78" x 86"
Block Size: 8" x 8"
Number of Blocks: 72

Materials

- 3/4 yard white floral print
- 1 yard each light blue print and pink plaid
- 1 1/2 yards each light green floral and yellow plaid
- 3 1/2 yards blue teacup print
- Backing 80" x 90"
- Batting 80" x 90"
- 9 1/2 yards self-made or purchased binding
- All-purpose thread to match fabrics
- Basic sewing tools and supplies

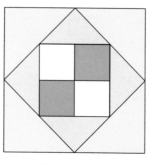

Four-Patch in a Square
8" x 8" Block

Triangles
8" x 8" Block

Making Four-Patch in a Square Blocks

Step 1. Cut five strips each white floral print and pink plaid 2 1/2" by fabric width.

Step 2. Sew a pink plaid strip to a white floral print strip with right sides together along length; press seams toward pink plaid. Repeat for five strip sets.

Step 3. Subcut strip sets into 2 1/2" segments; you will need 72 segments.

Step 4. Join two segments to make a Four-Patch unit as shown in Figure 1; repeat for 36 units.

Figure 1
Join 2 segments to make a Four-Patch unit.

Step 5. Cut seven strips light blue print 3 5/8" by fabric width; subcut strips into 3 5/8" square segments for A. You will need 72 A squares. Cut each square in half on one diagonal to make A triangles; you will need 144 A triangles.

Step 6. Sew an A triangle to each side of one Four-Patch unit as shown in Figure 2; repeat for all Four-Patch units. Press seams toward A.

Step 7. Cut nine strips light green floral 4 7/8" by fabric width; subcut strips into

Figure 2
Sew an A triangle to each side of 1 Four-Patch unit.

Figure 3
Sew a B triangle to each side of 1 pieced unit to complete 1 Four-Patch in a Square block as shown.

4 7/8" square segments for B. You will need 72 B squares. Cut each square in half on one diagonal to make B triangles; you will need 144 B triangles.

Step 8. Sew a B triangle to each side of one pieced unit to complete one Four-Patch in a Square block as shown in Figure 3; press seams toward B. Repeat for all pieced units to complete 36 blocks.

Making Triangles Blocks

Step 1. Cut four strips 4 1/2" x 78 1/2" blue teacup print; set aside for borders. **Note:** *For a one-way design fabric, cut the top and bottom strips across width of fabric and piece as needed to make the correct-length strip.*

Step 2. Cut five strips yellow plaid 9 1/4" by fabric width and nine strips blue teacup print 9 1/4" by remaining fabric width; subcut strips into 9 1/4" square segments for C. You will need 18 squares of each color.

Figure 4
Cut each square in half on both diagonals as shown.

Figure 5
Sew a blue teacup print C to a yellow plaid C.

Step 3. Cut each square in half on both diagonals as shown in Figure 4 to make C triangles; you will need 72 C triangles of each color.

Figure 6
Join 2 triangle units as shown to complete 1 Triangles block.

Step 4. Sew a blue teacup print C to a yellow plaid C as shown in Figure 5; repeat for 72 units. **Note:** *Take care here when piecing if fabric has a one-way design.* Press seams toward blue teacup print C triangles.

Step 5. Join two triangle units as shown in Figure 6 to complete one Triangles block; press seam in one direction. Repeat for 36 blocks.

Completing Quilt

Step 1. Join four Four-Patch in a Square blocks with four Triangles blocks to make an X row as shown in Figure 7; repeat for five X rows. Repeat to make a Y row as shown in Figure 8; repeat for four Y rows.

Figure 7
Join 4 Four-Patch in a Square blocks with 4 Triangles blocks to make an X row.

Figure 8
Join 4 Four-Patch in a Square blocks with 4 Triangles blocks to make a Y row.

Note: *If using a one-way-design fabric, be careful when piecing blocks in rows to keep blocks with design in an upright position.*

Step 2. Join the X and Y rows to complete the pieced center referring to the Placement Diagram for positioning of rows. Press seams in one direction.

Step 3. Cut and piece two strips each 1 1/2" x 66 1/2" and 1 1/2 x 72 1/2" pink plaid. Sew the longer strips

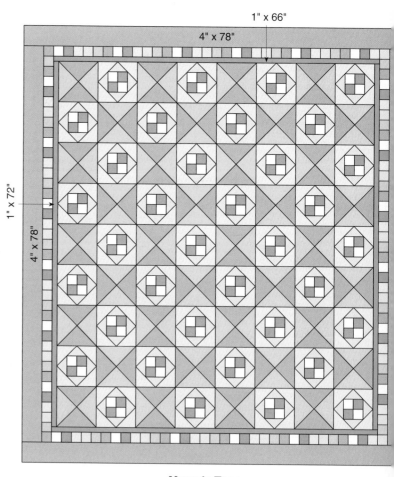

Mama's Teacups
Placement Diagram
78" x 86"

Continued on page 16

Arctic Star

By Holly Daniels

Dyed fabrics in different blue tones combine with white to make this large bed-size quilt.

Project Specifications

Skill Level: Intermediate

Quilt Size: 85" x 102"

Block Size: 12" x 12"

Number of Blocks: 4 Corner, 12 Schoolgirl's Puzzle and 14 Road to Oklahoma

Materials

- 1 1/2 yards medium light blue (B)
- 1 1/2 yards dark blue (D)
- 1 3/4 yards light blue (A)
- 2 3/4 yards medium dark blue (C)
- 4 yards white
- Backing 89" x 106"
- Batting 89" x 106"
- 11 yards self-made or purchased binding
- All-purpose thread to match fabrics
- Basic sewing tools and supplies

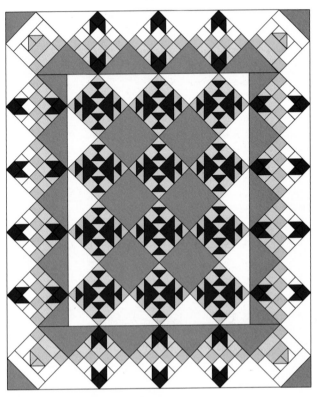

Arctic Star
Placement Diagram
85" x 102"

Making Schoolgirl's Puzzle Blocks

Step 1. Cut four strips 3 1/2" by fabric width fabric A; subcut each strip into 3 1/2" square segments to make 48 squares.

Step 2. Cut three strips each 3 7/8" by fabric width fabrics A and D; subcut each strip into 3 7/8" square segments to make 24 squares. Cut each square on one diagonal to make triangles.

Step 3. Sew an A triangle to a D triangle to make a A-D triangle/square unit as shown in Figure 1; repeat for 48 units.

Step 4. Join two A-D triangle/square units with two A squares as shown in Figure 2; repeat for 24 A-D units.

Schoolgirl's Puzzle
12" x 12" Block
Make 12

Figure 1
Sew an A triangle to a D triangle to make an A-D triangle/square unit.

Figure 2
Join an A-D triangle/square unit with 2 A squares as shown.

Step 5. Cut two strips 6 7/8" by fabric width fabric D; subcut each strip into 6 7/8" square segments to make 12 squares. Cut each square on one diagonal to make 24 large D triangles.

Step 6. Cut four strips fabric B and two strips fabric D 3 7/8" by fabric width; subcut each strip into 3 7/8" square segments. Cut each segment in half on one diagonal to make 72 B and 24 small D triangles.

Step 7. Sew a B triangle to a small D triangle to make a triangle/square unit as shown in Figure 3; repeat for 24 units.

Step 8. Sew two B triangles to a B-D unit to complete one B-B-D unit; repeat for 24 units.

Step 9. Sew a large D triangle to a B-B-D unit to complete one D-B-B-D unit as shown in Figure 4; repeat for 24 units.

Figure 3
Sew a B triangle to a small D triangle to make a triangle/square unit as shown.

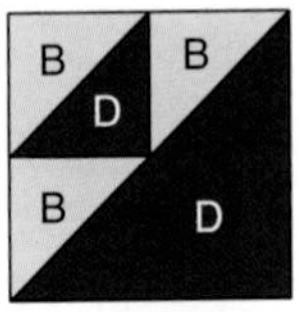

Figure 4
Sew a large D triangle to a B-B-D unit as shown.

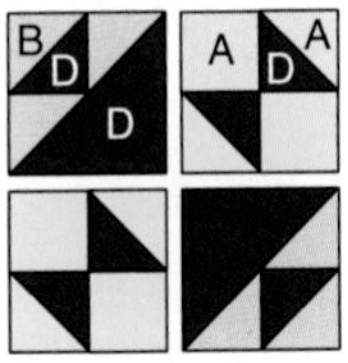

Figure 5
Join 2 A-D units with 2 D-B-B-D units to complete 1 Schoolgirl's Puzzle block.

Step 10. Join two A-D units with two D-B-B-D units to complete one Schoolgirl's Puzzle block referring to Figure 5; repeat for 12 blocks.

Making Road to Oklahoma Blocks

Step 1. Cut three fabric D, four fabric A, four white and five fabric B strips 3 1/2" by fabric width; subcut each strip into 3 1/2" square segments to make 28 D, 42 A, 42 white and 56 B squares.

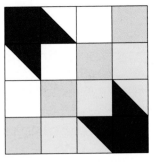

Road to Oklahoma
12" x 12" Block
Make 14

Step 2. Cut two strips each fabric A and white, and three strips fabric D 3 7/8" by fabric width; subcut into 3 7/8" square segments to make 14 A and white squares and 28 D squares. Cut each square in half on one diagonal to make 28 A and white triangles and 56 D triangles.

Step 3. Sew a D triangle to each A and white triangle to make 28 each D-A and D-white triangle/square units.

Step 4. Arrange the A, D, white and B squares in rows with the D-A and D-white units referring to Figure 6; join units in rows. Join rows to complete one Road to Oklahoma block; repeat for 14 blocks.

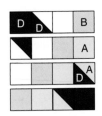

Figure 6
Arrange the A, D, white and B squares in rows with the D-A and D-white units; join to complete 1 Road to Oklahoma block.

Corner Blocks

Step 1. Cut two strips 3 1/2" by fabric width white; subcut into 12 1/2" segments for W; you will need four W pieces.

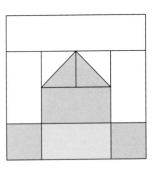

Corner
12" x 12" Block
Make 4

Step 2. Cut one strip each fabric A and B, and wo strips white 3 1/2" by fabric width; subcut into 6 1/2" segments to make four A, four B and eight white segments for X.

Step 3. Cut one strip fabric B 3 1/2" by fabric width; subcut strip into 3 1/2" square segments to make eight B squares.

Step 4. Cut one strip each white and fabric B 3 7/8" by fabric width; subcut into 3 7/8" square segments. Cut each square in half on one diagonal to make triangles. Sew a B triangle to a white triangle to make a B-white triangle/square unit; repeat for eight units.

Step 5. Arrange B, W and X and B-white units in rows referring to Figure 7; join units to complete one Corner block. Repeat for four Corner blocks.

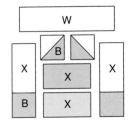

Figure 7
Arrange B, W and X and B-white units in rows to complete 1 Corner block.

Completing Quilt

Step 1. Cut five 18 1/4" x 18 1/4" squares white. Cut each square on both diagonals to make large M triangles; you will need 18 M triangles.

Step 2. Cut two 9 1/2" x 9 1/2" squares fabric C; cut on one diagonal to make N triangles.

Step 3. Cut five squares each fabric C and white 12 7/8" x 12 7/8"; cut each square on one diagonal to make 10 triangles each fabric. Join a fabric C triangle with a white triangle to make an O triangle/square unit; repeat for 10 units.

Step 4. Cut two 12 7/8" x 12 7/8" squares fabric C; Cut each square on one diagonal to make four triangles for P.

Step 5. Cut one square each fabric C and white 13 1/4" x 13 1/4"; cut each square on one diagonal to make triangles. Sew a white triangle to a C triangle to make a triangle/square unit; repeat for two units. Cut each of these triangle/square units on the diagonal to form Q triangle units as shown in Figure 8. Sew a Q triangle unit to a P triangle to make four Q-P units as shown in Figure 9.

Step 6. Cut six 12 1/2" x 12 1/2" squares fabric C for R squares.

Step 7. Arrange pieced blocks, R squares, Q-P and O units and M and N triangles in diagonal rows referring to Figure 10; join blocks in rows. Join the diagonal rows to complete the pieced top; press seams in one direction.

Figure 8
Cut each of these triangle/square units on the diagonal to form Q triangle units as shown.

Figure 9
Sew a Q unit to P.

Step 8. Prepare quilt top for quilting and finish referring to the General Instructions. **Note:** *The quilt shown was machine-quilted in a circular pattern in the pieced blocks and in a meandering design in the other areas.* ❖

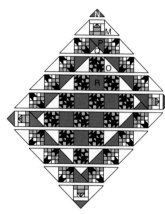

Figure 10
Arrange pieced blocks, R squares, Q-P and O units and M and N triangles in diagonal rows as shown; join blocks in rows.

Mama's Teacups
Continued from page 12

to opposite sides of the pieced center and the shorter strips to the top and bottom; press seams toward strips.

Step 4. Cut two strips 2 1/2" by fabric width from each fabric. Join one strip of each fabric with right sides together along length in the color order shown in Figure 9 to make a strip set. Press seams in one direction. Repeat for two strip sets.

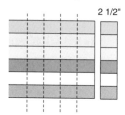
2 1/2"

Figure 9
Join 1 strip of each fabric with right sides together along length in the color order shown; subcut into 2 1/2" segments.

Step 5. Subcut strip sets into 2 1/2" segments; you will need 24 segments.

Step 6. Join six segments on short ends, repeating color order, to make a side strip as shown in Figure 10; remove one yellow plaid square from one remaining segment and add to one end of the strip; repeat for two strips.

Step 7. Sew these strips to opposite long sides of the

pieced center; press seams toward the pink plaid border strips.

Figure 10
Join 6 segments on short ends, repeating color order, to make a side strip as shown; remove 1 yellow square from 1 remaining segment and add to 1 end of the strip.

Step 8. Join five segments on short ends; add one five-square segment left from Step 6 as shown in Figure 11. Repeat for two strip sets.

Figure 11
Join 5 segments on short ends; add a 5-square segment as shown.

Step 9. Sew these strips to the top and bottom of the pieced center; press seams toward the pink plaid border strips.

Step 10. Sew a 4 1/2" x 78 1/2" blue teacup print border strip to each long side and to the top and bottom to complete the quilt top; press seams toward strips.

Step 11. Prepare quilt top for quilting and finish referring to the General Instructions. **Note:** *The quilt shown was machine-quilted in the ditch of seams and with a curving design and teacup design in the borders.* ❖

Four-Patch Posy Lap Quilt

By Pearl Louise Krush

Add a touch of spring to any room with this easy-to-make Four-Patch lap-size quilt.

Project Specifications

Skill Level: Intermediate

Quilt Size: 53" x 69"

Block Size: 8" x 8"

Number of Blocks: 9 B Blocks, 12 A Blocks and 14 C Blocks

Materials

- 1/2 yard each green and dark green prints
- 1 yard large floral print
- 1 1/8 yards pink print
- 1 3/4 yards white solid
- Backing 57" x 73"
- Batting 57" x 73"
- 7 1/4 yards self-made or purchased binding
- All-purpose thread to match fabrics
- 14 (3/4") dark rose buttons
- Basic sewing tools and supplies, rotary cutter, mat and ruler

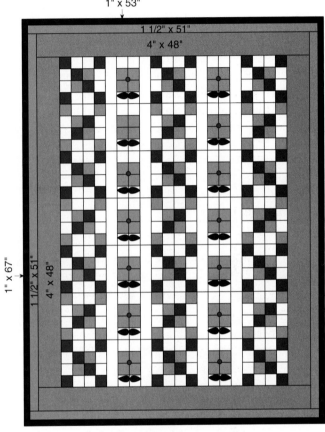

Four-Patch Posy Lap Quilt
Placement Diagram
53" x 69"

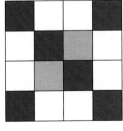

Block A
8" x 8" Block
Make 12

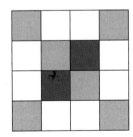

Block B
8" x 8" Block
Make 9

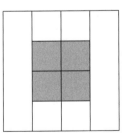

Block C
8" x 8" Block
Make 14

Instructions

Step 1. Cut six strips green print, nine strips pink print and 15 strips white solid 2 1/2" by fabric width.

Step 2. Sew a white solid strip to a green print strip with right sides together along length; press seams toward green print strip. Repeat for six strip sets.

Step 3. Subcut strip sets into 2 1/2" X segments; you will need 90 X segments.

Step 4. Sew a white solid strip to a pink print strip with right sides together along length; press seams toward pink print strip. Repeat for eight strip sets.

Step 5. Subcut strip sets into 2 1/2" Y segments; you will need 128 Y segments.

Step 6. Cut two strips white solid 8 1/2" by fabric width; subcut into 2 1/2" segments for Z. You will need 28 Z pieces.

Step 7. Join two X segments to make an X-X Four-Patch unit as shown in Figure 1; repeat for 24 X-X units.

Step 8. Join an X segment with a Y segment to make an X-Y Four-Patch unit as shown in Figure 2; repeat for 42 X-Y units.

Figure 1
Join 2 X segments to make an X-X Four-Patch unit as shown.

Figure 2
Join an X segment with a Y segment to make an X-Y Four-Patch unit as shown.

Figure 3
Join 2 Y units to make a Y-Y Four-Patch unit as shown.

Step 9. Join two Y units to make a Y-Y Four-Patch unit as shown in Figure 3; repeat for 18 Y-Y units.

Step 10. Join two X-X units and two X-Y units to

complete Block A as shown in Figure 4; repeat for 12 blocks.

Step 11. Join two X-Y units with two Y-Y units to complete Block B as shown in Figure 5; repeat for nine blocks.

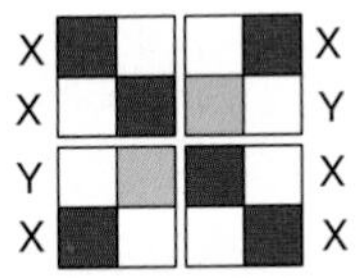

Figure 4
Join 2 X-X units and 2 X-Y units to complete Block A.

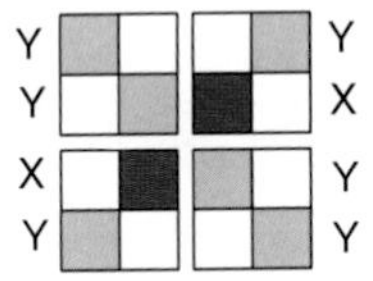

Figure 5
Join 2 X-Y units with 2 Y-Y units to complete Block B.

Step 12. Join four Y segments as shown in Figure 6; sew Z to opposite sides as shown in Figure 7 to complete one Block C; repeat for 14 blocks.

Step 13. Prepare leaf template using pattern given; cut as directed on pattern, adding a 1/4" seam allowance for hand appliqué.

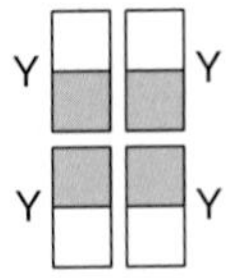

Figure 6
Join 4 Y segments as shown.

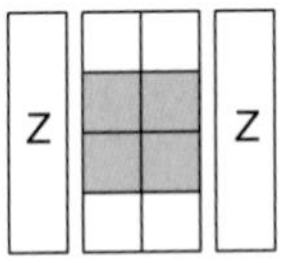

Figure 7
Sew Z to opposite sides of the Y unit to complete 1 Block C.

Step 14. Turn under edges of leaf shapes; baste to hold. Pin two leaf shapes to one Block C referring to Figure 8 for placement. Hand-appliqué in place.

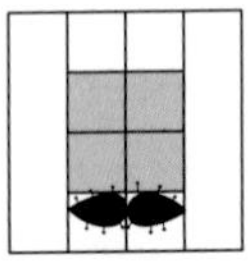

Figure 8
Pin 2 leaf shapes to 1 Block C.

Step 15. Join four A blocks with three B blocks to make a vertical row as shown in Figure 9; repeat for three rows. Press seams in one direction.

Step 16. Join seven C blocks to make a vertical row as shown in Figure 10; repeat for two rows. Press seams in one direction.

Step 17. Join the rows to complete the pieced center; press seams in one direction.

Step 18. Cut and piece two strips each 4 1/2" x 48 1/2" and 4 1/2" x 56 1/2" large floral print. Sew the

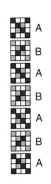

Figure 9
Join 4 A blocks with 3 B blocks to make a vertical row.

longer strips to opposite sides of the pieced center and shorter strips to the top and bottom; press seams toward strips.

Step 19. Cut and piece two strips each 2" x 51 1/2" and 2" x 64 1/2" pink print. Sew the longer strips to opposite sides of the pieced center and shorter strips to the top and bottom; press seams toward strips.

Step 20. Cut and piece two strips each 1 1/2" x 53 1/2" and 1 1/2" x 67 1/2" dark green print. Sew the longer strips to opposite sides of the pieced center and shorter strips to the top and bottom; press seams toward strips.

Step 21. Prepare quilt top for quilting and finish referring to the General Instructions. **Note:** *The quilt shown was machine-quilted diagonally through Blocks A and B and in a meandering pattern through white solid and border areas using all-purpose thread to match fabrics.*

Step 22. Sew a dark rose button in the center of each C block to complete the quilt. ❖

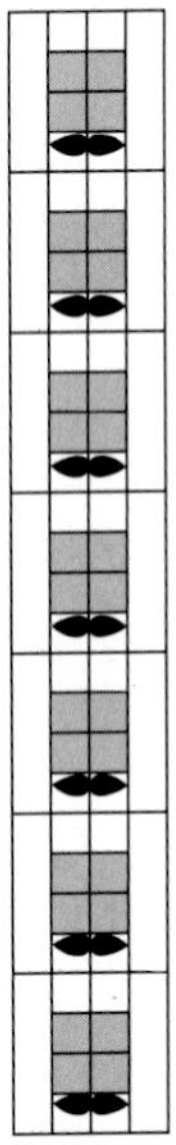

Figure 10
Join 7 C blocks to make a vertical row.

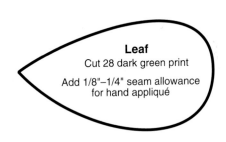

Leaf
Cut 28 dark green print

Add 1/8"–1/4" seam allowance for hand appliqué

Angel Table Runner & Stocking

By Judith Sandstrom

Four-Patch blocks form angel shapes on this runner and matching Christmas stocking.

Project Specifications

Skill Level: Intermediate

Runner Size: 14" x 49"

Stocking Size: 9 1/2" x 18 1/2"

Materials

- 1/8 yard each gold mottled and peach solid
- 1/4 yard white-on-cream and burgundy prints
- 1/2 yard Christmas print
- 1 yard green print
- Backing 18" x 53" and two 11" x 20"
- Batting 18" x 53" and two 11" x 20"
- 4 yards self-made or purchased binding
- All-purpose thread to match fabrics
- White quilting thread
- Basic sewing tools and supplies

Cutting

Step 1. Cut the following fabric-width strips from green print: four 3"—subcut into 13 A pieces 3" x 5 1/2" and 28 B squares 3" x 3"; one 1 3/4"—subcut into eight 1 3/4" x 3" C pieces and keep remainder as one piece; two 3 3/8"—subcut into 16 squares 3 3/8" cut on one diagonal to make 32 green D triangles; and one 4 3/4"—subcut into three 4 3/4" squares cut on both diagonals to make 12 G triangles.

Step 2. Cut the following fabric-width strips white-on-cream print: one 3"—subcut into eight 3" squares for E and one 3 3/8"—subcut into eight 3 3/8" squares cut on one diagonal to make 16 white D triangles.

Step 3. Cut one strip gold mottled 3 3/8" by fabric width; subcut into eight 3 3/8" square segments. Cut each segment on one diagonal to make 16 gold D triangles.

Step 4. Cut one strip peach solid 1 3/4" by fabric width; set aside.

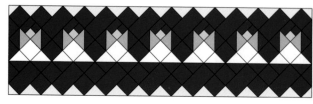

Angel Table Runner
Placement Diagram
14" x 49"

Step 5. From burgundy print cut the following fabric-width strips from Christmas print: one 4 3/4"—subcut into eight 4 3/4" square segments cut on both diagonals to make 30 F triangles; one 7 1/2" x 11" rectangle for stocking back; and two 2 3/4" x 2 3/4" squares cut on one diagonal to make four H corner triangles.

Step 6. From burgundy print cut two 4" x 7 1/2" pieces for stocking top front and back, and one 1" x

5" piece for hanging loop. Prepare piece J using pattern piece given; cut as directed on piece.

Piecing Blocks & Units

Step 1. Sew a gold D triangle to a green D triangle to make a triangle/square unit; repeat for 16 gold/green D units. Repeat with white D and green D triangles to make 16 white/green D units. Press seams toward darker fabric.

Step 2. Sew the remainder of the 1 3/4"-wide green print strip to the 1 3/4"-wide peach solid strip with right sides together along length; press seam toward green print strip. Subcut strip into 1 3/4" segments; you will need eight segments. Sew a C piece to one side of each segment to make eight C units.

Step 3. Join two gold/green D units with one C unit and one E square to complete one angel unit as shown in Figure 1; repeat for eight angel units.

Figure 1
Complete 1 angel
unit as shown.

Figure 2
Complete 1 skirt
unit as shown.

Figure 3
Complete 1 edge
unit as shown.

Step 4. Join two white/green D units with two B squares to complete one skirt unit as shown in Figure 2; repeat for six skirt units.

Step 5. Join one A, one B and two F pieces to make an edge unit as shown in Figure 3; repeat for 11 edge units.

Making the Runner

Step 1. Join one angel, one skirt and two edge units to make a diagonal strip as shown in Figure 4; repeat for four strips. Join the strips to complete the runner center section.

Step 2. Join one each A, F and B pieces with H to make one corner unit as shown in Figure 5. Join with

Figure 4
Join 1 angel, 1 skirt
and 2 edge units to
make a diagonal strip.

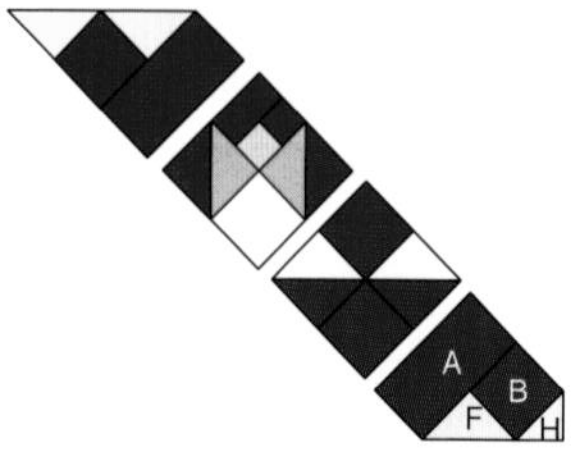

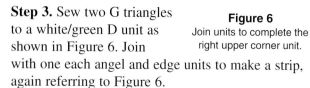

Figure 5
Join units to complete 1
right lower corner strip.

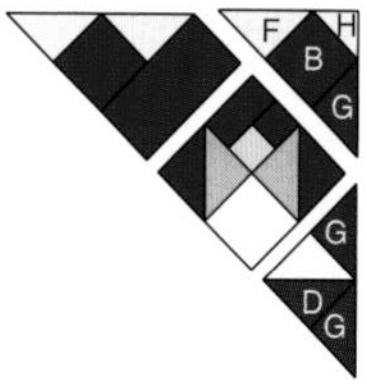

Figure 6
Join units to complete the
right upper corner unit.

one each angel, skirt and edge units to make a strip, again referring to Figure 5. Sew to the right end of the center section.

Step 3. Sew two G triangles to a white/green D unit as shown in Figure 6. Join with one each angel and edge units to make a strip, again referring to Figure 6.

Step 4. Join one each F, B, G and H pieces; sew to the pieced strip to make the right upper corner unit, again referring to Figure 6. Sew the pieced unit to the right end of the center section to complete one end.

Step 5. Join one each B, H and G pieces to make a unit as shown in Figure 7; join with one each angel, skirt and edge units to make a strip, again referring to Figure 7. Sew to the left end of the center section.

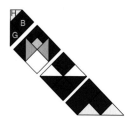

Figure 7
Join units to complete 1 left
upper corner strip.

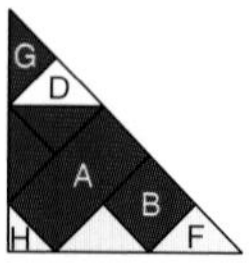

Figure 8
Complete the left lower
corner unit as shown.

Step 6. Join two each G and F pieces with one each A, B and H pieces and one white/green D unit to make the left lower corner unit as shown in Figure 8; add to the pieced section to complete the pieced runner and press.

Step 7. Prepare runner top for quilting and finish referring to the General Instructions. **Note:** *The project shown was hand-quilted 1/4" inside seams of green print pieces using white quilting thread.*

Making the Stocking

Step 1. Complete four corner units as shown in Figure 9.

Step 2. Sew a corner unit to each side of the remaining angel unit to complete the pieced section of stocking as shown in Figure 10.

Figure 9
Complete 4 corner
units as shown.

Figure 10
Sew a corner unit to each
side of the angel unit.

Step 3. Sew one 4 1/2" x 7 1/2" burgundy print rectangle to the top of the pieced section and J to the bottom as shown in Figure 11 to complete stocking front.

Figure 11
Sew a burgundy print rectangle to the
top of the pieced section and J to the
bottom to complete stocking front.

Step 4. Join the remaining burgundy print rectangle, the 7 1/2" x 11" rectangle Christmas print and the reversed J piece to complete stocking back.

Step 5. Cut two lining pieces and two batting pieces from rectangles listed using stocking front and back pieces as patterns.

Step 6. Layer the batting and lining right side up with stocking front right side down; pin and stitch across top edge only. Repeat with batting, lining and stocking back. Turn right side out; press top edge and pin layers together.

Step 7. Quilt each section as desired by hand or

machine. **Note:** *The stocking shown was hand-quilted 1/4" from seams in green print pieces using white quilting thread.*

Step 8. Fold the 1" x 6" burgundy print loop piece along length with right sides together; stitch. Turn right side out and press with seam on side. Fold with ends together and pin 3/4" from stitched top edge of one lining piece as shown in Figure 12; baste to hold.

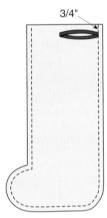

Figure 12
Pin loop piece 3/4"
from stitched top edge
of stocking lining.

Step 9. Place stocking back and front layers right sides together; stitch all around. Zigzag-stitch along raw edges to reinforce seam; turn right side out to finish. ❖

Angel Stocking
Placement Diagram
9 1/2" x 18 1/2"

J
Cut 2 burgundy print
(reverse 1)

Four-Patch Link

By Sandra L. Hatch

Matching pillowcases make this simple Four-Patch quilt a hit on any bed.

Four-Patch Link

Project Specifications

Skill Level: Intermediate

Quilt Size: 68" x 86"

Block Size: 6" x 6"

Number of Blocks: 48

Materials

- 3/4 yard brown print
- 3/4 yard light blue print
- 2 yards multicolored print
- 2 1/2 yards dark blue print
- 3 1/4 yards green print
- Backing 72" x 90"
- Batting 72" x 90"
- 8 3/4 yards self-made or purchased binding
- All-purpose thread to match fabrics
- Basic sewing tools and supplies

Instructions

Step 1. Cut 10 strips each brown and green prints 2" by fabric width.

Step 2. Sew a brown print strip to a green print strip along length with right sides together; press seams toward green print strip. Repeat with all green and brown print strips.

Step 3. Subcut strip sets into 2" segments; you will need 192 segments.

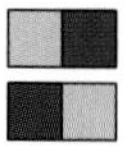

Step 4. Join two segments as shown in Figure 1 to make a Four-Patch unit; repeat for 96 units.

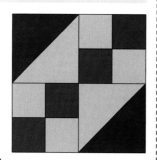

Four-Patch Link
6" x 6" Block

Figure 1
Join 2 segments to make a Four-Patch unit.

Step 5. Cut five strips each light blue and multicolored prints 3 7/8" by fabric width. Subcut each strip into 3 7/8" square segments; you will need 48 squares of each color. Cut each square in half to make a triangle; you will need 96 triangles of each color.

Step 6. Sew a light blue print triangle to a multicolored print triangle to complete a triangle/square unit as shown in Figure 2; repeat for 96 units.

Figure 2
Sew a light blue print triangle to a multicolored print triangle to complete a triangle/square unit.

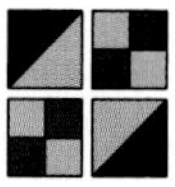

Figure 3
Join 2 triangle/square units with 2 Four-Patch units to complete 1 block.

Step 7. Join two triangle/square units with two Four-Patch units to complete one block as shown in Figure 3; repeat for 48 blocks.

Step 8. Cut two strips each 3 1/2" x 57 1/2" and 3 1/2" x 69 1/2" along length of dark blue print; set aside for borders.

Step 9. Cut eight strips 6 1/2" by remaining width and two strips across full width of the dark blue print; subcut into 3 1/2" segments for sashing strips. You will need 82 sashing strips.

Step 10. Cut two strips each 2" x 60 1/2" and 2" x 75 1/2" along length of green print for border strips; set aside.

Step 11. Cut four strips 3 1/2" by remaining fabric width green print; subcut strips into 3 1/2" square segments for sashing squares. You will need 35 sashing squares.

Step 12. Join six Four-Patch Link blocks with five sashing strips to make a block row as shown in Figure 4; press seams toward sashing strips. Repeat for eight block rows.

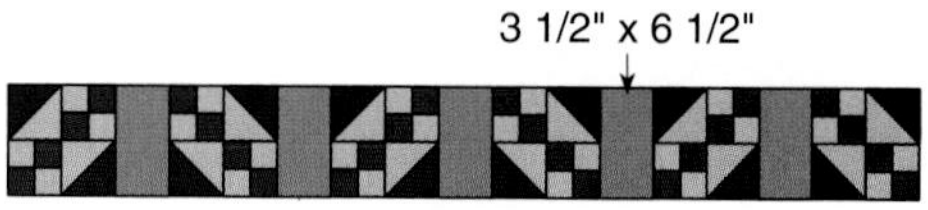

3 1/2" x 6 1/2"

Figure 4
Join 6 Four-Patch Link blocks with 5 sashing strips to make a block row.

Step 13. Join six sashing strips with five sashing squares to make a sashing row as shown in Figure 5; press seams toward sashing strips. Repeat for seven sashing rows.

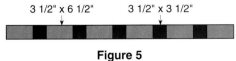

3 1/2" x 6 1/2"   3 1/2" x 3 1/2"

Figure 5
Join 6 sashing strips with 5 sashing squares to make a sashing row.

Step 14. Join the sashing rows with the block rows beginning and ending with block rows to complete the pieced center; press seams toward sashing rows.

Step 15. Sew the longer dark blue print border strips to opposite long sides of the pieced center; press seams toward strips. Sew the shorter dark blue print border strips to the top and bottom of the pieced center; press seams toward strips.

Step 16. Sew the longer green print border strips to

opposite long sides of the pieced center; press seams toward strips. Sew the shorter green print border strips to the top and bottom of the pieced center; press seams toward strips.

Step 17. Cut and piece two strips each multicolored print 4 1/2" x 68 1/2" and 4 1/2" x 78 1/2". Sew the longer strips to opposite long sides of the pieced center; press seams toward strips. Sew the shorter strips to the top and bottom of the pieced center; press seams toward strips.

Step 18. Prepare quilt top for quilting and finish referring to the General Instructions.

Four-Patch Link Pillowcases

Project Notes

The size of the pillowcase will vary. Make the unpieced section any length desired to fit double-, queen- or king-size pillows. The border strip finishes at 10" wide. The width of the pillowcase is determined by the width of the fabric used for the unpieced section. It should finish at least 20" wide on one side. The end pieces on the pieced strip are trimmed to match the width of the unpieced section to allow for varying fabric widths.

Project Specifications

Skill Level: Intermediate

Pillowcase Size: Size varies

Block Size: 6" x 6"

Number of Blocks: 5 per pillowcase

Fabric & Batting

- 1/4 yard dark blue print
- 3/8 yard each green and brown prints
- 1 yard multicolored print
- 2 yards light blue print

Supplies & Tools

- All-purpose thread to match fabrics
- Basic sewing tools and supplies

Instructions

Step 1. Cut two strips each brown and green prints 2" by fabric width.

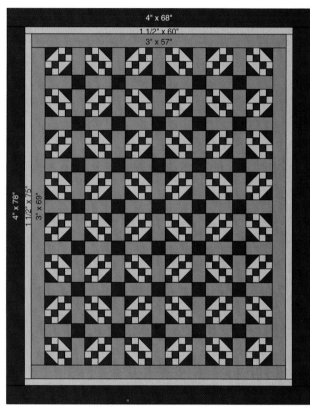

Four-Patch Link Quilt
Placement Diagram
68" x 86"

Step 2. Sew a brown print strip to a green print strip along length with right sides together; press seams toward green print strip. Repeat with the second green and brown print strips.

Step 3. Subcut strip sets into 2" segments; you will need 40 segments.

Step 4. Join two segments as shown in Figure 1 to make a Four-Patch unit; repeat for 20 units.

Step 5. Cut one strip each light blue and multicolored prints 3 7/8" by fabric width. Subcut strips into 3 7/8" square segments; you will need 10 squares of each color. Cut each square in half to make a triangle; you will need 20 triangles of each color.

Step 6. Sew a light blue print triangle to a multicolored print triangle to complete a triangle/square unit as shown in Figure 2; repeat for 20 units.

Step 7. Join two triangle/square units with two Four-Patch units to complete one block as shown in Figure 3; repeat for 10 blocks.

Step 8. Cut two rectangles 28 1/2" by fabric width light blue print. **Note:** *Shorter or longer pillowcases are made by varying the length of this strip.*

Step 9. Cut four strips each green and brown prints 1/2" by fabric width for border strips. Cut four strips 1/2" x 6 1/2" for sashing and two strips 3 1/2" x 1/2" for end pieces from dark blue print.

Step 10. Join five blocks with four sashing strips to make one long strip; sew a 3 1/2" x 6 1/2" end piece to each end of the strip as shown in Figure 6. Press seams toward strips.

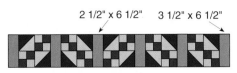

Figure 6
Join 5 blocks with 4 sashing strips
and 2 end pieces to make a strip.

Step 11. Sew a green print strip to a brown print strip with right sides together along length; press seams toward brown print strip. Repeat for four strip sets. Center and sew a strip set to each long side of the block strip with brown print strips on the outside; press seams toward strips.

Step 12. Cut one strip multicolored print 10 1/2" by fabric width for lining for pieced section. Press under one long edge 1/4".

Step 13. Center and pin unpressed edge of the lining right sides together with the pieced section; stitch. **Note:** At this point the ends of the pieced section and the lining may not match.

Step 14. Press lining and pieced section with seam toward lining piece and topstitch as shown in Figure 7.

Figure 7
Press lining and pieced section
with seam toward lining piece
and topstitch as shown.

Step 15. Center and stitch remaining raw edge of the pieced section to one end of one 8 1/2"-by-fabric-width rectangle of light blue print as shown in Figure 8. **Note:** Ends may not match, as shown in Figure 8.

Step 16. Trim edges of pieced section even with edges of the light blue

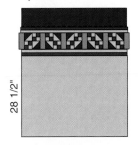

Figure 8
Center and stitch remaining raw
edge of the pieced section to 1 end
of 1 light blue print piece as shown;
ends may not be even.

print unpieced section or trim unpieced section even with strip as shown in Figure 9.

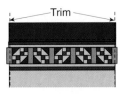

Figure 9
Trim edges of pieced section
even with edges of the light
blue print section.

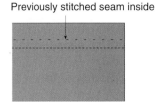

Figure 10
Stitch along the pressed-and-stitched
edge with a 3/8" seam allowance
to enclose previously stitched
seam as shown.

Step 17. Fold stitched piece with wrong sides together and raw edges even; stitch a 1/4" seam. Turn wrong side out; press seam flat.

Step 18. Stitch along the pressed-and-stitched edge with a 3/8" seam allowance to enclose previously stitched seam as shown in Figure 10. **Note:** This seam is called a French seam. It is a sturdy seam as there are no raw edges to wear.

Step 19. Fold the lining section to the inside to cover seam where pieced section and light blue print sections are joined; baste in place, carefully lining up edges as shown in Figure 11.

Figure 11
Fold the lining section to the inside to
cover seam where pieced section and light
blue print pieces are joined; baste in place,
carefully lining up edges as shown.

Step 20. From the right side, topstitch close to seam to catch basted section. Topstitch in the ditch between green print strips and pieced blocks to finish. Repeat Steps 10–20 for second pillowcase. ❖

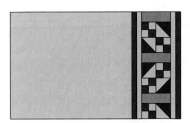

Four-Patch Link Pillowcase
Placement Diagram
Size Varies

Log Cabin Quilts

*Piece by piece,
lovingly built,
stitch by stitch,
a Log Cabin quilt!*

Antique Log Cabin

❖

Warm Neighbors

❖

Log Cabin Tree Skirt

❖

Courthouse Rounds

❖

Home Sweet Home

❖

Log Cabin Jacket

Antique Log Cabin

From the collection of Sue Harvey

Re-create this antique Log Cabin quilt using some of the reproduction fabrics available today, or take advantage of the pattern to use up your light scraps as the early quiltmaker did. Notice the unique border of this antique quilt.

Project Specifications

Skill Level: Beginner

Quilt Size: 84" x 84"

Block Size: 7" x 7"

Number of Blocks: 100

Materials

- 3/8 yard muslin for foundation
- 1/2 yard blue plaid
- 1 yard tan print
- 2 1/4 yards pink print
- 3 yards red solid
- 3 1/2 yards green print
- 3 1/2 yards total assorted light prints
- Backing 88" x 88"
- All-purpose thread to match fabrics
- Natural quilting thread
- Basic sewing tools and supplies

Instructions

Step 1. Cut four strips red solid 1 1/4" by fabric width; subcut into 1 1/4" square segments for center squares. You will need 100 center squares.

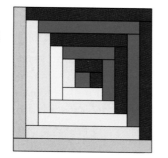

Log Cabin
7" x 7" Block

Step 2. Cut 42 strips red solid (R), 59 strips green print (G), 33 strips pink print (P) and 90 strips assorted light prints (L) 1 1/8" by fabric width.

Step 3. Sew a green print (G) strip to a center square; trim strip even with the center square as shown in Figure 1. Press seam toward the strip.

Step 4. Sew a green print (G) strip to the pieced unit, trim and press as shown in Figure 2.

Figure 1
Sew a green print strip to the center square; trim strip.

Figure 2
Sew a green print strip to the pieced unit; trim strip.

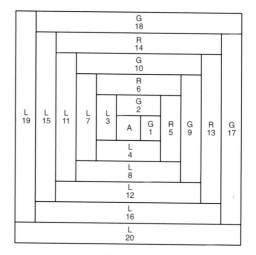

Figure 3
Add strips around the pieced unit in the order shown to complete 1 block.

Step 5. Continue adding strips around the pieced unit in the color and numerical order shown in Figure 3 to complete one block; repeat for 100 blocks, cutting additional 1 1/8" strips if necessary. **Note:** *Strips in positions 15 and 16 are pink print and in positions 19 and 20 are light print in 50 Log Cabin A blocks as shown in Figure 4. The fabric positions are reversed in the remaining 50 Log Cabin B blocks, again as shown in Figure 4.*

Figure 4
Make Log Cabin A and B blocks as shown.

Step 6. Join two A blocks with three B blocks to make a row as shown in Figure 5; repeat for three rows.

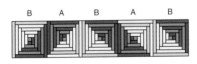

Figure 5
Join 2 A blocks with 3 B
blocks to make a row.

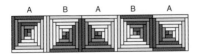

Figure 6
Join 3 A blocks with 2 B
blocks to make a row.

Step 7. Join three A
blocks with two B
blocks to make a row
as shown in Figure 6;
repeat for two rows.

Step 8. Join the rows
to make a quarter unit
as shown in Figure 7.
Repeat to make four
quarter units.

Step 9. Join the four
quarter units to complete the pieced center
as shown in Figure 8; press.

Figure 7
Join rows to make
a quarter unit.

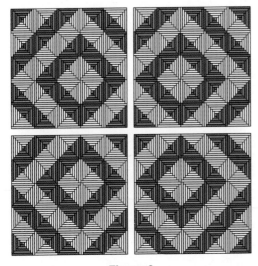

Figure 8
Join the 4 quarter units to
complete the pieced center.

Step 10. Cut 10 strips each red solid (R1) and pink print (P1) 1 3/8" by fabric width.

Step 11. Cut 20 red solid (R2), 25 green print (G), 15 pink print (P2), 20 tan print (T) and 10 blue plaid (B) strips 1 1/8" by fabric width.

Step 12. Join strips as shown in Figure 9 to make a red/green strip set and a pink strip set; repeat for five strip sets of each combination.

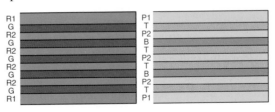

Figure 9
Make red/green and pink strip sets as shown.

Step 13. Prepare template for C using pattern piece given; transfer seam lines to template.

Step 14. Place C along length of a red/green strip set to cut nine red/green C pieces from each strip set, aligning lines on template with seams of strip set as shown in Figure 10. Repeat to cut 44 red/green C pieces.

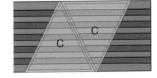

Figure 10
Cut 9 C pieces from each strip set.

Step 15. Repeat Step 14 with pink strip sets to cut 40 pink C pieces.

Step 16. Join 11 red/green C pieces with 10 pink C pieces to make a border strip as shown in Figure 11; repeat for four border strips.

Step 17. Sew a border strip to each side of the pieced center with pink C pieces against Log Cabin blocks; press seams toward border strips.

Step 18. Prepare four muslin-foundation D pieces; transfer seam lines to each piece.

Step 19. Cut one strip each pink print, blue plaid and tan print 1 1/4" by fabric width.

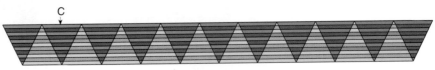

Figure 11
Join 11 red/green and 10 pink C pieces to make a border strip.

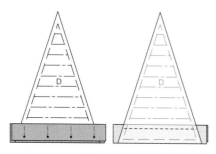

Figure 12
Place the pink print and tan print
strips on the muslin foundation;
stitch on the 1-2 line.

Step 20. Place the pink print strip on stripe 1 of the wrong side of one muslin foundation. Place the tan print strip right sides together with the pink print strip as shown in Figure 12 and pin in place. Turn the piece over and stitch along the line between stripe 1 and 2, again referring to Figure 12. Trim seam allowance and flip the tan print strip down; press. Continue to add strips in numerical order and in colors designated in Figure 13; repeat for four D pieces.

Step 21. Set a D piece into each corner to complete the pieced top; press.

Step 22. Place the pieced top on the prepared backing piece with wrong sides together; pin or baste to hold.

Step 23. Quilt as desired. **Note:** *The antique quilt shown was hand-quilted in the ditch of seams between blocks and C pieces with white quilting thread. There is no batting in the quilt.*

Step 24. Remove pins or basting. Cut nine strips green print 2 1/4" by fabric width. Join strips on short ends to make a long strip. Fold in half along length with wrong sides together; press to make binding strip. Bind edges of quilt to finish. ❖

Figure 13
Complete the D
piece as shown.

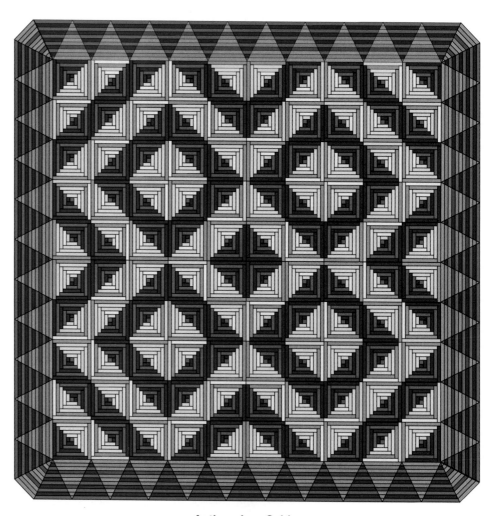

Antique Log Cabin
Placement Diagram
84" x 84"

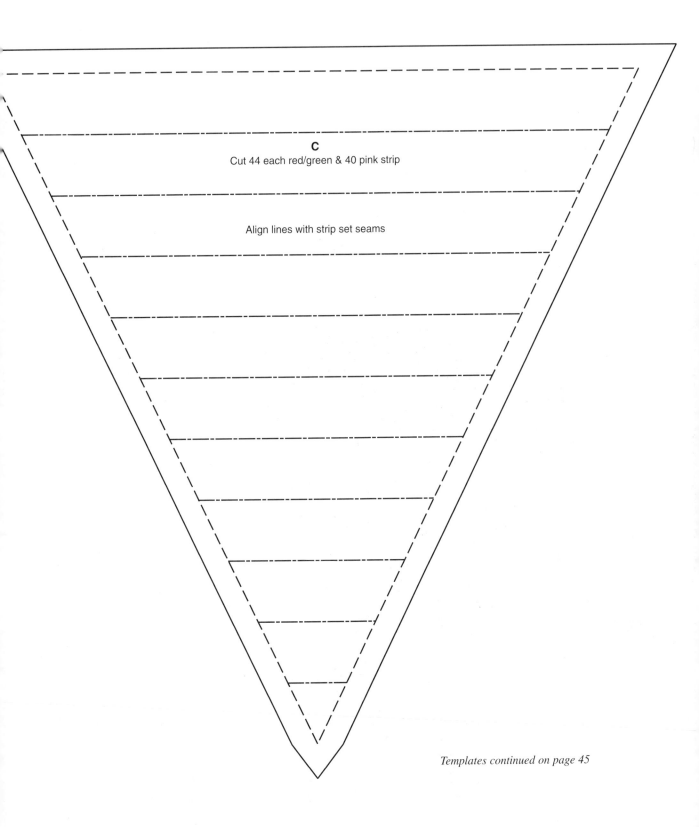

C

Cut 44 each red/green & 40 pink strip

Align lines with strip set seams

Templates continued on page 45

Warm Neighbors

By Pearl Louise Krush

*The Cabin, Tree and Log Cabin blocks create a warm and inviting
feeling wherever you hang this cozy wall quilt.*

Project Specifications

Skill Level: Intermediate

Quilt Size: 53" x 53"

Block Size: 8" x 8"

Number of Blocks: 4 Tree, 4 Cabin and 8
   Log Cabin

Materials

- 1 1/2" x 14" strip salmon print
- 1/8 yard cream print
- 1/4 yard dark brown print
- 1/4 yard beige print
- 1/3 yard light brown print
- 3/8 yard medium brown print
- 3/8 yard blue mottled
- 3/4 yard gold, green and rust prints
- 1 1/3 yards darkest brown print
- Backing 57" x 57"
- Batting 57" x 57"
- 6 1/4 yards self-made or purchased binding
- All-purpose thread to match fabrics
- Basic sewing tools and supplies, rotary
   cutter, mat and ruler

Cabin Blocks

Step 1. Cut the following
pieces from blue mottled:
four 2 7/8" x 2 7/8" squares
for B and twelve 1 1/2" x
2 1/2" rectangles for A.

Step 2. Cut the following
pieces from medium brown
print: four 2 7/8" x 2 7/8"
squares for B and twelve
1 1/2" x 4 1/2" rectangles
for C.

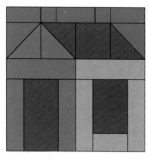

Cabin
8" x 8" Block

Step 3. Cut the following pieces from light brown

print: four 1 1/2" x 2 1/2" rectangles for E and twelve
1 1/2" x 4 1/2" rectangles for D.

Step 4. Cut the following from darkest brown print:
four 2 7/8" x 2 7/8" squares for B; four 2 1/2" x 2 1/2"
squares for F; four 2 1/2" x 3 1/2" rectangles for G;
and four 2 1/2" x 4 1/2" rectangles for H.

Step 5. Cut eight 1 1/2" x 1 1/2" squares salmon print
for J.

Step 6. To piece one Cabin
block, sew A to J to A to J to
A to piece the chimney row
as shown in Figure 1.

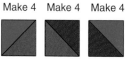

Figure 1
To piece 1 Cabin block,
sew A to J to A to J to A to
piece the chimney row.

Step 7. Draw a diagonal line on each B square; layer
colors as follows: blue mottled on medium brown
print, medium brown print on darkest brown print and
blue mottled on darkest brown print. Stitch 1/4" on
each side of the line as shown in Figure 2. Cut on the
drawn line; open each unit to reveal triangle/square
units as shown in Figure 3. For each block you need
one each blue/medium brown, blue/darkest brown and
medium brown/darkest brown units.

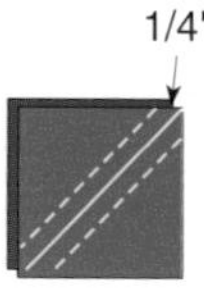

1/4"

Figure 2
Stitch 1/4" on each side
of the line as shown.

Make 4   Make 4   Make 4

Figure 3
Cut on the drawn line;
open each unit to reveal
triangle/square units as shown.

Step 8. Join one of
each color version of
the triangle/square
units with an F square
to complete one roof
row as shown in Figure 4.

B   F

Figure 4
Join 1 of each color version of
the triangle/square units with an
F square to complete 1 roof row.

Step 9. Sew C to each long side of H; add C to the
top to make a door unit as shown in Figure 5.

Step 10. Sew E to one short side of G; add D to
opposite long sides and to the top to complete one
window unit as shown in Figure 6.

Figure 5
Sew C to each side of H; add C to the top to make a door unit.

Figure 6
Sew E to 1 short side of G and add D to opposite long sides and D to the top to complete 1 window unit.

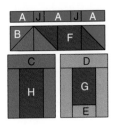

Figure 7
Join the units as shown to complete 1 Cabin block.

Step 11. Join the chimney, roof, door and window units as shown in Figure 7 to complete one Cabin block; repeat for four blocks.

Tree Blocks

Step 1. Cut four 2 1/2" x 2 1/2" squares darkest brown print for F.

Step 2. Cut the following from blue mottled fabric: twelve 2 7/8" x 2 7/8" squares for B; eight 2 1/2" x 2 1/2" squares for F; eight 2 1/2" x 3 1/2" rectangles for G; and eight 1 1/2" x 2 1/2" rectangles for K.

Step 3. Cut the following from green print: twelve 2 7/8" x 2 7/8" squares for B and twelve 2 1/2" x 2 1/2" squares for F.

Step 4. Create 24 triangle/square units using blue mottled and green print B squares as in Step 7 for

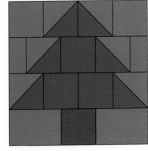

Tree
8" x 8" Block

Cabin blocks. You will need six blue/green B triangle/square units for one block.

Step 5. Join two blue mottled F squares with two B units to make the treetop row as shown in Figure 8.

Step 6. Join two K pieces with one green print F square and two B units to make the tree center row as shown in Figure 9.

Step 7. Join two B units with two green print F squares to make the tree bottom row as shown in Figure 10.

Step 8. Join two G pieces with the darkest brown print

Figure 8
Join F and B units to complete treetop row.

Figure 9
Join F, B and K to make tree center row.

Figure 10
Join F and B units to make tree bottom row.

Figure 11
Join G with F to make tree trunk row.

F to complete the tree trunk row as shown in Figure 11.

Step 9. Join the rows to complete one Tree block as shown in Figure 12; repeat for four Tree blocks.

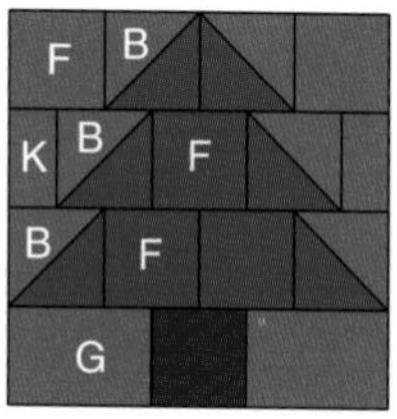

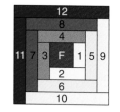

Figure 12
Join rows to complete
1 Tree block.

Log Cabin Blocks

Step 1. Cut eight 1 1/2"-wide rectangles of each length from fabrics as listed: cream—2 1/2" (1) and 3 1/2" (2); light brown—3 1/2" (3) and 4 1/2" (4); beige—4 1/2" (5) and 5 1/2" (6); medium brown—5 1/2" (7) and 6 1/2" (8); gold—6 1/2" (9) and 7 1/2" (10); and dark brown—7 1/2" (11) and 8 1/2" (12).

Step 2. Cut eight squares rust print 2 1/2" x 2 1/2" for block centers (F).

Step 3. Referring to Figure 13, sew pieces around center F square in numerical order, pressing seams toward newly added strip as you sew; repeat for eight blocks.

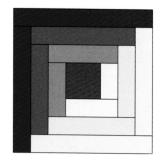

Log Cabin
8" x 8" Block

Figure 13
Sew pieces around center F
square in numerical order.

Completing Quilt

Step 1. Cut 24 strips green print 1 1/2" x 8 1/2" for sashing. Join blocks in rows with sashing strips referring to Figure 14. Press seams toward sashing strips.

Step 2. Cut nine 1 1/2" x 1 1/2" squares rust print for sashing squares. Join four sashing strips and three sashing squares to make a sashing row as shown in Figure 15; repeat for three sashing rows. Press seams toward sashing squares.

Step 3. Join the block rows with the sashing rows to complete the pieced center.

Step 4. Cut two strips each rust print 3 1/2" x 35 1/2" and 3 1/2" x 41 1/2". Sew the shorter strips to opposite sides of the pieced center and the longer strips to the top and bottom; press seams toward strips.

Step 5. Cut (and piece) two strips each gold print

2 1/2" x 41 1/2" and 2 1/2" x 45 1/2". Sew the shorter strips to the top and bottom and longer strips to opposite sides of the pieced center; press seams toward strips.

Step 6. Cut and piece two strips each darkest brown print 4 1/2" x 45 1/2" and 4 1/2" x 53 1/2". Sew the shorter strips to the top and bottom and longer strips to opposite sides of the pieced center; press seams toward strips.

Step 7. Prepare quilt top for quilting and finish referring to the General Instructions. **Note:** *The quilt shown was machine quilted in a meandering design using all-purpose thread to match fabrics.* ❖

Figure 14
Join blocks in rows with sashing strips.

1 1/2" x 8 1/2"   1 1/2" x 1 1/2"

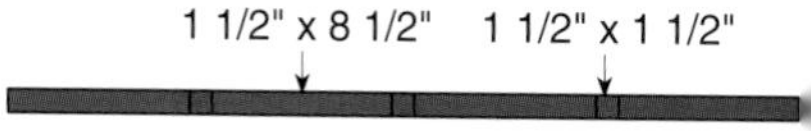

Figure 15
Join 4 sashing strips and 3 sashing
squares to make a sashing row.

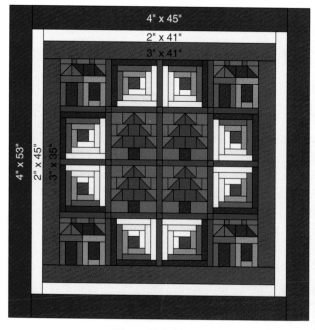

Warm Neighbors
Placement Diagram
53" x 53"

Log Cabin Tree Skirt

By Phyllis Dobbs

Half Log Cabin blocks make perfect triangle points for a decorative holiday tree skirt.

Project Specifications

Skill Level: Intermediate

Project Size: Approximately 43 1/2" diameter

Block Size: 9" x 9" x 12 3/4"

Number of Blocks: 8

Materials

- 1/8 yard medium green print (1)
- 1/8 yard red plaid (2)
- 1/8 yard red-and-green print (3)
- 1/8 yard dark green print (4)
- 1/4 yard red-on-red print (A)
- 1 yard beige mottled
- Backing 48" x 48"
- Batting 48" x 48"
- 5 1/2 yards self-made or purchased bias binding
- Neutral color all-purpose thread
- Basic sewing tools and supplies

Instructions

Step 1. Prepare templates for A and B pieces using pattern pieces given. To make full-size B pieces, add 5" between marked lines on pattern and connect lines as shown in Figure 1. Cut as directed on each piece.

Log Cabin Tree Skirt
Placement Diagram
Approximately 43 1/2" Diameter

Step 2. Cut two strips medium green print 1 3/4" by fabric width. Sew one short side of each A triangle to the strip, leaving 1 1/2" between A pieces as shown in Figure 2.

Step 3. Press seam toward medium green print strips. Lay stitched strips on flat surface and using a ruler, trim ends of strip even with A to make an A/green unit; repeat for eight units.

Step 4. Cut two strips each 1 1/2" by fabric width of each of the remaining red and green prints. Sew the A unit to the strips in numerical order as given in the materials list, press and trim as in Step 3 to complete eight Half Log Cabin blocks as shown in Figure 3.

Step 5. Sew a completed block to the wide end of one

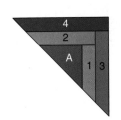

Figure 3
Sew the A unit to the strips
in numerical order as
shown; press and trim.

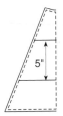

Figure 1
To make full-size B pieces,
add 5" between marked
lines on pattern and
connect lines.

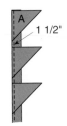

Figure 2
Sew 1 short side of each
A triangle to the strip, leaving
1 1/2" between A pieces as shown.

B piece as shown in Figure 4; repeat for eight units.

Step 6. Join the units, leaving one seam open to complete the tree skirt top as shown in Figure 5; press seams in one direction.

Step 7. Prepare top for quilting and finish referring to the General Instructions. ❖

Figure 4
Sew a completed
block to the wide end
of 1 B piece as shown.

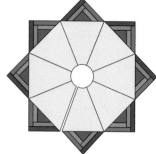

Figure 5
Join the units, leaving 1
seam open to complete the
tree skirt top as shown.

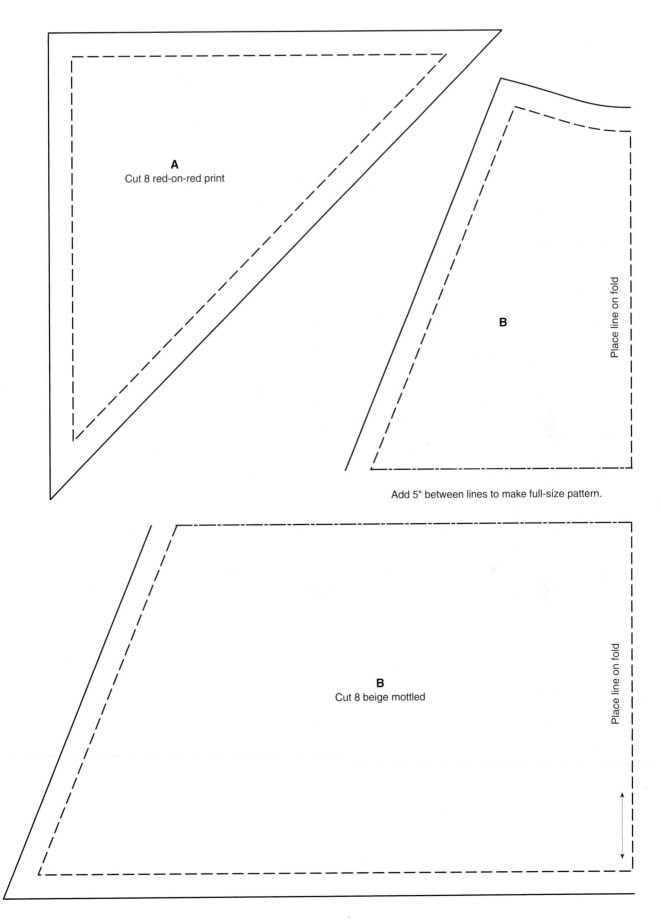

A
Cut 8 red-on-red print

B

Place line on fold

Add 5" between lines to make full-size pattern.

B
Cut 8 beige mottled

Place line on fold

Courthouse Rounds

By Sue Harvey

The traditional Courthouse Steps block takes on a contemporary look with careful placement of color.

Project Specifications

Skill Level: Beginner

Quilt Size: 85" x 92"

Block Size: 13" x 13"

Number of Blocks: 12

Materials

- 3/8 yard each blue, red, green and gold tonal prints
- 1/2 yard each blue, red, green and gold florals
- 2 yards cream print
- 5 yards black floral
- Batting 89" x 96"
- Backing 89" x 96"
- All-purpose thread to match fabrics
- Basic sewing tools and supplies, rotary cutter, mat and ruler

Instructions

Step 1. Cut two strips 3 1/2" by fabric width black floral; subcut into 3 1/2" square segments for A. You will need 18 A squares.

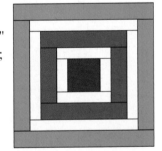

Courthouse Steps
13" x 13" Block

Step 2. Cut the following fabric-width strips cream print: two 3 1/2"—subcut into 1 1/2" segments for B; two 5 1/2"—subcut into 1 1/2" segments for C; one 8 1/2"—subcut into 1 1/2" segments for F; and one 10 1/2"—subcut into 1 1/2" segments for G.

Step 3. Cut two strips 2" by fabric width blue floral; subcut strips into six 5 1/2" segments for D and six 8 1/2" segments for E. Repeat with red, green and gold florals.

Step 4. Cut four strips 2" by fabric width blue tonal print; subcut strips into six 10 1/2" segments for H and six 13 1/2" segments for I. Repeat with red, green and gold tonal prints.

Step 5. To piece one Courthouse Steps block, sew B to opposite sides of A, and C to the remaining sides as shown in Figure 1.

Figure 1
Sew B to opposite sides of A; add C.

Figure 2
Add D and E, F and G, and H and I strips to complete 1 block.

Step 6. Continue to add D and E, F and G, and H and I strips as shown in Figure 2 to complete one block. **Note:** *Use same-color D and E and H and I strips. Repeat to make three blocks of each color.*

Step 7. Repeat step 5 to make six sashing squares.

Step 8. Cut three strips 13 1/2" by fabric width black floral; subcut into 5 1/2" segments to make sashing strips. You will need 17 sashing strips.

Step 9. Join three blocks with two sashing strips to make a block row as shown in Figure 3; repeat to make four block rows referring to the Placement Diagram for color placement.

5 1/2" x 13 1/2"

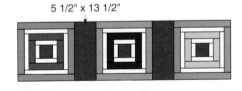

Figure 3
Join 3 blocks with 2 sashing strips to make a block row.

Step 10. Join two sashing squares with three sashing strips to make a sashing row as shown in Figure 4; repeat to make three sashing rows.

Step 11. Join the block rows with the sashing rows, beginning and ending with a block row and referring to the Placement Diagram for positioning of block rows.

5 1/2" x 13 1/2"

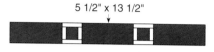

Figure 4
Join 2 sashing squares with 3 sashing
strips to make a sashing row.

Step 12. Cut and piece one strip each 5 1/2" x 59 1/2" and 7 1/2" x 59 1/2" and two strips 5 1/2" x 67 1/2" black floral.

Step 13. Sew the longer strips to opposite sides and the shorter strips to the top and bottom of the pieced center; press seams toward strips.

Step 14. Cut 14 strips 1 1/2" by fabric width cream print. Cut four strips 2" by fabric width each blue, red, green and gold florals.

Step 15. Join two strips each floral with seven cream print strips to make a strip set as shown in Figure 5; repeat for two strip sets.

6 1/2"

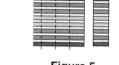

Figure 5
Join strips to make a strip set;
cut into 6 1/2" segments.

Step 16. Cut each strip set into 6 1/2" segments, again referring to Figure 5. You will need 11 strip segments.

Step 17. Cut two strips 6 1/2" by fabric width black floral; subcut strips into ten 3 1/2" segments for J and two 6 1/2" segments for K.

Step 18. Join four strip segments with four J pieces to make a strip as shown in Figure 6; repeat. Trim each strip on the strip segment end to measure 79 1/2" long as shown in Figure 7. Sew a strip to opposite long sides of the pieced center.

Figure 6
Join 4 strip segments with 4 J pieces to make a strip.

79 1/2"

Figure 7
Trim strip to measure 79 1/2".

Step 19. Join three strip segments with two J pieces to make a strip as shown in Figure 8. Trim 2" from each end to make a 59 1/2"-long strip.

Figure 8
Join 3 strip segments with
2 J pieces to make a strip.

Step 20. Sew a K square to each end of the pieced strip. Sew to the bottom of the pieced center. **Note:** *The 5 1/2" black floral border is the bottom edge.*

Step 21. Cut and piece three strips 7 1/2" x 85 1/2" black floral. Sew a strip to opposite long sides and the bottom of the pieced center; press seams toward strips.

Step 22. Prepare quilt top for quilting and quilt referring to the General Instructions. **Note:** *The sample shown was professionally machine-quilted in an allover meandering design.*

Step 23. Prepare 10 1/2 yards self-made black floral binding and bind edges referring to the General Instructions. ❖

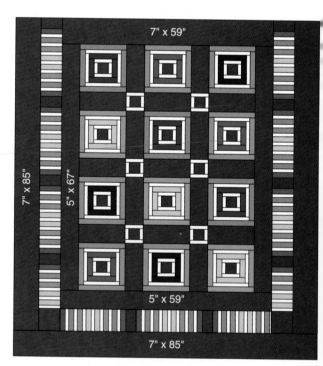

Courthouse Rounds
Placement Diagram
85" x 92"

Home Sweet Home

By Mary Ayres

A one-block project can be used as a pillow top, small wall quilt or a centerpiece for a small table.

Project Specifications

Skill Level: Intermediate
Project Size: 12" x 12"
Block Size: 8" x 8"
Number of Blocks: 1

Materials

- Scraps green and red textured fabrics
- Scraps 3 light, 3 dark and 3 medium plaid homespuns
- Scrap gold plaid homespun
- 1/8 yard blue textured fabric
- Backing 12 1/2" x 12 1/2"
- Batting 12 1/2" x 12 1/2"
- Neutral color all-purpose thread
- 1 1/2 yards black jumbo rickrack
- Black 6-strand embroidery floss
- 7/8" flat blue heart button
- Basic sewing tools and supplies and water-erasable marker or pencil

Home Sweet Home
Placement Diagram
12" x 12"

Instructions

Step 1. Cut one 2 1/2" x 3 1/2" rectangle red textured fabric for door.

Step 2. Cut all log strips for house 1 1/2" wide. Cut a 3 1/2"-long strip from dark plaid homespun; stitch to left side of door piece. Press seam toward door piece.

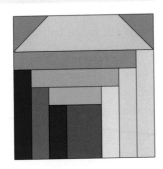

Log Cabin
8" x 8" Block

Step 3. Cut a 3 1/2" -long strip medium plaid homespun; sew to the top of the pieced section as shown in Figure 1. Press seam toward strip.

Step 4. Cut a 4 1/2"-long strip light plaid homespun; sew to the right side of the door piece. Press seam toward strips.

Step 5. Cut plaid homespun strips in lengths as follows for consecutive rows: 4 1/2" and 5 1/2" dark; 5 1/2" and 7 1/2" medium; and 5 1/2" and 6 1/2" light.

Step 6. Sew the strips to the left side, top and right side of the pieced segment referring to Figure 2 for size placement and order of stitching. Press all seams toward outside strip after each stitching.

Figure 1
Sew the 3 1/2"-long medium plaid homespun strip to the top of the pieced section.

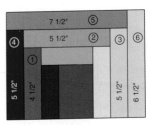

Figure 2
Sew strips to pieced section in order and lengths as shown.

Step 7. Cut one 2 1/2" x 8 1/2" rectangle gold plaid homespun for roof. Cut two 2 1/2" x 2 1/2" squares blue textured fabric. Place a square on each

end of the roof section; stitch on the diagonal of each square as shown in Figure 3; cut excess 1/4" beyond seam. Press remaining fabric up to make corner triangles.

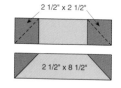

Figure 3
Place a square on each end of the roof section; stitch on the diagonal of each square as shown.

Step 8. Sew the roof section to the top of the pieced section to complete the Log Cabin block; press seam toward roof section.

Step 9. Cut one strip blue textured fabric 2 1/2" x 8 1/2" and two strips 2 1/2" x 10 1/2". Sew the shorter strip to the left side, one longer strip to the top and the remaining strip to the right side of the pieced block; press seams toward strips.

Step 10. Cut one strip green textured fabric 2 1/2" x 12 1/2" for grass; sew to the bottom of the pieced section to complete the pieced top.

Step 11. Center and transfer letters to green strip with top of letters 1/2" down from seam using a water-erasable marker or pencil. Embroider letters using 3 strands black embroidery floss and a stem stitch.

Step 12. Baste batting piece to the wrong side of the pieced top.

Step 13. Sew the black jumbo rickrack around the sides of the pieced top 1/4" from edge, beginning and ending in a bottom corner.

Step 14. Place the backing piece right sides together with the pieced top; sew together along stitching line for rickrack, leaving a 4" opening on the bottom. Turn right side out through opening; press. Hand-stitch opening closed. Quilt as desired by hand or machine.

Step 15. Sew heart button to the center of the door using 3 strands of black embroidery floss, stitching through all layers. ❖

Letters

Antique Log Cabin

Continued from page 33

Pink
11

Tan
10

Pink
9

Blue
8

Tan
7

Pink
6

D
Cut 4 muslin

Tan
5

Blue
4

Pink
3

Tan
2

Pink
1

Log Cabin Jacket

By Willow Ann Sirch

Blues, violets and purples give the traditional Log Cabin block a more contemporary appearance in this quilted jacket.

Project Notes

This project uses a commercial, collarless patchwork jacket pattern with two front pieces, two side pieces, two sleeve pieces and a single back piece with lining. This version is made without batting and is unquilted. The Log Cabin blocks for this jacket feature a tiny "picture" for the center of each block. You can get the same effect by selecting a fabric that features a repeating print 1-inch or smaller and cutting out each square so the picture is centered.

If you haven't tried paper piecing, this is a good project to start you off. Accuracy is important when creating paper-piecing patterns. You can photocopy the foundation papers for the Log Cabin blocks, but keep in mind that a photocopy machine may distort the image slightly. In addition, bond paper, like that used in photocopy machines, does not tear away as easily as tracing paper. For those reasons, it is recommended that you trace the Log Cabin patterns onto tracing paper or water-soluble paper specially designed for foundation piecing. Note that no seam allowances are given for the individual pieces in foundation work. You will need to cut fabric larger than the template "logs" in order to allow for this.

If you prefer to make the Log Cabin blocks freehand, that is, not using the paper-piecing technique, that is okay, too. Iron and measure the blocks when they are finished to be sure they are exactly the right size before proceeding with the project.

Project Specifications

Skill Level: Intermediate

Project Size: Size varies

Block Size: 7" x 7"

Number of Blocks: 10

Materials

- 1/4 yard "picture" print for center square
- 1/2 yard light purple/blue mottled
- 3/4 yard total dark prints
- 3/4 yard total light prints
- 1 yard purple/blue batik for jacket
- 2 1/2 yards lining fabric
- 5 yards self-made or purchased bias binding
- Neutral color all-purpose thread
- Basic sewing supplies and tools and tracing paper

Instructions

Step 1. Copy the Log Cabin paper-piecing pattern onto tracing paper to make 10 foundation papers. Number the sections on each foundation paper as on the pattern. The numbers indicate the order of sewing. The letters D and L indicate whether the log is dark or light print.

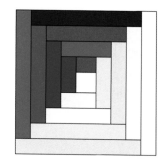

Log Cabin
7" x 7" Block

Step 2. Cut 10 center squares 1 1/2" x 1 1/2" from the "picture" print centering a motif in each square.

Step 3. Cut fifteen 1 1/2"-wide strips of dark prints and the same of light prints. Strips may be 18" or longer in length.

Step 4. Place piece 1 (the center square) right side up on the unmarked side of one foundation paper. Hold the foundation paper up to a light source to check that piece 1 covers the area marked 1 and includes a 1/4" seam allowance beyond the marked square all around as shown in Figure 1.

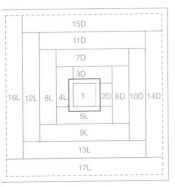

Figure 1
Be sure that piece 1 covers the area marked 1 and includes a 1/4" seam allowance beyond the marked square all around as shown.

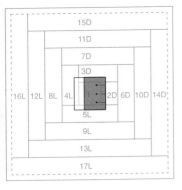

Figure 2
Pin piece 2 on piece 1 with right sides together as shown.

Step 5. Select a dark print strip. Cut a length from the strip that extends 1/4" beyond each end of the area marked 2D. Check that piece 2 covers the area marked 2D and includes at least 1/4" for seam allowance all around. Pin piece 2 on piece 1 with right sides together as shown in Figure 2.

Step 6. Flip the foundation paper so the marked side is up. Sew on the line between pieces 1 and 2 as shown in Figure 3. Fold piece 2 down, checking that it covers all of area 2 with seam allowance as shown in Figure 4; press. Trim excess seam allowance between the pieces to 1/4".

Step 7. Continue adding pieces to the paper foundation in numerical order to complete one Log Cabin

Figure 3
Sew on the line between pieces 1 and 2.

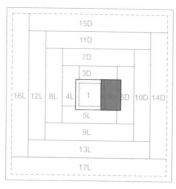

Figure 4
Fold piece 2 down, checking that it covers all of area 2 with seam allowance as shown.

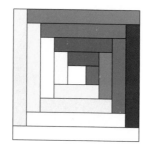

Figure 5
Continue adding pieces to the paper foundation in numerical order to complete 1 Log Cabin block as shown.

block as shown in Figure 5; press. Repeat to make 10 blocks.

Step 8. Join three blocks to make the right front panel as shown in Figure 6. Repeat to make the left front panel.

Step 9. Join four blocks to make the back panel as shown in Figure 7.

Step 10. Add pieces to the top, bottom and one side of each front panel to make suitable for cutting jacket front pattern pieces as shown in Figure 8. Repeat with back panel as shown in Figure 9.

Step 11. Construct jacket referring to commercial pattern instructions, binding edges with self-made or purchased binding. ❖

Figure 6
Join 3 blocks to make the front panels.

Figure 7
Join 4 blocks to make back panel as shown.

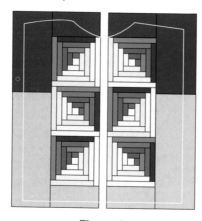

Figure 8
Add pieces to the top, bottom and 1 side of each front panel to make suitable for cutting jacket front pattern pieces.

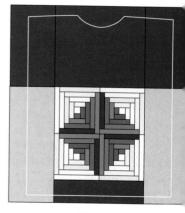

Figure 9
Add pieces to the top, bottom and side of back panel to make suitable for cutting jacket back pattern pieces.

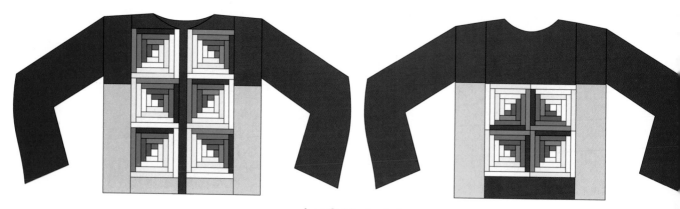

Log Cabin Jacket
Placement Diagram
Size Varies

15D

11D

7D

3D

14D | 10D | 6D | 2D | 1 | 4L | 8L | 12L | 16L

5L

9L

13L

17L

Basket Quilts

A tisket, a tasket,
A pretty quilted basket!

Antique Flower Basket

From the collection of Sue Harvey

This 19th-century quilt displays the quilting mastery of its early maker. The setting squares were quilted with a veritable sampler of patterns including feathered heart wreaths, pineapples and flowers. It is a lasting tribute to her love of quilting.

Project Specifications

Skill Level: Intermediate

Quilt Size: 73 3/4" x 87"

Block Size: 9 3/8" x 9 3/8"

Number of Blocks: 30

Materials

- 1/4 yard pink solid
- 1 yard green print
- 1 1/4 yards rose print
- 1 1/2 yards pink print
- 5 yards white solid
- Backing 78" x 91"
- Batting 78" x 91"
- 9 1/2 yards self-made or purchased white binding
- All-purpose thread to match fabrics
- White quilting thread
- Basic sewing tools and supplies

Antique Flower Basket
Placement Diagram
73 3/4" x 87"

Instructions

Step 1. Prepare templates for A and the appliqué pieces; cut as directed on patterns, adding a 1/8"–1/4" seam allowance all around each appliqué piece. Prepare flower and leaf pieces for appliqué referring to the General Instructions.

Flower Basket
9 3/8" x 9 3/8" Block

Step 2. Cut six strips pink print and nine strips rose print 2 3/4" by fabric width; subcut each strip into 2 3/4" square segments. Cut each square on one diagonal to make 180 pink and 270 rose B triangles.

Step 3. Cut four strips white solid 6 1/8" by fabric width; subcut into 2 3/8" segments for C. You will need 60 C rectangles.

Step 4. Cut two strips white solid 4 5/8" by fabric width; subcut into 4 5/8" square segments. Cut each square on one diagonal to make 30 D triangles.

Step 5. Cut three strips white solid 8 3/8" by fabric width; subcut into 8 3/8" square segments. Cut each square on one diagonal to make 30 E triangles.

Step 6. Cut five strips white solid 9 7/8" by fabric width; subcut into 9 7/8" square segments for F. You will need 20 F squares.

Step 7. Cut five squares 14 1/2" x 14 1/2" white solid; cut each square on both diagonals to make G triangles. You will need 18 G triangles.

Step 8. Cut two squares 7 1/2" x 7 1/2" white solid; cu

each square on one diagonal to make four H triangles.

Step 9. Cut 14 yards 3/4"-wide bias strips from green print; join strips on short ends to make a long strip. Fold under both long edges 1/4"; press to make 1/4" bias for handles and stems.

Step 10. Cut 30 pieces bias 10" long for handles, 30 pieces 2 1/2" long for center stems and 60 pieces 2" long for side stems.

Step 11. Sew a pink B to a rose B along the diagonal to make a B unit as shown in Figure 1; repeat for 150 B units.

Step 12. To piece one Flower Basket block, join two B units as shown in Figure 2; add a rose and a pink B triangle, again referring to Figure 2.

Step 13. Join two B units and add a rose B triangle as shown in Figure 3.

Figure 1
Sew a pink B
to a rose B.

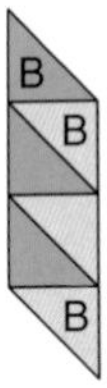

Figure 2
Join 2 B units;
add a rose and A
pink B triangle.

Figure 3
Join 2 B units;
add a rose B.

Step 14. Join a B unit with two rose B triangles as shown in Figure 4.

Step 15. Join the pieced units to complete the basket section as shown in Figure 5.

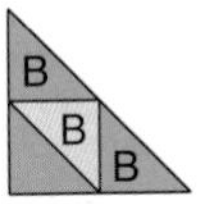

Figure 4
Join a B unit with
2 rose B triangles.

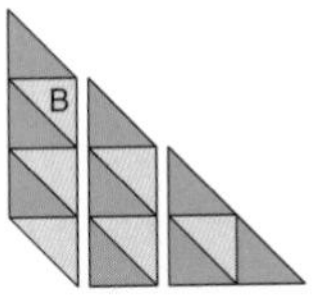

Figure 5
Join the pieced units to
complete the basket section.

Step 16. Sew C to opposite sides of the basket section as shown in Figure 6; set A into the C end and add D, again referring to Figure 6.

Step 17. Place a bias handle piece on E as shown in Figure 7; appliqué in place.

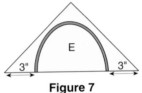

Figure 7
Place a bias handle on E.

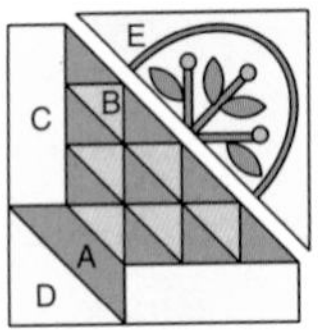

Step 18. Place a center stem and two side stems on E referring to the block drawing for positioning; appliqué in place. Add three flowers and four leaves. Repeat on all E pieces.

Step 19. Sew the appliquéd E pieces to the top edge of the basket section as shown in Figure 8 to complete 30 Flower Basket blocks.

Step 20. Join the blocks in diagonal rows with the F squares and G and H triangles as shown in Figure 9; join

Continued on page 79

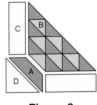

Figure 6
Add A, C and D pieces
to the basket section.

Figure 8
Complete 1 Flower Basket
block as shown.

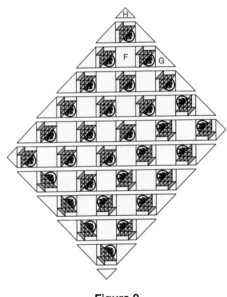

Figure 9
Join blocks, F squares and G
and H triangles in diagonal rows.

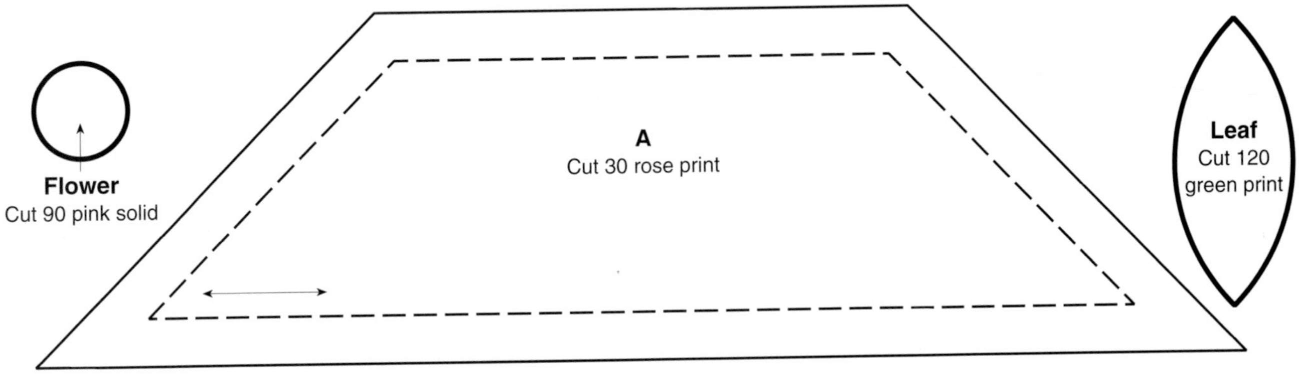

Flower
Cut 90 pink solid

A
Cut 30 rose print

Leaf
Cut 120
green print

Serendipity Table Runner

By Pearl Louise Krush

Three-dimensional flowers made from fabric yo-yos
fill the baskets on this colorful table runner.

Project Specifications

Skill Level: Intermediate

Runner Size: 40" x 16"

Block Size: 12" x 12"

Number of Blocks: 2 basket; 1 wreath

Materials

- 1 fat quarter each red, deep blue and medium blue prints
- 1 fat quarter each gold, green and bright blue mottleds
- 1/2 yard black print
- 2/3 yard cream print
- All-purpose thread to match fabrics
- Backing 44" x 20"
- Batting 44" x 20"
- Off-white machine-quilting thread
- Basic sewing tools and supplies

Instructions

Step 1. Cut a 12 1/2" by fabric width piece cream print. Subcut the strip into one 12 1/2" center square and two 6 1/2" x 12 1/2" A segments. Cut four each 3 1/2" x 4 1/2" B rectangles and 2 1/2" x 3 1/2" C rectangles and eight 2 1/2" x 2 1/2" D squares referring to Figure 1.

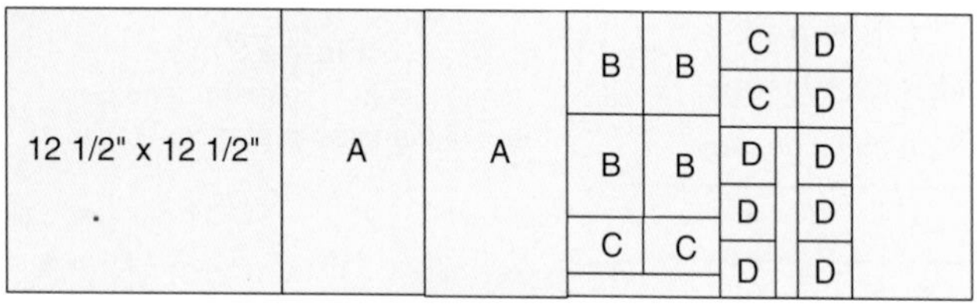

12 1/2" x 12 1/2"	A	A	B	B	C	D
					C	D
			B	B	D	D
					D	D
			C	C	D	D

Figure 1
Cut the 12 1/2" by fabric width strip cream print as shown.

Step 2. Cut two 1 1/4" x 16 1/2" bias strips for basket handles and two 2 1/2" x 6 1/2" E rectangles bright blue mottled.

Step 3. Cut four 2 1/2" x 6 1/2" F rectangles and four 2 1/2" x 2 1/2" G squares from medium blue print.

Wreath
12" x 12" Block

Serendipity Basket
12" x 12" Block

Step 4. Turn under 1/4" on each long side of each 1 1/4" x 16 1/2" bias strip; press.

Step 5. To piece one Serendipity Basket block, pin one end of one bias strip 1 1/4" in from each end of A for basket handle referring to Figure 2. Smooth and pin flat; handstitch in place.

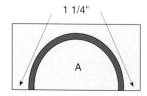

Figure 2
Pin 1 end of 1 bias strip 1 1/4" from each end of A for basket handle.

Step 6. Draw a diagonal line on the wrong side of each D and G square. Place a marked D square on one end of F as shown in Figure 3; stitch on marked line. Trim excess seam beyond stitching to 1/4" as shown in Figure 4; fold back D and press. Repeat on opposite corner to complete one D-F unit as shown in Figure 5; repeat for one D-E unit.

Figure 3
Place a marked D square on 1 end of F.

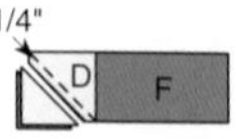

Figure 4
Trim excess seam beyond stitching to 1/4"; fold back D and press.

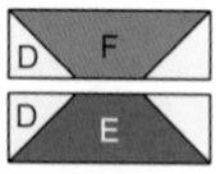

Figure 5
Complete 1 D-F and 1 D-E unit as shown.

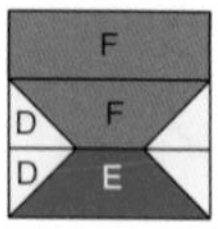

Figure 6
Join D-F and D-E; add F.

Step 7. Join the D-F and D-E units and add F as shown in Figure 6.

Step 8. Complete two C-G units as in Step 6 and

Figure 7
Complete 2 C-G units;
add B to the C side.

referring to Figure 7. Sew B to the C side of each unit, again referring to Figure 7.

Step 9. Sew a B-C unit to each side of the basket base as shown in Figure 8; sew to the appliquéd A piece to complete one block as shown in Figure 9. Repeat for two blocks; set aside.

Figure 8
Sew B-C to each side of the
basket base as shown.

Figure 9
Sew the basket base to the appliquéd
A piece to complete 1 block.

Step 10. Place a 9" dinner plate in the center of the 12 1/2" x 12 1/2" cream print square and trace to make a circle.

Step 11. Cut 2" x 2" squares for flowers as follows: 50 red print and 45 deep blue print. Prepare templates for yo-yo circles and leaf; cut as directed on each piece (adding a 1/8"–1/4" seam allowance to leaf shape for hand appliqué).

Step 12. To make a flower, fold each 2" x 2" square on the diagonal with wrong sides together; knot the end of a double strand of matching all-purpose thread. Stitch large gathering stitches from one raw edge end of each folded square to the other as shown in Figure 10.

Step 13. Pull the thread to gather the bottom as shown in Figure 11; continue stitching with the same thread on another folded square and pull to gather. Continue until there are five gathered petals on the same thread as shown in Figure 12; join the end petals to make a circle for

Figure 10
Stitch large gathering stitches
from 1 raw edge end of each
folded square to the other.

Figure 11
Pull the thread to
gather the bottom.

Figure 12
Continue until there are 5 gathered petals
on the same thread as shown; join the end
petals to make a circle for flower.

flower, again referring to Figure 12. Repeat for nine deep blue print and 10 red print petal flowers.

Step 14. Fold over the edge of each yo-yo circle 1/4" knot the end of a double strand of thread and baste around folded edge as shown in Figure 13. Pull thread at end to gather to make a yo-yo as shown in Figure 14; secure end of thread. Repeat for 19 small and 17 large yo-yos.

Figure 13
Baste around folded edge as shown

Figure 14
Pull thread at end to
gather to make a yo-yo.

Figure 15
Hand-stitch a cream
print yo-yo to the center
of each flower.

Step 15. Hand-stitch a cream print yo-yo to the center of each petal flower as shown in Figure 15.

Step 16. Turn under seam allowance on leaf shapes; baste in place. Arrange seven leaves, six red print flowers, three deep blue print flowers and nine gold mottled yo-yos around drawn line on the 12 1/2" x 12 1/2" cream print square referring to the block drawing for placement of pieces; hand-stitch in place using matching all-purpose thread.

Step 17. Arrange five leaves, two red print flowers, three deep blue print flowers and four gold mottled yo-yos on each basket block referring to the block drawing for placement of pieces; hand-stitch in place using matching all-purpose thread.

Step 18. Join the two Serendipity Basket blocks with the Wreath block to make runner center referring to Figure 16; press.

Step 19. Cut two strips 2 7/8" by fabric width each from cream and black prints; subcut each strip into

Figure 16
Join the 2 Serendipity
Basket blocks with the
Wreath block to make
runner center.

2 7/8" square segments. You will need 24 squares of each fabric.

Step 20. Draw a diagonal line on the wrong side of each cream print square. Place right sides together with each black print square; stitch 1/4" on each side of the drawn line as shown in Figure 17. Cut apart on drawn line and press open; repeat for 48 border units.

Figure 17
Stitch 1/4" on each side of the drawn line.

Step 21. Join 18 border units to make a side strip as shown in Figure 18; repeat for two side strips. Sew a strip to each long side of the pieced center; press seams toward strips.

Figure 18
Join 18 border units to make a side strip.

Step 22. Join six border units to make an end strip as shown in Figure 19; repeat for two end strips. Cut four 2 1/2" x 2 1/2" squares red print; sew a square to each end of each end strip. Sew the end strips to the short ends of the runner; press seams toward strips.

Figure 19
Join 6 border units to make an end strip.

Step 23. Prepare the finished top for quilting and quilt. Prepare 3 1/2 yards black print straight-grain binding and finish edges referring to the General Instructions. *Note: The project shown was machine-quilted with off-white machine-quilting thread in a meandering design* ❖

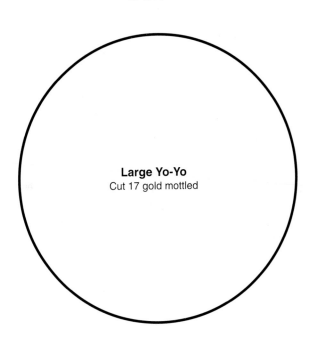

Serendipity Table Runner
Placement Diagram
40" x 16"

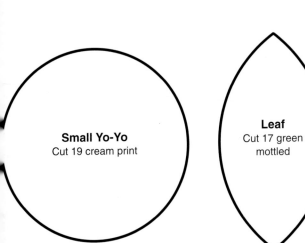

Small Yo-Yo
Cut 19 cream print

Leaf
Cut 17 green mottled

Large Yo-Yo
Cut 17 gold mottled

Grandma's Baskets Quilt

By Julie Weaver

It is hard to tell a vintage quilt made in the 1930s from a quilt made today using reproduction prints. If you like quilts from this time period, try this pretty basket pattern using your favorite fabrics.

Project Notes

Basket handles on the sample were made using bias strips and hand-appliquéd to the background. An alternative method would be to cut out and fuse each handle piece. Yardages are given for either method. Appliquéd shapes were fused and finished with a machine buttonhole stitch. If hand appliquéing, add a 1/4" seam allowance around each shape when cutting. Because the binding matches the sashing used in the quilt, yardages given include fabric for self-made binding.

Project Specifications

Skill Level: Intermediate

Quilt Size: 50" x 50"

Block Size: 8" x 8"

Number of Blocks: 16

Instructions

Step 1. Cut two 6 7/8" by fabric width strips cream-on-cream print; subcut into eight 6 7/8" square segments for A. Cut each A square in half on one diagonal to make 16 A triangles.

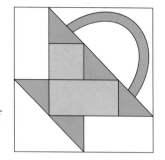

Grandma's Basket
8" x 8" Block

Step 2. Cut one 4 7/8" by fabric width strip cream-on-cream print; subcut into eight 4 7/8" squares for B. Cut each square in half on one diagonal to make 16 B triangles.

Step 3. Cut three 2 7/8" x 2 7/8" squares from each of the 16 different basket prints for C; cut each square in half on one diagonal to make six half-square triangles. Discard one.

Materials

- 1/8 yard 16 different 1930s prints for baskets and handles (fused) or 1/4 yard 16 different prints for baskets and handles (bias) including yellow and green prints
- 1/8 yard each 16 different 1930s prints for basket heart centers
- 1 1/4 yards green 1930s print for sashing and binding
- 2 yards cream-on-cream print for background, sashings and borders
- Backing 54" x 54"
- Batting 54" x 54"
- All-purpose thread to match fabrics
- Off-white machine-quilting thread
- 1/2 yard fusible transfer web (for machine appliqué)
- Basic sewing tools and supplies

Step 4. Cut four 2 1/2" by fabric width strips cream-on-cream print for F; subcut into thirty-two 4 1/2" rectangles for F.

Step 5. For bias handle, cut a 1 1/2" x 10" bias strip from each of the 16 different prints. Fold in half along length with right sides together; stitch. Turn right side out; press with seam centered on the backside. *Note: For fused handles, trace handle pattern on paper side of fusible transfer web; fuse to fabric. Cut out on traced line; remove paper backing.*

Step 6. Hand-stitch the bias handle 2 1/4" from straight-edge seam allowance on A as shown in Figure 1. *Note: For fusible handle, position handle on A referring to Figure 1 and fuse in place. Machine-appliqué in place using a narrow zigzag stitch with all-purpose thread to match fabrics.*

Step 7. Cut one 2 1/2" x 2 1/2" square for D and one 2 1/2" x 4 1/2" rectangle for E from each of the 16 different prints for the heart center.

Figure 1
Hand-stitch the bias handle 1/4" from straight-edge seam allowance on A as shown.

Step 8. To piece one block, sew C to one end of D, E and F pieces as shown in Figure 2. Join the pieced segments with A, B and the remaining C triangle, again referring to Figure 2 to complete one block; repeat for 16 different blocks.

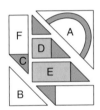

Figure 2
Piece 1 block as shown.

Step 9. Cut nine 1 1/2" by fabric width strips cream-on-cream print and 21 strips 1" by fabric width green sashing print. Sew a cream-on-cream print strip between two green print strips; press seams toward green print strips. Repeat for nine strip sets.

Step 10. Subcut strip sets into forty 8 1/2" sashing strips and twenty-five 1 1/2" G segments as shown in Figure 3.

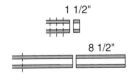

Figure 3
Subcut strip sets into 8 1/2" sashing strips and 1 1/2" G segments as shown.

Figure 4
Sew H to opposite sides of each G segment to make sashing squares.

Step 11. Subcut the remaining green print strips into 2 1/2" segments; you will need 50 segments for H.

Step 12. Sew H to opposite sides of each G segment to make sashing squares as shown in Figure 4; repeat for 25 sashing squares.

Step 13. Join four blocks and five sashing strips to make a block row referring to Figure 5; press seams toward sashing strips. Repeat for four block rows referring to the Placement Diagram for positioning of blocks.

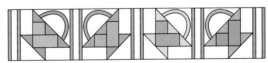

Figure 5
Join 4 blocks and 5 sashing strips to make a block row.

Figure 6
Join 4 sashing strips with 5 sashing squares to make a sashing row.

Step 14. Join four sashing strips with five sashing squares to make a sashing row referring to Figure 6; repeat for five sashing rows. Press seams toward sashing squares.

Step 15. Join the block rows with the sashing rows to complete the pieced center referring to the Placement

Diagram for positioning of rows; press seams toward sashing rows.

Step 16. Prepare templates for appliquéd flowers and leaves using patterns given. Prepare for fusible, machine appliqué referring to the General Instructions.

Step 17. Cut (and piece) two strips each cream-on-cream print 4 1/2" x 42 1/2" and 4 1/2" x 50 1/2". Sew the shorter strips to opposite sides and longer strips to the top and bottom of the pieced center. Press seams toward strips.

Step 18. Arrange one large and two small flower motifs on two opposite corners referring to the Placement Diagram for positioning. Machine-appliqué pieces in place referring to the General Instructions and using off-white machine-quilting thread and a machine buttonhole stitch.

Continued on page 69

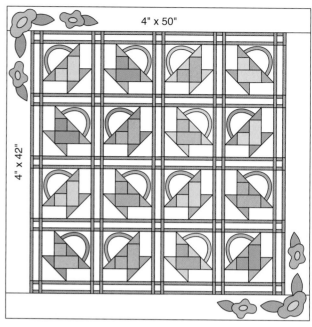

Grandma's Baskets Quilt
Placement Diagram
50" x 50"

Large Flower
Cut 2 different prints

Large Flower Center
Cut 2 yellow print

Handle
Cut 16 different basket prints

Large Leaf
Cut 4 green print

Garden Basket Wall Quilt

By Ruth Swasey

Scraps of bright colors make up the baskets and borders of this simple wall quilt.

Project Specifications

Skill Level: Intermediate

Quilt Size: 49 1/8" x 49 1/8"

Block Size: 5 3/8" x 5 3/8"

Number of Blocks: 13

Materials

- Scraps assorted pastel prints
- 1 fat quarter bright plaid
- 13 fat quarters bright prints
- 1/2 yard white-on-white print
- 1 1/4 yards pale green floral
- 1 1/4 yards white floral
- Backing 53" x 53"
- Batting 53" x 53"
- 6 yards self-made or purchased binding
- All-purpose thread to match fabrics
- Yellow machine-quilting thread
- Basic sewing tools and supplies

Instructions

Step 1. Prepare templates using patterns given; cut as directed on each piece for one block. Repeat for 13 blocks.

Step 2. To piece one block, sew B to two adjacent sides of C; sew A to the B sides of B-C unit to complete one triangle half of the block as shown in Figure 1.

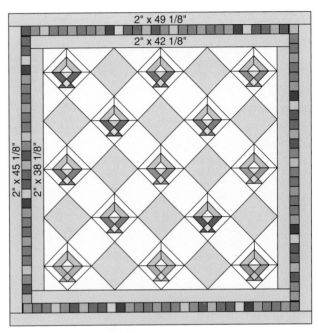

Garden Basket Wall Quilt
Placement Diagram
49 1/8" x 49 1/8"

Step 3. Sew E to C and ER to F; sew E-C to ER-F. Sew G to the straight end of D; repeat with DR and sew to the E-F-C unit as shown in Figure 2. Add H to complete the bottom half of the block.

Step 4. Join the pieced units as shown in Figure 3 to complete one block; repeat for 13 blocks.

Figure 3
Join the pieced units as shown to complete 1 block.

Step 5. Cut 16 squares white floral and 12 squares pale green floral 5 7/8" x 5 7/8". Cut four 9" x 9" squares white floral; cut each square in half on both diagonals to make 16 side J triangles. Cut two squares white floral 4 3/4" x 4 3/4"; cut each square in half on one diagonal to make four corner K triangles.

Step 6. Arrange the pieced blocks in diagonal rows with pale green and white floral squares, and J and K triangles referring to Figure 4; join in rows. Join rows to complete the pieced center; press seams in one direction.

Figure 1
Sew A to the B sides of B-C unit to complete 1 triangle half of the block.

Figure 2
Sew the D-G units to the E-F-C unit as shown; add H.

Step 7. Cut (and piece) two strips each 2 1/2" x 38 5/8" and 2 1/2" x 42 5/8" pale green floral.
Sew the shorter strips to opposite sides and the longer strips to the top and bottom of the pieced center; press seams toward strips.

Step 8. Cut one strip each 2" by fabric width from bright print and bright plaid fat quarters. Join strips along length in any order to form a strip set; cut strip set into 2" segments as shown in Figure 5.

Step 9. Join segments to make two strips each 42 5/8" and 45 5/8" as shown in Figure 6. *Note: Trim excess as necessary and use to piece remaining strips.*

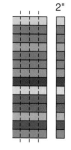

Figure 5
Cut strip set into
2" segments.

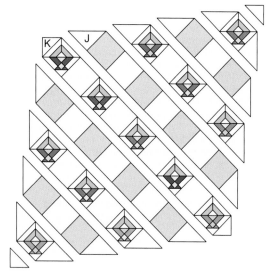

Figure 4
Arrange the pieced blocks in diagonal rows
with pale green and white floral squares and
J and K triangles; join in rows.

45 5/8"

Figure 6
Join segments to make border strips as shown.

Step 10. Sew the shorter pieced strips to opposite sides and the longer pieced strips to the top and bottom of the pieced center; press seams away from the pieced strips.

Step 11. Cut and piece two strips each pale green floral 2 1/2" x 45 5/8" and 2 1/2" x 49 5/8". Sew the shorter strips to opposite sides and the longer strips to the top and bottom of the pieced center; press seams toward strips.

Step 12. Prepare the finished top for quilting, quilt and bind edges with self-made or purchased binding referring to the General Instructions. *Note: The quilt shown was professionally machine-quilted with yellow machine-quilting thread in an allover design.* ❖

Garden Basket
Placement Diagram
5 3/8" x 5 3/8"

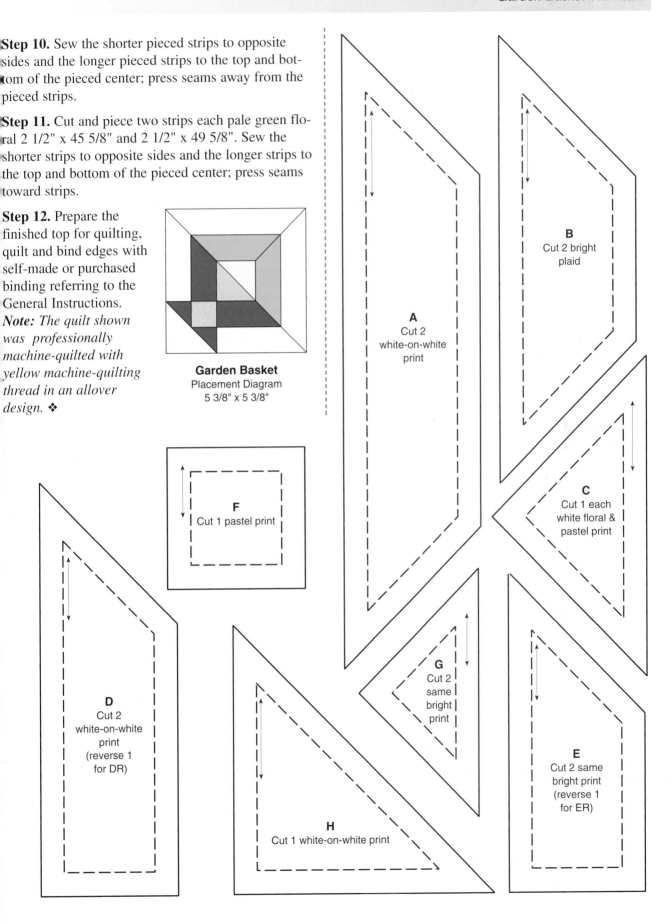

F
Cut 1 pastel print

B
Cut 2 bright plaid

A
Cut 2 white-on-white print

C
Cut 1 each white floral & pastel print

D
Cut 2 white-on-white print (reverse 1 for DR)

G
Cut 2 same bright print

E
Cut 2 same bright print (reverse 1 for ER)

H
Cut 1 white-on-white print

Cottage-Style Basket Pillows

By Jill Reber

Create a soft and subtle country-cottage look with this pair of basket-pattern pillows.

Project Specifications

Skill Level: Beginner

Pillow Size: 20" x 20", excluding trim

Block Size: 16" x 16"

Number of Blocks: 1 for each pillow

Materials

- 1/4 yard fabric 1
- 1/2 yard fabric 2
- 1/2 yard background fabric
- 1 yard border and backing fabric
- 1 1/2 yards lining fabric
- Two 20 1/2" x 20 1/2" squares batting (optional)
- All-purpose thread to match fabrics
- White quilting thread
- Two 20" x 20" pillow forms
- Two 20" zippers to match backing fabric
- 4 2/3 yards trim to coordinate with fabrics
- Basic sewing tools and supplies

Instructions

Step 1. Cut the following from background fabric: one 8 7/8" x 8 7/8" square—cut square on one diagonal to make A triangles; one 12 7/8" x 12 7/8" square—cut square on one diagonal to make B triangles; two 4 7/8" x 4 7/8" squares—cut each square on one diagonal to make C triangles; two 4 1/2" x 4 1/2" squares for D and four 4 1/2" x 8 1/2" rectangles for E.

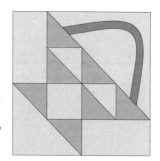

Flower Basket
16" x 16" Block

Step 2. Cut seven 4 7/8" x 4 7/8" squares from fabric 1; cut each square on one diagonal to make C triangles.

Step 3. Cut one 2 1/2" x 20" bias strip from fabric 2 for handle.

Step 4. To piece one block, join two background C triangles with three fabric 1 C triangles to make a row as shown in Figure 1.

Figure 1
Join 2 background C triangles with 3 fabric 1 C triangles to make a row.

Figure 2
Sew 2 fabric 1 C triangles to 2 adjacent sides of a D square.

Step 5. Sew two fabric 1 C triangles to two adjacent sides of a D square as shown in Figure 2.

Step 6. Sew the C-D unit to the C unit to complete basket base as shown in Figure 3.

Figure 3
Sew the C-D unit to the C unit to complete basket base as shown.

Figure 4
Sew a fabric 2 C to 1 end of E; repeat as shown.

Step 7. Sew a fabric 2 C to one end of E; repeat as shown in Figure 4; sew the C-E unit to the basket base unit and add A as shown in Figure 5.

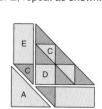

Figure 5
Sew the C-E units to the basket base unit and add A.

Step 8. Fold 3/4" in on each long edge of the bias strip; press. Measure in 3" from the seam allowance on the longest side of B as shown in Figure 6; pin ends of bias strip at that point. Ease a smooth shape for handle and hand-stitch in place.

Step 9. Sew B to the pieced unit to complete one block as shown in Figure 7.

Figure 6
Measure in 3" from the seam allowance on the longest side of B as shown.

Figure 7
Sew B to the pieced unit to complete 1 block.

Step 10. Cut two strips each 2 1/2" x 16 1/2" and 2 1/2" x 20 1/2" border fabric. Sew the shorter strips to opposite sides and longer strips to remaining sides of the pieced block to complete one pillow top; press seams toward strips. Repeat for second pillow top.

Step 11. If quilting pillow tops, cut two 20 1/2" x 20 1/2" lining and batting pieces.

Step 12. Sandwich one batting piece between one lining piece and one pillow top; pin or baste layers together to hold flat.

Step 13. Quilt as desired by hand or machine. When quilting is complete, trim edges even.

Step 14. Pin and stitch trim around all sides of each pillow top, overlapping and turning under beginning ends.

Step 15. Cut two pieces each backing fabric and lining 3 3/4" x 20 1/2" and 19 1/4" x 20 1/2". Pin a matching-size lining piece to the wrong side of each backing piece; machine-baste to hold layers together. Turn under one 20 1/2" edge of each layered piece 1"; press.

Step 16. Insert and stitch zipper between folded edges referring to zipper manufacturer's instructions and leaving a 1/2" overlap to cover zipper to complete pillow back; repeat for two pillow backs.

Step 17. Place an unzipped pillow back right

sides together with a pillow front; stitch all around. Turn right side out through zipper opening. Insert pillow form and zip closed to finish. Repeat for second pillow. ❖

Cottage-Style Basket Pillow
Placement Diagram
20" x 20" without trim

Welcome Basket

By Marian Shenk

*Fill your fabric basket with appliquéd flowers and hang
to welcome visitors to your home.*

Project Specifications
Skill Level: Intermediate
Project Size: Approximately 14" x 22 3/4"

Materials
- Scraps beige, brown, yellow and green prints or solids
- 12" x 12" square dark green print
- 1 strip orange solid 4" x 6"
- 1/2 yard white-on-cream print
- Backing 18" x 27"
- Batting 18" x 27"
- All-purpose thread to match fabrics
- White quilting thread
- 1/4 yard fusible transfer web
- 1/4 yard fabric stabilizer
- 2 packages 1/2"-wide dark brown bias tape
- 1 gold tassel
- Basic sewing tools and supplies

Instructions

Step 1. Cut a 14 5/8" x 18 1/2" rectangle white-on-cream print for top background.

Step 2. Cut an 18 1/2" length 1/2"-wide dark brown bias tape for handle; pin ends 2" from each outside edge on one 14 5/8" end of the background piece as shown in Figure 1. Smooth and hand-appliqué in place using matching all-purpose thread.

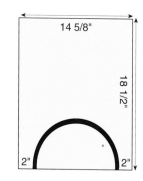

Figure 1
Place handle 2" in from each outside edge on one 14 5/8" end of the background piece.

Step 3. Prepare templates for letters and flower center using patterns given. Prepare pieces for fused, machine appliqué referring to the General Instructions and to patterns for color and number to cut. Set aside flower centers.

Step 4. Evenly space letters across the top half of the background piece 7" from top edge as shown in Figure 2. Fuse in place.

Step 5. Cut a piece of fabric stabilizer to fit behind the letters; pin in place. Using all-purpose thread to match the letters, stitch letters in place using a narrow

Figure 2
Evenly space letters across the top half of the background piece 7" from top edge.

machine zigzag stitch. When stitching is complete, remove fabric stabilizer.

Step 6. Prepare templates for remaining pieces using patterns given. Cut A–D as directed. Cut appliqué shapes as directed, adding a 1/8"–1/4" seam allowance to each shape when cutting for hand appliqué.

Step 7. To piece the bottom basket shape, join A squares in rows as shown in Figure 3. Add B triangles, again referring to Figure 3.

Figure 3
Join A squares in rows as shown;
add B triangles.

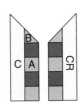

Figure 4
Sew C and CR to
the 4-unit rows.

Step 8. Sew C and CR to the four-unit rows as shown in Figure 4.

Step 9. Sew a brown D to a white-on-cream print D along the diagonal and sew to the end of one A-B-C unit. Join the pieced units as shown in Figure 5 to complete the basket base; press.

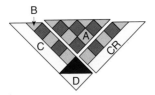

Figure 5
Join the pieced units as shown
to complete the basket base.

Step 10. Center stem for center flower on the bottom edge of the top background piece; hand-appliqué in place using all-purpose thread to match fabric. Arrange the center flower motif with leaves and the remaining two stems around center stem and hand-appliqué in place using matching all-purpose thread.

Step 11. Sew the basket base to the top background piece; press.

Step 12. Appliqué remaining two flower shapes and leaves to the top background, extending part of each flower onto the basket base referring to the Placement Diagram for positioning.

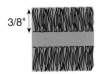

3/8"

Figure 6
Fray both long sides of
each strip about 3/8".

Figure 7
Gather and stitch in the
center of each flower.

Step 13. To make fringed flower centers, cut three 1" x 6" strips orange solid. Fray both long sides of each strip about 3/8" in as shown in Figure 6. Fold the fringed strip in half along length and run a basting stitch along the fold. Pull tight to form a circle. Place the circle in the center of each flower; stitch in place by hand or machine referring to Figure 7. Repeat for three flowers.

Step 14. Fuse the flower centers over the center of the fringed orange piece to cover gathering stitches. Machine-appliqué flower centers in place with matching all-purpose thread.

Step 15. Prepare the finished top for quilting, quilt and bind edges (except top edge) with 1/2"-wide dark brown bias tape referring to the General Instructions. *Note: The quilt shown was hand-quilted in the background using the quilting design given, around each appliqué shape and in the ditch of seams in basket base using white quilting thread.*

Step 16. Turn top edge under 1/4"; press and turn 2" to the backside; hand-stitch in place to form sleeve for hanging. Hand-stitch gold tassel to bottom point to finish. ❖

Stems
Cut 1 each green scrap

A
Cut 6 beige &
8 brown scraps

Welcome Basket
Placement Diagram
Approximately 14" x 22 3/4"

Letters
Cut 2 E's & 1 each remaining
letters dark green print

C
2 white-on-
cream print
(reverse 1 for
CR)

D
Cut 1 each brown scrap
& white-on-cream print

B
Cut 6 beige
scrap

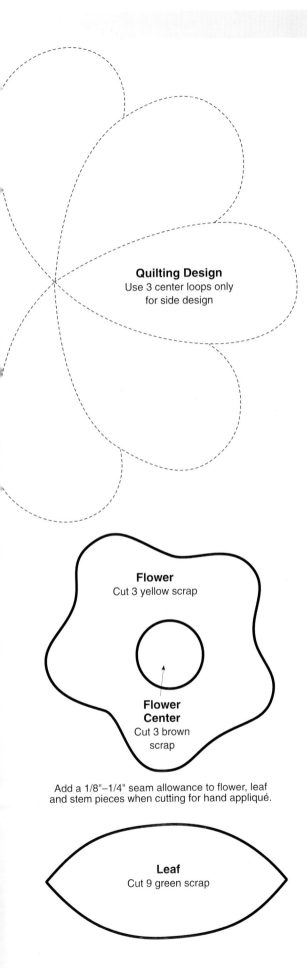

Quilting Design
Use 3 center loops only
for side design

Flower
Cut 3 yellow scrap

**Flower
Center**
Cut 3 brown
scrap

Add a 1/8"–1/4" seam allowance to flower, leaf
and stem pieces when cutting for hand appliqué.

Leaf
Cut 9 green scrap

Grandma's Baskets Quilt

Continued from page 60

Step 19. Sandwich batting between the pieced top and prepared backing piece; pin or baste layers together to hold flat.

Step 20. Quilt as desired by hand or machine. *Note: The quilt shown was machine-quilted in a meandering pattern using off-white machine-quilting thread.*

Step 21. Remove pins or basting; trim backing even with top.

Step 22. Prepare 6 yards self-made green 1930s print binding and bind edges referring to the General Instructions to finish. ❖

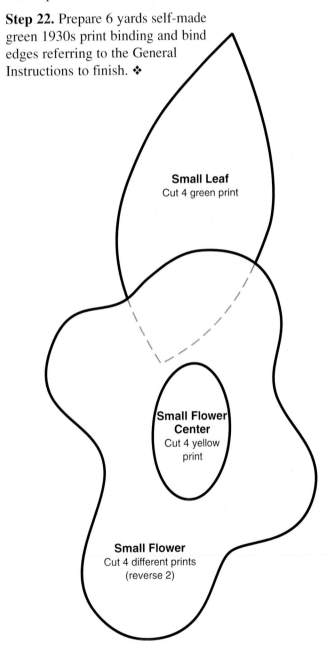

Small Leaf
Cut 4 green print

**Small Flower
Center**
Cut 4 yellow
print

Small Flower
Cut 4 different prints
(reverse 2)

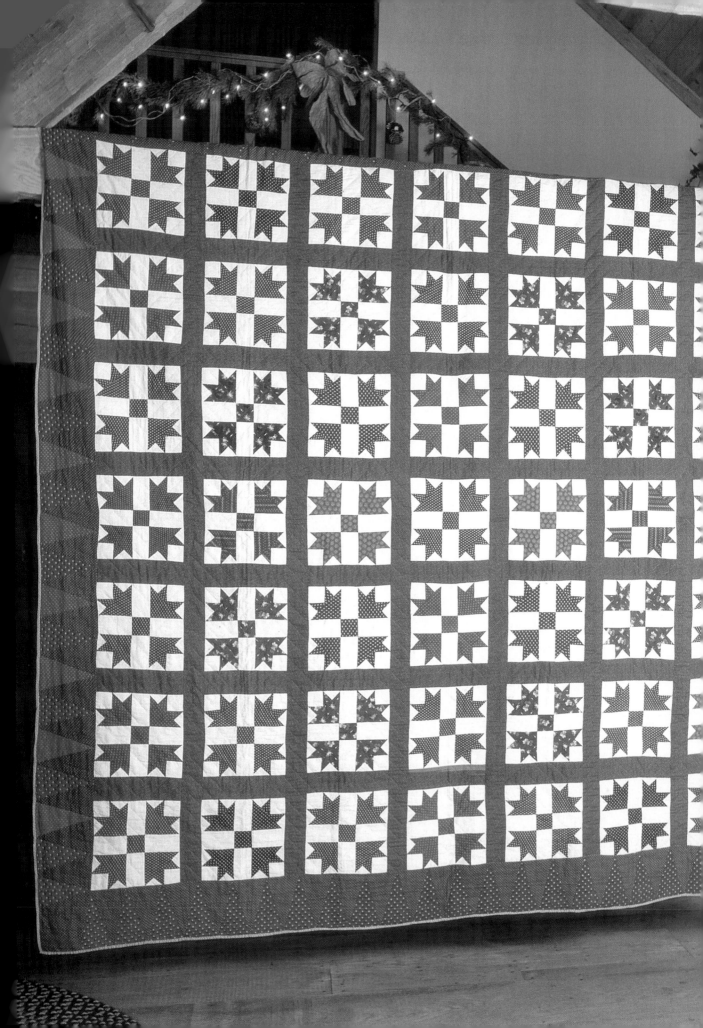

Nine-Patch Quilts

Sing a song of Nine-Patch,
A quilt to catch your eye!

Goose Tracks

From the collection of Sue Harvey

The Goose Tracks block was introduced by the Ladies Art Co. before 1895. The fabrics used in this quilt were very popular during that era and have been reproduced today. Use some of these to make your version of this antique beauty.

Project Specifications

Skill Level: Intermediate

Quilt Size: 98" x 98"

Block Size: 10" x 10"

Number of Blocks: 49

Materials

- 1 yard total brown prints for blocks
- 2 1/2 yards total green prints for blocks and border
- 3 yards total red prints for blocks and border
- 2 1/2 yards green print for sashing
- 3 1/2 yards muslin
- Backing 102" x 102"
- 11 1/4 yards self-made or purchased binding
- All-purpose thread to match fabrics
- White quilting thread
- Basic sewing tools and supplies

Instructions

Step 1. For each block, cut the following brown, green or red print: two squares 3 1/4" x 3 1/4"—cut on both diagonals to make print A triangles; one square 2 1/2" x 2 1/2" for B and two squares 4 7/8" x 4 7/8"—cut on one diagonal to make C triangles. Repeat for 12 brown, 12 green and 25 red blocks.

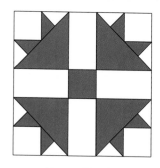

Goose Tracks
10" x 10" Block

Step 2. Cut eight strips muslin 3 1/4" by fabric width; subcut into 3 1/4" square segments. Cut each square on both diagonals to make 392 muslin A triangles.

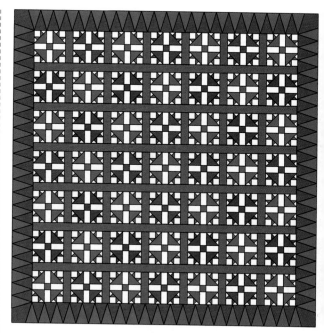

Goose Tracks
Placement Diagram
98" x 98"

Step 3. Cut 13 strips muslin 2 1/2" by fabric width; subcut into 196 muslin B squares 2 1/2" x 2 1/2".

Step 4. Cut 13 strips muslin 4 1/2" by fabric width; subcut into 196 D rectangles 2 1/2" x 4 1/2".

Step 5. To piece one block, sew a print A to a muslin A as shown in Figure 1; repeat for eight A units.

Step 6. Sew an A unit to adjacent sides of a muslin B as shown in Figure 2; add C. Repeat for four A-B-C units.

Step 7. Join two pieced units with D to make a row as shown in Figure 3; repeat.

Make 4   Make 4

Figure 1
Sew a print A to
a muslin A.

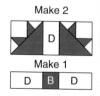

Figure 2
Sew an A unit to
adjacent sides
of B; add C.

Make 2

Make 1

Figure 3
Make block rows
as shown.

Step 8. Join two D rectangles with a print B square to make a row, again referring to Figure 3.

Step 9. Join the rows to complete one Goose Tracks block; repeat to make 12 brown, 12 green and 25 red blocks as shown in Figure 4.

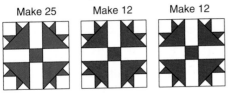

Figure 4
Make Goose Tracks blocks in colors as shown.

Step 10. Cut six strips 3" x 85 1/2" along length of green print for sashing to make sashing rows.

Step 11. Cut six strips 10 1/2" by remaining width green print for sashing; subcut each strip into 3" segments to make 42 sashing strips.

Step 12. Join blocks with sashing strips to make rows 1–4 as shown in Figure 5.

Step 13. Join block rows with sashing rows as shown in Figure 6 to complete the pieced center.

Step 14. Prepare templates for E and F pieces; cut as directed on each piece.

Row 1
Make 2

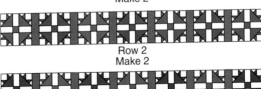

Row 2
Make 2

Row 3
Make 2

Row 4
Make 1

Figure 5
Join blocks with sashing strips to make rows as shown.

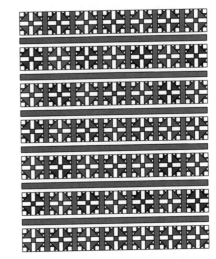

Figure 6
Join block rows with sashing rows.

E
Cut 84 green & 88 red prints

Figure 7
Join E pieces to make a border strip.

Step 15. Join 21 green and 22 red E pieces to make a border strip as shown in Figure 7; repeat for four border strips.

Step 16. Sew a border strip to each side of the pieced center, referring to the Placement Diagram for positioning of strips.

Step 17. Set an F piece into each corner to complete the pieced top.

Step 18. Place the pieced top on the prepared backing piece with wrong sides together; pin or baste to hold.

Step 19. Quilt as desired. ***Note:*** *The antique quilt shown was hand-quilted in the ditch of sashing seams and in diagonal lines through blocks with white quilting thread. There is no batting in the quilt.*

Step 20. Remove pins or basting; trim backing even with top. Bind edges of quilt to finish. ❖

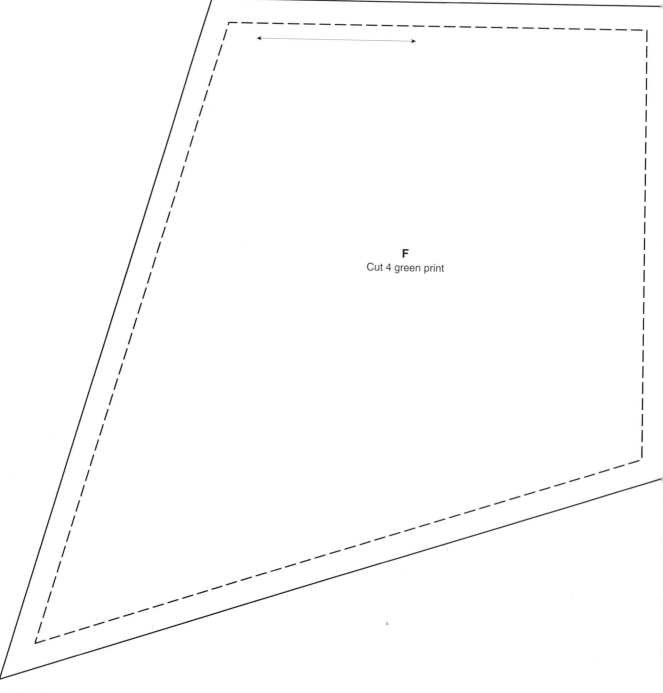

F
Cut 4 green print

Bunnies in the Clover

By Janice Loewenthal

These bunnies are hopping around the garden looking for their favorite snacks—carrots and clover.

Project Specifications

Skill Level: Beginner

Quilt Size: 44" x 44"

Block Size: 6" x 6"

Number of Blocks: 6 appliquéd and 36 pieced

Materials

- 1/4 yard green-and-white print
- 3/4 yard peach mottled
- 3/4 yard carrot print
- 1 1/4 yards green print
- 1 1/4 yards white-on-cream print
- Backing 48" x 48"
- Batting 48" x 48"
- All-purpose thread to match fabrics
- Green machine-embroidery thread
- Cream machine-quilting thread
- 1/2 yard fusible transfer web
- 1/2 yard fabric stabilizer
- Basic sewing tools and supplies

Bunnies in the Clover
Placement Diagram
44" x 44"

Green Nine-Patch
6" x 6" Block

Bunny
6" x 6" Block

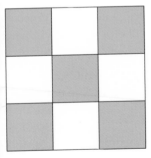

Peach Nine-Patch
6" x 6" Block

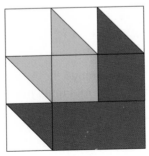

Flower Bud
6" x 6" Block

Instructions

Step 1. Cut six 6 1/2" x 6 1/2" squares white-on-cream print for appliqué background squares; fold and crease to mark center.

Step 2. Prepare template for bunny shape using pattern given. Prepare for fusible, machine appliqué referring to the General Instructions.

Step 3. Center a bunny shape on each background square. Machine-appliqué pieces in place referring to the General Instructions and using green machine-embroidery thread and a machine buttonhole stitch; set aside blocks.

Step 4. To make Nine-Patch blocks, cut three 2 1/2"

Step 8. Join two peach/cream/peach segments with one cream/peach/cream segment to make a Peach Nine-Patch block, again referring to Figure 2; repeat for eight blocks.

Step 9. Cut three strips white-on-cream and two strips each green print and peach mottled 2 7/8" by fabric width. Subcut each strip into 2 7/8" square segments. Cut each segment in half on one diagonal to make A triangles. You will need 40 A triangles each green print and peach mottled, and 80 white-on-cream print.

Make 40   Make 40

Figure 3
Sew a colored A to a
white-on-cream print A
to make A units.

by fabric width strips each green print and peach mottled and six strips 2 1/2" by fabric width white-on-cream print.

Step 5. Sew a white-on-cream print strip between two green print strips with right sides together along length; press seams toward darker fabric. Repeat with a white-on-cream print strip between two peach mottled strips, a green print strip between two white-on-cream print strips and a peach mottled strip between two white-on-cream print strips.

Step 6. Subcut each strip set into 2 1/2" segments as shown in Figure 1.

Step 7. Join two green/cream/green segments with one cream/green/cream segment to make a Green Nine-Patch block as shown in Figure 2; repeat for eight blocks.

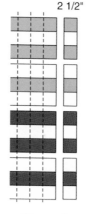

2 1/2"

Figure 1
Subcut each strip set
into 2 1/2" segments.

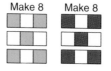

Make 8   Make 8

Figure 2
Join segments as shown to
make Nine-Patch blocks.

Step 10. Sew a colored A to a white-on-cream print A to make A units as shown in Figure 3.

Step 11. Cut two strips 2 1/2" by fabric width each white-on-cream print, green print and peach mottled; subcut strips into 2 1/2" square segments for B. You will need 20 B squares of each fabric.

Step 12. Cut two 4 1/2" by fabric width strips green print; subcut into 2 1/2" segments for C. You will need 20 C pieces.

Step 13. Arrange the A units with B and C as shown in Figure 4; join units in rows. Join rows to complete one Flower Bud block; repeat for 20 blocks. Press blocks with seams in one direction.

Figure 4
Complete 1 Flower Bud
block as shown.

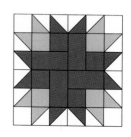

Figure 5
Join 4 Flower Bud
blocks as shown.

Step 14. Join four Flower Bud blocks as shown in Figure 5; press.

Step 15. Cut two strips each 3 1/2" x 12 1/2" and 3 1/2" x 18 1/2" carrot print. Sew the shorter strips to opposite sides and longer strips to the top and bottom of the pieced block unit to complete the quilt center unit.

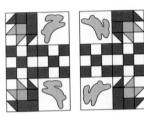

Figure 6
Join blocks to make 2 side units.

Step 16. Arrange two Bunny blocks with two Flower Bud and two Green Nine-Patch blocks as shown in Figure 6; join blocks in rows. Join the rows to complete a side unit; repeat for two side units.

Step 17. Sew a side unit to two opposite sides of the center unit as shown in Figure 7; press seams away from center unit.

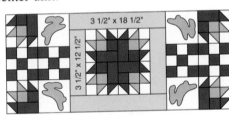

Figure 7
Sew a side unit to opposite sides of the center unit.

Step 18. Arrange blocks in rows as shown in Figure 8; join blocks in rows. Press seams in one direction.

Figure 8
Join blocks in rows.

Step 19. Join rows with the center unit to complete the pieced center referring to the

Placement Diagram for positioning of rows; press seams in one direction.

Step 20. Cut and piece four strips 1 1/2" x 48" green print. Fold each strip with wrong sides together along length; press.

Step 21. Cut and piece four strips carrot print 2 1/2" x 48". Place a folded green strip on each carrot print strip with raw edges aligned; baste 1/8" from edge. *Note: These strips do not add size to the completed top. They are added as a 3-D trim.*

Step 22. Center and sew a layered strip to each side of the pieced center; miter corner and trim excess. Press seams toward strips.

Step 23. Prepare the finished top for quilting and quilt referring to the General Instructions stopping quilting 1 1/4" from all outside edges. *Note: The quilt shown was machine-quilted in the ditch of seams with cream machine-quilting thread.*

Step 24. When quilting is complete, trim backing and batting 1 1/4" smaller than the quilt top all around. Turn under outside edge of each border strip 1/4" and press 1" to the backside of the quilt for binding. Hand- or machine-stitch in place on the backside to finish. ❖

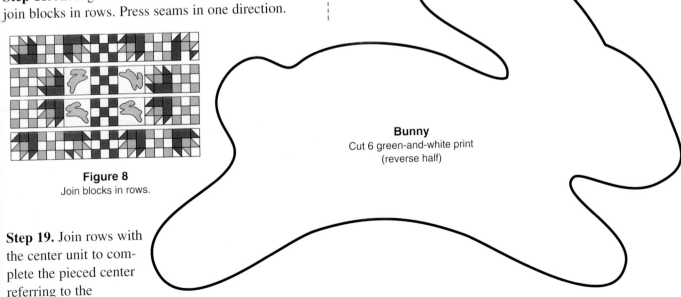

Bunny
Cut 6 green-and-white print
(reverse half)

Bear Pillow

By Mary Ayres

Cut a bear shape from a Nine-Patch block to create a simple pillow shape.

Project Specifications

Skill Level: Beginner

Pillow Size: 8" x 7 1/2"

Block Size: 9" x 9"

Number of Blocks: 1

Materials

- 1/8 yard white solid
- 1/4 yard blue print
- All-purpose thread to match fabrics
- 3/8 yard 1"-wide blue satin ribbon
- Polyester fiberfill
- Basic sewing tools and supplies

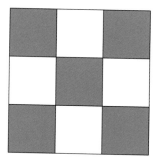

Nine-Patch
9" x 9" Block

Figure 1
Arrange the squares 3
across and 3 down,
alternating fabrics.

Instructions

Step 1. Cut five squares blue print and four squares white solid 3 1/2" x 3 1/2".

Step 2. Arrange the squares three across and three down, alternating fabrics referring to Figure 1. Join squares in rows; join rows and press to complete the block.

Step 3. Prepare template for bear pattern; cut as directed.

Step 4. Pin and sew bear front to bear back with right sides together, leaving a 3" opening on bottom center as marked on pattern. Clip curves; turn right side out through opening.

Step 5. Stuff polyester fiberfill through opening until bear shape is firm, distributing evenly inside bear; hand-stitch opening closed.

Step 6. Tie the 1"-wide blue satin ribbon in a bow; trim ends to a V shape as shown in Figure 2; securely hand-stitch to bear at X marked on pattern, sewing through to the backside of the bear, pulling tightly to indent bear at ribbon location to finish. ❖

Figure 2
Trim ribbon ends to a
V shape as shown.

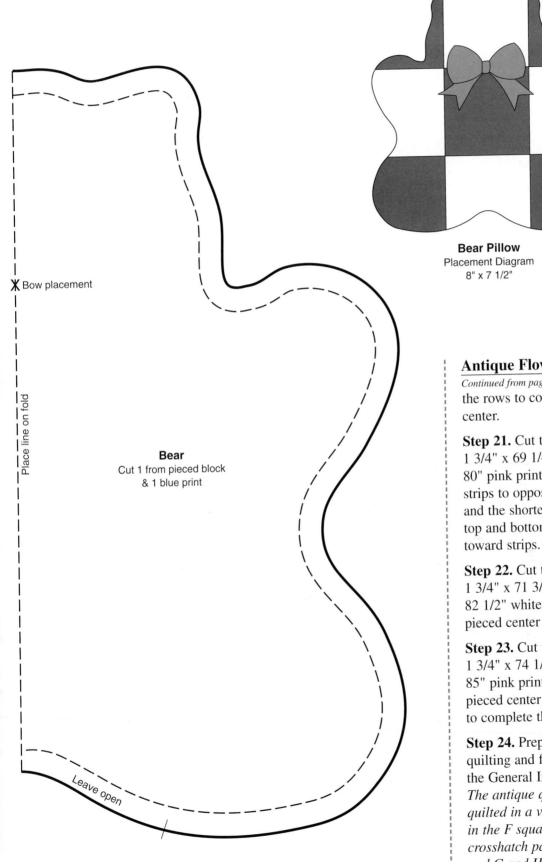

Bear Pillow
Placement Diagram
8" x 7 1/2"

✗ Bow placement

Place line on fold

Bear
Cut 1 from pieced block
& 1 blue print

Leave open

Antique Flower Basket

Continued from page 53

the rows to complete the pieced center.

Step 21. Cut two strips each 1 3/4" x 69 1/4" and 1 3/4" x 80" pink print. Sew the longer strips to opposite long sides and the shorter strips to the top and bottom; press seams toward strips.

Step 22. Cut two strips each 1 3/4" x 71 3/4" and 1 3/4" x 82 1/2" white solid. Add to the pieced center as in Step 21.

Step 23. Cut two strips each 1 3/4" x 74 1/4" and 1 3/4" x 85" pink print. Add to the pieced center as in Step 21 to complete the top.

Step 24. Prepare quilt top for quilting and finish referring to the General Instructions. *Note: The antique quilt was hand-quilted in a variety of designs in the F squares and in a 1/2" crosshatch pattern in the blocks and G and H triangles.* ❖

Spanish Tile

By Judith Sandstrom

Two simple blocks combine to make a pattern resembling a tile floor design.

Project Specifications

Skill Level: Beginner

Quilt Size: 78 3/4" x 101 1/4"

Block Size: 11 1/4" x 11 1/4"

Number of Blocks: 35

Materials

- 1 1/4 yards black print
- 1 1/2 yards tan print
- 1 1/2 yards multifloral print
- 1 3/4 yards cream-on-cream print
- 2 1/4 yards rust print
- 2 1/2 yards blue print
- Backing 83" x 105"
- Batting 83" x 105"
- All-purpose thread to match fabrics
- Cream quilting thread
- Basic sewing tools and supplies

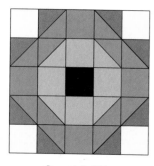

Spanish Tile
11 1/4" x 11 1/4" Block

4X Star
11 1/4" x 11 1/4" Block

Instructions

Step 1. Cut 12 cream-on-cream, 14 black and 13 each rust, blue and tan print strips 2 3/4" by fabric width; set aside seven cream-on-cream, eight black and eight each rust, blue and tan print strips. Subcut remaining strips into 2 3/4" square segments for A to make 68 each cream-on-cream, blue and tan, 72 rust and 89 black A squares.

Step 2. Cut six cream-on-cream, 11 rust, eight blue and three tan print strips 3 1/8" by fabric width. Subcut each strip into 3 1/8" square segments for B; cut each B square in half on one diagonal to make 144 cream-on-cream, 280 rust, 204 blue and 68 tan print B triangles.

Step 3. To make one 4X Star block, sew a 2 3/4"-wide cream-on-cream print strip between two same-size black print strips with right sides together along length; press seams toward black print strips. Repeat for three strip sets; subcut strip sets into 2 3/4" segments. You will need 44 segments.

Step 4. Sew a 2 3/4"-wide black print strip between two same-size cream-on-cream print strips with right sides together along length; press seams toward black print strips. Repeat for two strip sets; subcut strip sets into 2 3/4" segments. You will need 22 segments.

Step 5. Join one cream/black/cream segment with two black/cream/black segments to make a Nine-Patch unit as shown in Figure 1; repeat for 22 units. Set aside four Nine-Patch units for borders.

Figure 1
Join segments to
make a Nine-Patch
unit as shown.

Figure 2
Complete a
rust B unit
as shown.

Figure 3
Join 2 B units with
a rust print A
square to make an
A-B side unit.

Step 6. Sew a rust print B to a cream-on-cream print B along the diagonal to make a rust B unit as shown in Figure 2; repeat for 144 units.

Step 7. Join two B units with a rust print A square to make an A-B side unit as shown in Figure 3.

Step 8. Sew an A-B side unit to opposite sides of a Nine-Patch unit; press. Sew a black print A square to each end of two A-B side units and sew to the pieced Nine-Patch unit to complete one 4X Star block as shown in Figure 4; repeat for 18 blocks.

Figure 4
Complete 1 4X
Star block as shown.

Step 9. To complete Spanish Tile blocks, join one

black and two each tan and blue print A squares to make the center row referring to Figure 5; repeat for 17 units.

Figure 5
Join A squares to make the center row.

Figure 6
Complete tan and rust B units as shown.

Step 10. Sew a tan print B triangle to a blue print B triangle along the diagonal to make a tan B unit as shown in Figure 6; repeat for 68 units. Repeat with rust and blue print B triangles to make 136 rust B units.

Figure 7
Join A squares with 2 rust B units to make a rust A-B row.

Figure 8
Join 1 tan print A square with 2 tan and 2 rust A-B units to make a tan A-B row.

Step 11. Join one blue and two cream-on-cream print A squares with two rust B units to make a rust A-B row as shown in Figure 7; repeat for 34 rust A-B rows.

Step 12. Join one tan print A square with two tan and two rust A-B units to make a tan A-B row as shown in Figure 8; repeat for 34 tan A-B rows.

Step 13. Join one center row with two each tan and rust A-B rows to complete one Spanish Tile block as shown in Figure 9; repeat for 17 blocks.

Figure 9
Join 1 center row with 2 each tan and rust A-B rows to complete 1 Spanish Tile block.

Step 14. Join three 4X Star blocks with two Spanish Tile blocks to make a row as shown in Figure 10; repeat for four rows. Join three Spanish Tile blocks with two 4X Star blocks to make a row, again referring to Figure 10; repeat for three rows. Press seams in one direction.

Make 4

Make 3

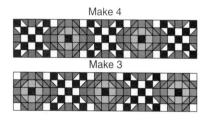

Figure 10
Join blocks to make rows as shown.

Step 15. Join the rows referring to the Placement Diagram to complete the pieced top; press seams in one direction.

Step 16. Using 2 3/4"-wide strips set aside in Step 1, sew a blue print strip to a tan print strip to a rust print strip with right sides together along length; press seams in one direction. Subcut strip set into 7 1/4" segments as shown in Figure 11; repeat for eight strip sets to make 40 segments for borders.

7 1/4"

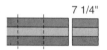

Figure 11
Subcut strip set into
7 1/4" segments.

Figure 12
Join 12 border segments to make a
side border strip as shown; remove
1 rust strip from each strip.

Step 17. Join 12 border segments to make a side border strip as shown in Figure 12; repeat for two border strips. Remove one rust strip from one end of each border strip and set aside.

Step 18. Cut and piece four strips each 2 3/4" x 79 1/4" multifloral print. Sew a strip to opposite long sides of each side border strip as shown in Figure 13; press seams toward multifloral print strips.

2 3/4" x 79 1/4"

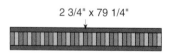

Figure 13
Sew a strip to opposite long
sides of the side border strip.

Step 19. Join eight border segments to make a top strip; repeat for a bottom strip. Sew one rust strip removed from the side border strips in Step 17 to one end of each strip.

Step 20. Cut eight 2 3/4" x 7 1/4" strips multifloral print; sew a strip to each end of the top and bottom strips; press.

Step 21. Sew a Nine-Patch unit to each end of each top and bottom strip as shown in

Figure 14
Sew a Nine-Patch unit to each
end of each top and bottom strip.

Figure 14; press. Sew the remaining 7 1/4" strips multifloral print to each end of each strip.

Step 22. Cut and piece four strips multifloral print 2 3/4" x 79 1/4". Sew a strip to opposite sides of the top and bottom strips; press seams toward strips.

Step 23. Sew a pieced-and-bordered strip to the top and bottom of the pieced center; press seams toward strips.

Step 24. Prepare the finished top for quilting and quilt referring to the General Instructions. *Note: The quilt shown was hand-quilted 1/4" from seams of some pieces and in diagonal lines through all black print squares using cream quilting thread.*

Step 25. When quilting is complete, prepare quilt for binding and finish edges with 10 1/2 yards self-made, blue print, straight-grain binding referring to the General Instructions. ❖

Spanish Tile
Placement Diagram
78 3/4" x 101 1/4"

Snowball Friends

By Pearl Louise Krush

Hand-appliqué a happy snowman shape to the center of the Snowball blocks and combine them with Nine-Patch blocks to make a neat wintertime wall quilt.

Project Specifications

Skill Level: Beginner

Quilt Size: 41" x 51"

Block Size: 9" x 9"

Number of Blocks: 6 pieced and 6 appliquéd

Materials

- 1/8 yard red dot
- 1/4 yard green plaid
- 1/4 yard white-on-white print
- 3/8 yard red plaid
- 1/2 yard each blue and green prints
- 1 yard blue dot
- 1 yard red-and-green print
- Backing 45" x 55"
- Batting 45" x 55"
- All-purpose thread to match fabrics
- Black and orange 6-strand embroidery floss
- Variety of 18 different buttons
- Basic sewing tools and supplies

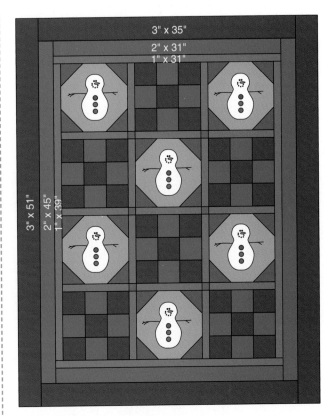

Snowball Friends
Placement Diagram
41" x 51"

Figure 1
Place a marked square
on each corner of a
blue dot square.

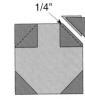

Figure 2
Stitch along the drawn line
on each small square; trim
excess beyond seam to
1/4" as shown.

Nine-Patch
9" x 9" Block

Snowball
9" x 9" Block

Instructions

Making Snowball Blocks

Step 1. Cut six 9 1/2" x 9 1/2" squares blue dot.

Step 2. Cut two 3 1/2" by fabric width strips green plaid; subcut strips into 3 1/2" squares. You will need 24 squares.

Step 3. Draw a diagonal line on each green plaid square. Place a marked square on each corner of a blue dot square as shown in Figure 1.

Step 4. Stitch along the drawn line on each small square; trim excess beyond seam to 1/4" as shown in Figure 2.

embroidery floss, buttonhole-stitc around each snowman shape, satin-stitch eyes, make French knots for mouth and outline-stitch around nose. Satin-stitch nose using 3 strands orange embroidery floss.

Step 9. Mark stick arms from snowman shape; stem-stitch on marked lines using 3 strands black embroidery floss. Set aside completed blocks.

Making Nine-Patch Blocks

Step 1. Cut three 3 1/2" by fabric width strips each red plaid and red-and-green print. Sew a red-and-green print strip between two red plaid strips with right sides together along length. Press seams toward red plaid strips.

Step 2. Sew a red plaid strip between two red-and-green print strips with right sides together along length. Press seams toward red plaid strip.

Step 3. Subcut strip sets into 3 1/2" square segments.

Step 4. Join two print/plaid/print segments with one plaid/print/plaid segment to complete one Nine-Patch block; repeat for six blocks.

Assembling Quilt

Step 1. Cut one strip 9 1/2" by fabric width blue print; subcut into 1 1/2" segments for sashing strips. You will need 17 sashing strips.

Step 2. Cut six 1 1/2" x 1 1/2" squares red dot for sashing squares.

Step 3. Join two Nine-Patch blocks with one Snowball block and two sashing strips to make a row as shown in Figure 4; repeat for two rows.

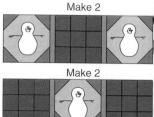

Figure 4
Join blocks with sashing strips to make rows as shown.

Step 5. Prepare template for snowman shape using pattern given, cut as directed, adding a 1/8"–1/4" seam allowance when cutting for hand appliqué. Transfer detail lines to fabric.

Step 6. Turn under seam allowance on snowman shapes; baste in place.

Step 7. Baste snowman shapes to the center of each pieced unit as shown in Figure 3.

Step 8. Using 3 strands black

Figure 3
Baste snowman shapes to the center of each pieced unit.

ress seams toward sashing strips.

Step 4. Join two Snowball blocks with one Nine-Patch block and two sashing strips to make a row, again referring to Figure 4; repeat for two rows. Press seams toward sashing strips.

Step 5. Join three sashing strips with two sashing squares to make a sashing row as shown in Figure 5; repeat for three sashing rows. Press seams toward sashing squares.

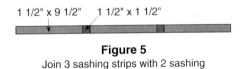

1 1/2" x 9 1/2"   1 1/2" x 1 1/2"

Figure 5
Join 3 sashing strips with 2 sashing
squares to make a row.

Step 6. Join the block rows with the sashing rows referring to the Placement Diagram for positioning of rows; press seams toward sashing rows.

Step 7. Cut two strips each 1 1/2" x 31 1/2" and 1 1/2" x 39 1/2" blue print.

Sew the longer strips to opposite long sides and shorter strips to the top and bottom; press seams toward strips.

Step 8. Cut (and piece) two strips each 2 1/2" x 31 1/2" and 2 1/2" x 45 1/2" green print. Sew the shorter strips to the top and bottom and longer strips to opposite long sides; press seams toward strips.

Step 9. Cut (and piece) two strips each 3 1/2" x 35 1/2" and 3 1/2" x 51 1/2" red-and-green print. Sew the shorter strips to the top and bottom and longer strips to opposite long sides; press seams toward strips.

Step 10. Prepare the finished top for quilting, quilt and bind edges with 5 1/4 yards self-made blue dot, straight-grain binding referring to the General Instructions. *Note: The quilt shown was machine-quilted with tan machine-quilting thread in a meandering pattern.*

Step 11. Hand-stitch three buttons on each snowman shape referring to the X's on the pattern for placement. ❖

X

X

Snowman
Cut 6 white-on-white print

X

Independence Square Picnic Quilt

By Holly Daniels

If you can't bear to cut up your favorite print, use it as the center of a picnic quilt and purchase coordinating fabrics for the blocks.

Project Specifications

Skill Level: Beginner

Quilt Size: 51" x 51"

Block Size: 9" x 9"

Number of Blocks: 16

Materials

- 1 yard red-white-and-blue print
- 1 yard blue print
- 1 1/8 yards gold-on-white print
- 1 1/4 yards red print
- Backing 55" x 55"
- Batting 55" x 55"
- All-purpose thread to match fabrics
- Clear nylon monofilament
- Basic sewing tools and supplies

Instructions

Step 1. Cut four gold-on-white and five red print 1 1/2" by fabric width strips. Sew strips with right sides together along length to make two A and one B strip sets as shown in Figure 1.

Independence Square
9" x 9" Block

Step 2. Subcut each strip set into 1 1/2" A and B segments, again referring to Figure 1. You will need 32 A segments and 16 B segments.

Figure 1
Subcut strip sets into 1 1/2" A and B segments.

Step 3. Join one B segment with two A segments to complete one Nine-Patch unit as shown in Figure 2; repeat for 16 Nine-Patch units. Press seams toward B segments.

Figure 2
Join A and B segments to complete 1 Nine-Patch unit as shown.

Figure 3
Subcut strip sets into 3 1/2" C segments.

Step 4. Cut six strips each red and blue prints and 16 gold-on-white print 1 1/2" by fabric width; set aside 10 gold-on-white print strips.

Step 5. Sew a gold-on-white print strip between a blue print and red print strip with right sides together along length to make a C strip set; press seams toward dark strips. Repeat for six C strip sets. Subcut strip sets into 3 1/2" C segments as shown in Figure 3; you will need 64 C segments.

Step 6. Cut four 2 1/2" by fabric width strips red print. Sew a strip to one of the reserved gold-on-white print strips from Step 4 with right sides together along length to make a D strip set; repeat for four D strip sets. Subcut strip sets into 2 1/2" D segments as shown in Figure 4; you will need 64 D segments.

Figure 4
Subcut strip sets into 3 1/2" D segments

Figure 5
Sew the D segments to the remaining 6 gold-on-white print strips.

Figure 6
Cut strip even with D units to complete E units.

Step 7. Sew the D segments to the remaining six gold-on-white print strips as shown in Figure 5; press seam away from D units. Cut strip even with D units to complete E units as shown in Figure 6. You will need 64 E units.

Step 8. Arrange Nine-Patch units with C and E units in rows referring to Figure 7; join units in rows.

Figure 7
Arrange Nine-Patch units with C and E units in rows and join to complete 1 block.

Join rows to complete one Independence Square block; repeat for 16 blocks. Press seams in one direction.

Step 9. Cut two strips blue print 9 1/2" by fabric width. Cut each strip into 1 1/2" segments to form 48 sashing strips.

Step 10. Cut two strips gold-on-white print 1 1/2" by fabric width. Cut each strip into 1 1/2" segments for 32 sashing squares.

Step 11. Cut a 29 1/2" x 29 1/2" square red-white-and-blue print for center square.

Step 12. Join three sashing strips with two sashing squares to make a short sashing row as shown in Figure 8; repeat for four

1 1/2" x 1 1/2"   1 1/2" x 9 1/2"

Figure 8
Join 3 sashing strips with 2 sashing squares to make a short sashing row.

sashing rows. Press seams toward sashing strips.

Step 13. Join two sashing strips with three blocks to make a short block row as shown in Figure 9; repeat for two blocks rows for sides. Press seams toward sashing strips.

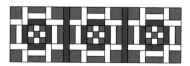

Figure 9
Join 2 sashing strips with 3 blocks
to make a short block row.

Step 14. Sew a short sashing row to opposite long sides of each short block row as shown in Figure 10; press seams toward sashing rows.

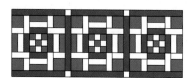

Figure 10
Sew a short sashing row to opposite
long sides of each short block row.

Step 15. Sew a short block/sashing row to two opposite sides of the center square; press seams toward square.

Step 16. Join five sashing strips with six sashing squares to make a long sashing row as shown in Figure 11; repeat for four sashing rows. Press seams toward sashing strips.

1 1/2" x 1 1/2"   1 1/2" x 9 1/2"

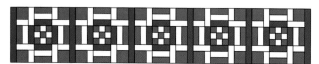

Figure 11
Join 5 sashing strips with 6 sashing squares to make a long sashing row.

Step 17. Join six sashing strips with five blocks to make a long block row as shown in Figure 12; repeat for two long block rows. Press seams toward sashing strips.

Figure 12
Join 6 sashing strips with 5 blocks to make a long block row.

Step 18. Sew a long sashing row to opposite long sides of each long block row as shown in Figure 13; press seams toward sashing rows.

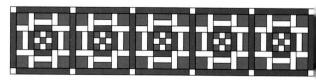

Figure 13
Sew a long sashing row to opposite long sides of each long block row.

Step 19. Sew the long block/sashing rows to the remaining sides of the center square; press seams toward square.

Step 20. Prepare the finished top for quilting and quilt referring to the General Instructions. *Note: The quilt shown was machine-quilted in the meandering design using clear nylon monofilament in the top of the machine and all-purpose thread in the bobbin.*

Step 21. When quilting is complete, prepare 6 1/4 yards red print, straight-grain binding and bind edges to finish referring to the General Instructions. ❖

Independence Square Picnic Quilt
Placement Diagram
51" x 51"

Chicken Place Mat & Runner

By Connie Kauffman

Hen, chicken and rooster motifs are popular decorative themes. Look for some prints using these designs to create this simple kitchen set.

Place Mat

Project Specifications

Skill Level: Beginner

Place Mat Size: 16" x 12"

Block Size: 3" x 3"

Number of Blocks: 4

Materials

Note: Fabrics given are for 1 place mat

- 1/8 yard cream chicken-wire print
- 1/8 yard tan basket-weave print
- 1/8 yard black solid
- 1/4 yard red chicken print
- Backing 16 1/2" x 12 1/2"
- Batting 16 1/2" x 12 1/2"
- All-purpose thread to match fabrics
- Basic sewing tools and supplies

Instructions

Step 1. Cut two strips each black solid and red chicken print 1 3/4" x 16". Cut one strip each black solid and tan basket-weave print 1" x 16".

Mini Chicken Wire Nine-Patch
3" x 3" Block

Step 2. Sew the 1"-wide strip black solid between two strips red chicken print; press seams toward black solid strip.

Step 3. Subcut strip into 1 3/4" segments; you will need eight segments.

Step 4. Sew the tan basket-weave print strip between two 1 3/4"-wide black solid strips; press seams toward black solid strips. Subcut into four 1" segments.

Step 5. Sew a 1" segment between two 1 3/4" segments to complete one block as shown in Figure 1; repeat for four blocks.

Step 6. Cut one 1" by fabric width strip black solid

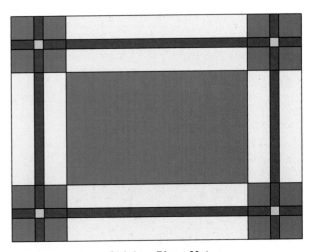

Chicken Place Mat
Placement Diagram
16" x 12"

1 3/4" 1" 1 3/4"

Figure 1
Sew a 1" segment between two 1 3/4" segments to complete 1 block.

6 1/2"   6 1/2"   10 1/2"   10 1/2"

Figure 2
Cut the strip into two 6 1/2" and two 10 1/2" segments.

and two 1 3/4" by fabric width strips cream chicken-wire print. Sew the black solid strip between the two cream chicken-wire print strips with right sides together along length; press seams away from center strip.

Step 7. Cut the strip into two 6 1/2" and two 10 1/2" segments as shown in Figure 2.

Step 8. Cut a 6 1/2" x 10 1/2" rectangle red chicken print; sew a 6 1/2" segment to the 6 1/2" sides of the rectangle. Press seams away from the rectangle. Sew a pieced block to each end of the two 10 1/2" segments and sew these to opposite long sides of the rectangle; press seams away from the rectangle.

Step 9. Pin the pieced top right sides together with the prepared backing piece; pin batting to the backing side. Stitch all around, leaving a 3" opening on one side; turn right side out through opening. Pull out corners and press.

Step 10. Machine-quilt in the ditch of seams using all-purpose thread to match fabrics to finish.

Table Runner

Project Specifications

Skill Level: Beginner

Place Mat Size: Approximately 30" x 10"

Block Size: 7" x 7"

Number of Blocks: 3

Materials

- 1/8 yard tan basket-weave print
- 1/4 yard cream chicken-wire print
- 1/4 yard black solid
- 1/8 yard red chicken print
- Backing 30 1/2" x 10 1/2"
- Batting 30 1/2" x 10 1/2"
- All-purpose thread to match fabrics
- Basic sewing tools and supplies

Instructions

Step 1. Cut one strip red chicken print 3 1/2" by fabric width; cut strip in half to make two shorter strips. Cut one strip black solid 1 1/2" x 21 1/4".

Step 2. Sew the black solid strip between the red chicken print strips with right sides together along length; press seams toward black solid strip. Subcut strip set into 3 1/2" segments; you will need six segments.

Step 3. Cut one strip tan basket-weave print 1 1/2" x 8" and two strips black solid 3 1/2" x 8". Sew the tan basket-weave print strip between the two black solid strips with right sides together along length; press seams toward black solid strips. Subcut strip set into three 1 1/2" segments.

Step 4. Join two 3 1/2"-wide segments with one 1 1/2"-wide segment to complete one block as shown

Chicken Wire Nine-Pat
7" x 7" Block

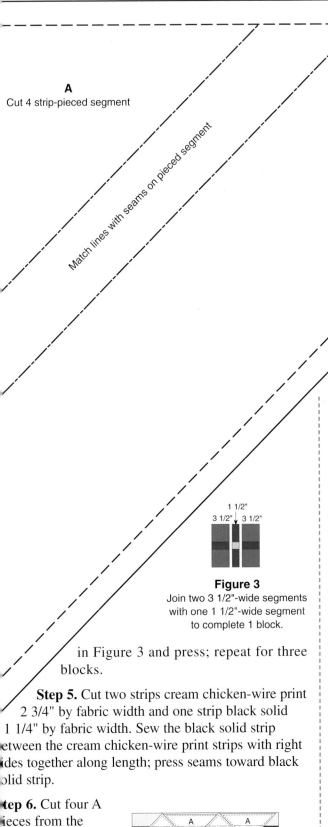

A
Cut 4 strip-pieced segment

Match lines with seams on pieced segment

Step 7. Join the A segments with the pieced blocks referring to Figure 5; press seams away from blocks. *Note: The black solid strips in the A segment should match with the black solid strips in the blocks.*

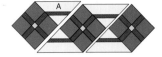

Figure 5
Join the A segments with the pieced blocks.

Step 8. Cut the backing and batting pieces to match the pieced top, using the pieced top as a pattern.

Step 9. Pin the pieced top right sides together with the prepared backing piece; pin batting to the backing side. Stitch all around, leaving a 3" opening on one side; turn right side out through opening. Pull out corners and press.

Step 10. Machine-quilt in the ditch of seams using all-purpose thread to match fabrics to finish. ❖

1 1/2"
3 1/2"   3 1/2"

Figure 3
Join two 3 1/2"-wide segments
with one 1 1/2"-wide segment
to complete 1 block.

in Figure 3 and press; repeat for three blocks.

Step 5. Cut two strips cream chicken-wire print 2 3/4" by fabric width and one strip black solid 1 1/4" by fabric width. Sew the black solid strip between the cream chicken-wire print strips with right sides together along length; press seams toward black solid strip.

Step 6. Cut four A pieces from the strip set, matching lines on A with seams on strip as shown in Figure 4.

A   A   A
A   A

Figure 4
Cut 4 A pieces from the strip set, matching
lines on A with seams on strip as shown.

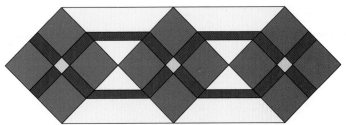

Chicken Runner
Placement Diagram
Approximately 30" x 10"

Wedding Ring Quilts

*With this ring
I thee wed.
A quilt stitched with love
to adorn your bed!*

**Antique Double
Wedding Ring**

❖

**Nine-Patch Wedding
Ring**

❖

Winter Wedding

❖

Wedding Ring Purse

❖

Circle of Love

Antique Double Wedding Ring

From the collection of Sandra L. Hatch

The melon shapes create large circles of color and give this wonderful old quilt from the 1930s a soft, appealing look.

Project Note

The quilt shown uses white background prints to match the solid colors used in the pieced units. For example, the pink solid units used a white-with-pink print. We refer to these prints as white prints to match the solids. Purchase 1/2 yard of each fabric, if using five different prints.

Project Specifications

Skill Level: Experienced

Quilt Size: Approximately 80" x 96"

Materials

- 3/4 yard each yellow, green, purple, pink and blue solids
- 2 1/2 yards total white prints to match solids
- 6 1/2 yards white solid
- Backing 85" x 101"
- Batting 85" x 101"
- 13 yards self-made or purchased pink bias binding
- All-purpose thread to match fabrics
- White hand-quilting thread
- Basic sewing tools and supplies

Instructions

Step 1. Prepare templates using pattern pieces given; cut as directed on each piece.

Step 2. Join seven pink solid and seven white print A pieces to make an A unit as shown in Figure 1;

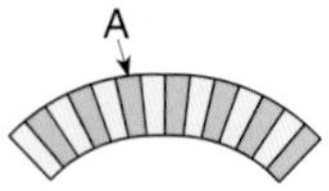

Figure 1
Join 7 pink solid and 7 white print A pieces to make an A unit.

Figure 2
Join 4 D segments to make a Four-Patch unit.

repeat for 18 pink, 17 yellow, 19 green and 22 each purple and blue A units.

Step 3. Join two each white print and white solid D squares to make a Four-Patch unit as shown in Figure 2; repeat for 98 Four-Patch units.

Step 4. Center and sew a pink A unit to one side of B as shown in Figure 3, clipping curves; press seam toward B.

Step 5. Sew a Four-Patch unit to each end of a purple A unit as shown in Figure 4.

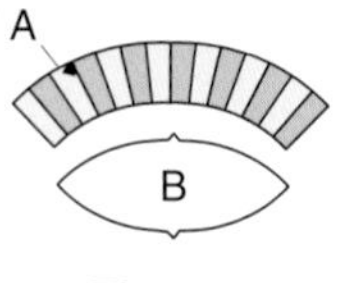

Figure 3
Center and sew a pink A unit to 1 side of B.

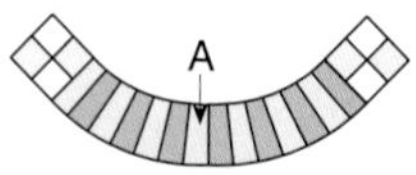

Figure 4
Sew a Four-Patch unit to each end of a purple A unit.

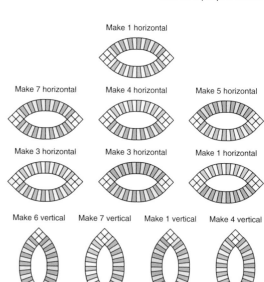

Make 1 horizontal

Make 7 horizontal   Make 4 horizontal   Make 5 horizontal

Make 3 horizontal   Make 3 horizontal   Make 1 horizontal

Make 6 vertical   Make 7 vertical   Make 1 vertical   Make 4 vertical

Make 1 vertical   Make 4 vertical   Make 2 vertical

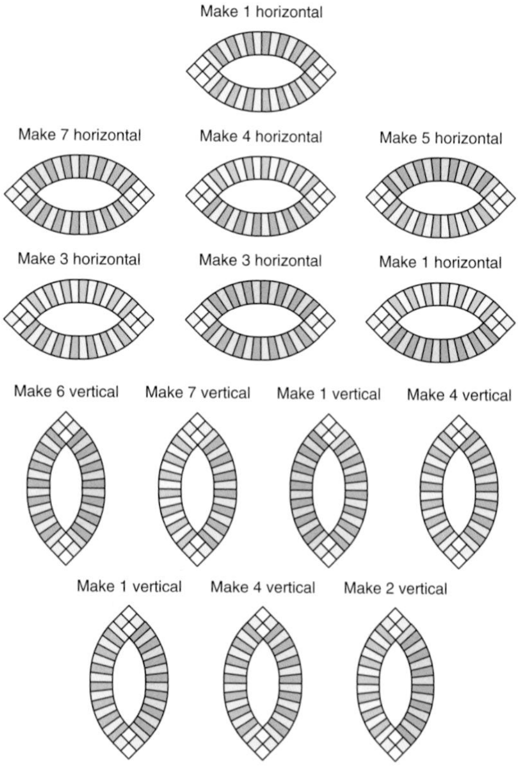

Figure 5
Make melon units as shown.

Step 6. Sew the Four-Patch/A unit to the remaining side of the A-B unit to complete one horizontal pink/purple melon unit as shown in Figure 5. Repeat to make 24 horizontal melon units and 25 vertical melon units, again referring to Figure 5 for placement of A unit colors and positioning of Four-Patch units.

Step 7. Join five vertical melon units with four C pieces referring to Figure 6 for color placement of melon units. Clip seam allowance curves as shown in Figure 7; repeat for five C rows.

Step 8. Arrange four horizontal melon units in a row referring to Figure 8 for color placement; repeat for six melon rows.

Step 9. Set the melon rows into the C rows beginning and ending with a melon row and referring to the Placement Diagram for positioning of rows.

Step 10. Set an E piece into the intersection of two melon units as shown in Figure 9; repeat with three E pieces each on the top and bottom and four E pieces each on opposite sides to complete the top.

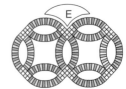

Figure 9
Set an E piece into the intersection of 2 melon units.

Step 11. Prepare quilt top for quilting and finish referring to the General Instructions. *Note: This quilt was hand-quilted in the center of each C piece using the quilting designs given, through the center of each A piece, in a 3/4" crosshatch pattern on B and E pieces and in the ditch of seams using white hand-quilting thread.* ❖

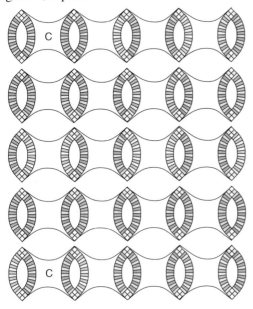

Figure 6
Join vertical melon units with 4 C pieces.

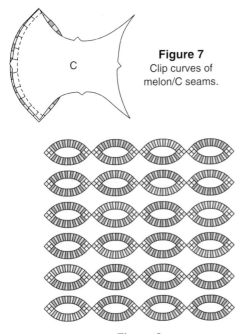

Figure 7
Clip curves of melon/C seams.

Figure 8
Arrange horizontal melon units in rows.

Antique Double Wedding Ring
Placement Diagram
Approximately 80" x 96"

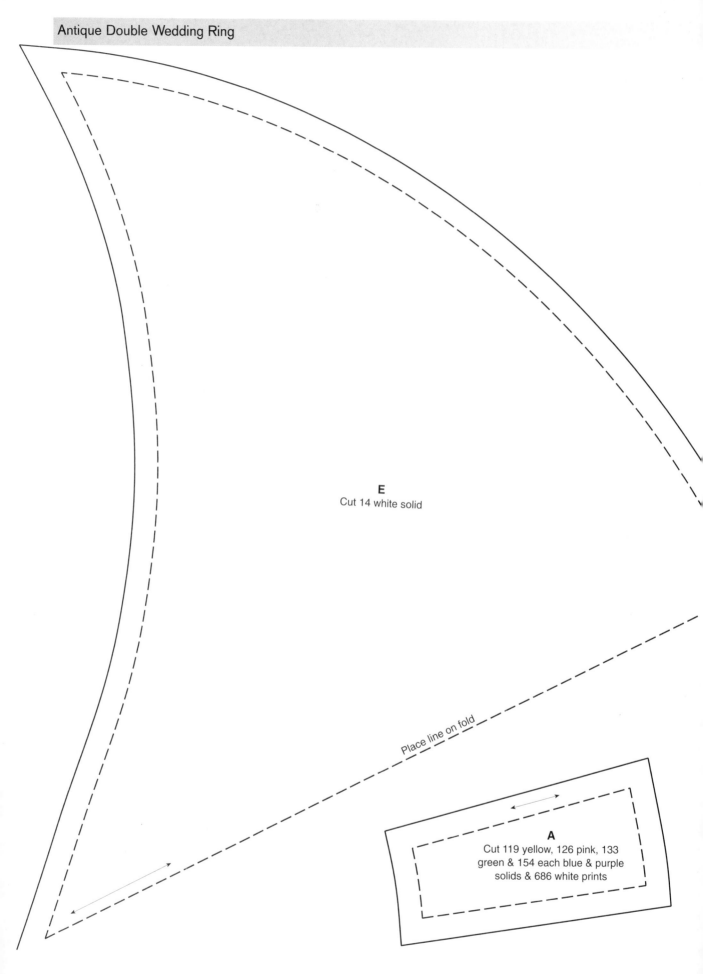

E
Cut 14 white solid

Place line on fold

A
Cut 119 yellow, 126 pink, 133
green & 154 each blue & purple
solids & 686 white prints

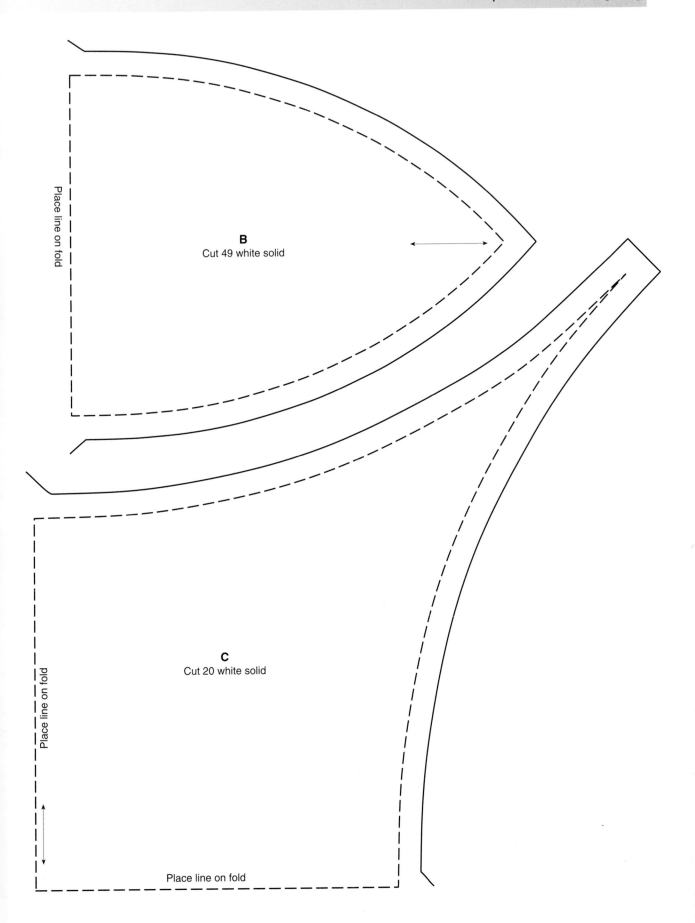

B
Cut 49 white solid

Place line on fold

C
Cut 20 white solid

Place line on fold

Place line on fold

Wreath Quilting Design

Bud Quilting Design

D
Cut 196 each white
prints & white solid

Nine-Patch Wedding Ring

By Judith Sandstrom

Combine scrap-pieced Nine-Patch blocks with Snowball blocks to create an unusual wedding ring design.

Project Specifications

Skill Level: Beginner

Quilt Size: 70" x 88"

Block Size: 9" x 9"

Number of Blocks: 31 Snowball;
  32 Nine-Patch

Materials

- 1/8 yard each 31 different prints
- 1 yard black print
- 2 1/2 yards cream-on-cream print
- Backing 74" x 92"
- Batting 74" x 92"
- 9 1/4 yards self-made or purchased binding
- All-purpose thread to match fabrics
- White hand-quilting thread
- Basic sewing tools and supplies

Nine-Patch Wedding Ring
Placement Diagram
70" x 88"

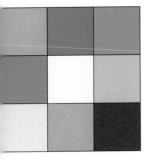

Nine-Patch
9" x 9" Block

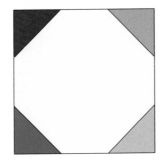

Snowball
9" x 9" Block

Cutting

Step 1. Cut eight strips 9 1/2" by fabric width cream-on-cream print; subcut into 9 1/2" squares. You will need 31 squares.

Step 2. Cut three strips 3 1/2" by fabric width cream-on-cream print.

Step 3. Cut one strip each 3 1/2" by fabric width of 24 different prints.

Step 4. Cut one 3 7/8" by fabric width strip from each of the remaining seven prints. Subcut each strip into 3 7/8" square segments. Cut each square in half on one diagonal to make triangles. You will need 124 triangles.

Step 5. Cut (and piece) two strips each 4" x 63 1/2" and 4" x 88 1/2" black print; set aside for borders.

Nine-Patch Blocks

Step 1. Randomly select three 3 1/2"-wide print strips; join the three strips with right sides together along length. Repeat for six strip sets; press seams in one direction. Subcut strip sets into 3 1/2" A units as shown in Figure 1.

Figure 1
Subcut strip sets
into 3 1/2" A units.

Step 2. Sew one 3 1/2"-wide cream-on-cream print strip between two different 3 1/2"-wide print strips with right sides together along length; repeat for three strip sets. Subcut strip sets into 3 1/2" B units as shown in Figure 2.

Figure 2
Subcut strip sets
into 3 1/2" B units.

Figure 3
Sew a B unit
between 2 A units
to complete 1
Nine-Patch block.

Step 3. Sew a B unit between two A units to complete one Nine-Patch block as shown in Figure 3; repeat for 32 blocks.

Snowball Blocks

Step 1. Select four different print triangles; pin a triangle to a 9 1/2" x 9 1/2" cream-on-cream print square 3 1/8" from the corners of the square; stitch 1/4" from edge of triangle as shown in Figure 4.

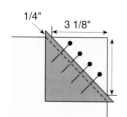

Figure 5
Sew triangles to remaining
corners to complete 1
Snowball block.

Figure 4
Pin a triangle
to a cream-on-cream print
square 3 1/8" from the corner
of the square; stitch 1/4" from
edge of triangle as shown.

Step 2. Repeat Step 1 on remaining corners to complete one Snowball block as shown in Figure 5; press seams toward triangles. *Note: You may trim the underneath layer to the seam allowance or leave it for extra stabilization of the block.* Repeat for 31 Snowball blocks.

Quilt Assembly

Step 1. Join four Nine-Patch blocks with three Snowball blocks to complete a row; repeat for five rows. Press seams in one direction.

Step 2. Join four Snowball blocks with three Nine-Patch blocks to complete a row; repeat for four rows. Press seams in one direction.

Step 3. Join the rows referring to the Placement Diagram for positioning; press seams in one direction.

Step 4. Sew the previously cut 4" x 63 1/2" black print border strips to the top and bottom of the pieced top; press seams toward strips. Sew the longer black print border strips to opposite sides; press seams toward strips.

Step 5. Prepare quilt top for quilting and finish referring to the General Instructions. *Note: This quilt was hand-quilted in the center of the Snowball block using the butterfly design, and 1/4" from seams, in the ditch of seams of the center square in each Nine-Patch block, in each cream-on-cream print piece in blocks and in the ditch of border strip seams using white hand-quilting thread.* ❖

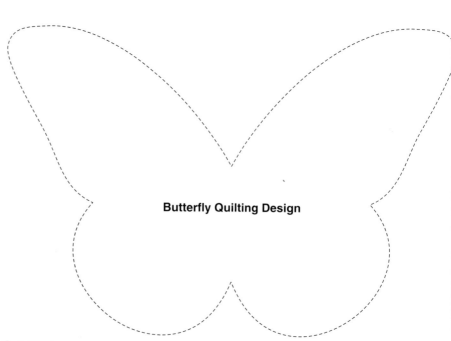

Butterfly Quilting Design

Winter Wedding

By Johanna Wilson

Blue batik appears like a snowy winter sky in this simple wall quilt.

Project Specifications

Skill Level: Beginner

Quilt Size: 35" x 35"

Block Size: 9" x 9"

Number of Blocks: 4

Materials

- 1/4 yard tan check
- 3/4 yard white-on-cream print
- 1 yard blue batik
- Backing 39" x 39"
- Batting 39" x 39"
- 4 1/3 yards self-made or purchased binding
- All-purpose thread to match fabrics
- Cream and blue machine-quilting thread
- Basic sewing tools and supplies

Instructions

Step 1. Cut twelve 3 1/2" x 9 1/2" rectangles for A and sixty-four 2" x 2" squares white-on-cream print for B.

Step 2. Cut twenty-nine 3 1/2" x 3 1/2" squares blue batik for C.

Step 3. Cut two strips each 2" by fabric width white-on-cream print and blue batik. Sew a white strip to a blue strip with right sides together along length; repeat. Press seams toward blue batik. Subcut strip sets into 3 1/2" segments for D units; you will need 16 D units.

Step 4. Draw a diagonal line on each B square; place a B square on C and stitch on marked line as shown in Figure 1; repeat on all four corners of B as shown in Figure 2. Trim seams to 1/4"; press seams away from C. Repeat for 16 B-C units.

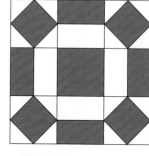

Single Wedding Ring
9" x 9" Block

Figure 1
Place a B square on C and stitch on marked line.

Figure 2
Sew B to each corner of C as shown. Trim and press to make B-C units.

Step 5. Arrange four B-C units with four D units and one C square in rows as shown in Figure 3; join units in rows. Join rows to complete one block; press. Repeat for four blocks.

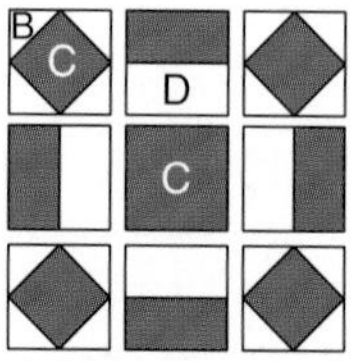

Figure 3
Arrange 4 B-C units with 4 D units and 1 C square in rows.

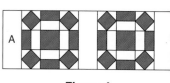

Figure 4
Join 2 blocks with 3 A rectangles to make a block row.

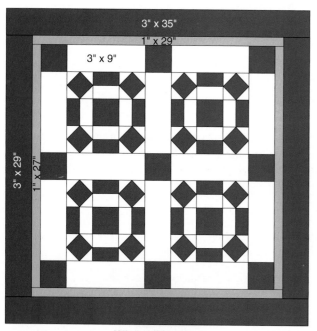

Winter Wedding
Placement Diagram
35" x 35"

Step 6. Join two blocks with three A rectangles to make a block row as shown in Figure 4; press seams toward A. Repeat for two rows.

Step 7. Join two A rectangles with three C squares to make a sashing row as shown in Figure 5; press seams toward C squares. Repeat for three sashing rows.

Step 8. Join sashing rows and block rows to complete the pieced center; press seams toward sashing rows.

Figure 5
Join 2 A rectangles with 3 C squares to make a sashing row.

Step 9. Cut two strips each 1 1/2" x 27 1/2" and 1 1/2" x 29 1/2" tan check;

sew the shorter strips to opposite sides and longer strips to the top and bottom of the pieced center. Press seams toward strips.

Step 10. Cut two strips each 3 1/2" x 29 1/2" and 3 1/2" x 35 1/2" blue batik; sew the shorter strips to opposite sides and longer strips to the top and bottom of the pieced center. Press seams toward strips.

Step 11. Prepare quilt top for quilting and finish referring to the General Instructions. *Note: This quilt was machine-quilted 1/4" from seams in each white-on-cream print piece in blocks, in a curved S design in the sashing strips and in the ditch of border seams using machine-quilting thread to match fabrics.* ❖

Wedding Ring Purse

By Holly Daniels

The wedding ring design is the perfect shape for a large fabric purse.

Project Specifications

Skill Level: Intermediate

Purse Size: Approximately 17" x 17" x 1 1/2"

Materials

- Scraps of a variety of green prints
- 3/8 yard cream-on-cream print
- 3/4 yard green mottled
- 3/4 yard lining fabric
- 2 squares batting 18" x 18"
- 1 strip each 2" x 42" and 1" x 42" thin batting
- All-purpose thread to match fabrics
- Cream machine-quilting thread
- 10" green zipper
- Basic sewing tools and supplies and machine zipper foot attachment

Instructions

Step 1. Prepare templates using pattern pieces given; cut as directed on each piece.

Step 2. Join four A pieces as shown in Figure 1; press seams in one direction. Repeat for seven A units.

Step 3. Sew B and BR to ends of each unit as shown in Figure 2.

Figure 1
Join 4 A pieces.

Figure 2
Sew B and BR to ends of each unit.

Figure 3
Sew C to opposite ends of 4 A-B units.

Step 4. Sew C to opposite ends of four A-B units as shown in Figure 3.

Step 5. Sew an A-B unit to one side and an A-B-C unit to the opposite side of D to complete one melon unit as shown in Figure 4. *Note: Center the units on D, matching notch to center A seam, and work from*

Figure 4
Sew an A-B unit to 1 side and an A-B-C unit to the opposite side of D.

the center to the outside when pinning. Clip curves on D when stitching is complete; press seams away from D. Repeat for three melon units.

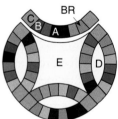

Figure 5
Sew the 3 melon units and the remaining A-B-C unit to E.

Step 6. Sew the three melon units and the remaining A-B-C unit to E as shown in Figure 5. *Note: Center the units on E and work from the center to the outside when pinning, again matching notches on E to center* *seam.* Clip curves on E when stitching is complete; press seams away from E.

Step 7. Place a batting square behind the completed ring unit; pin layers to hold. Quilt as desired by hand or machine. ***Note:*** *The sample shown was machine-quilted with cream machine-quilting thread in a 1/4" echo design on pieces D and E.*

Step 8. When quilting is complete, trim batting even with quilted front; remove pins.

Step 9. Cut two pieces lining fabric, one batting and one purse back piece from green mottled using quilted front piece as a pattern. Baste the purse back and batting pieces together; quilt as desired. Set aside lining pieces. ***Note:*** *The sample shown has no quilting on the purse back. If you prefer a two-sided purse, make a second ring unit as in Steps 1–8.*

Step 10. Cut one 2" x 42" strip each green mottled and lining fabric for side gusset. Baste the green mottled and 2" x 42" batting pieces together; quilt as desired. Set aside lining piece.

Step 11. Cut two strips green mottled 2" x 11 1/4". Baste the two strips with right sides together along length with a 1/2" seam allowance; press seam open. Place unopened zipper right sides against the seam line; baste to hold. Attach zipper foot to your machine; stitch along sides and across ends of zipper as shown in Figure 6; remove basting. Trim completed zipper placket to 2" wide with zipper centered.

Figure 6
Stitch along sides and across ends of zipper.

Step 12. Pin the zipper placket to the short curve of the purse front; stitch as shown in Figure 7. Align with purse back and stitch to connect front and back as shown in Figure 8.

Figure 7
Pin the zipper placket to the short curve of the purse front; stitch as shown.

Figure 9
Pin handle stops to upper sides of purse with top edges even with side gusset.

Figure 8
Align zipper placket with purse back and stitch to connect front and back.

Step 13. Center and pin the 2" x 42" quilted gusset strip right sides together with the purse front, starting at one top edge and ending on the opposite edge; stitch. Repeat with purse back. Sew the 2" ends of the zipper placket to the ends of the gusset piece; trim excess gusset.

Step 14. Join two F handle stop pieces with right sides together, leaving top edges open; repeat for two units. Turn right side out; press. Turn open edge under 1/4"; press to complete handle stops.

Step 15. Cut one 2 3/4" x 42" (or desired length) strip green mottled for handle. Press one long side of fabric strip under 1/4"; press remaining long side under 1/2". Insert 1" x 42" batting strip under the 1/2" flap. Fold remainder of fabric over batting, covering batting and 1/2" flap; hand-stitch along edge to secure.

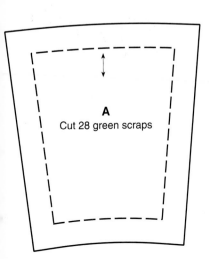

A
Cut 28 green scraps

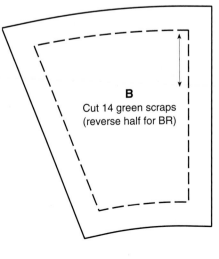

B
Cut 14 green scraps
(reverse half for BR)

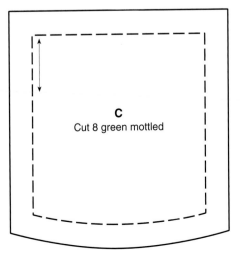

C
Cut 8 green mottled

Topstitch 1/4" from each long side.

Step 16. Insert ends of strap 1/2" into handle stops; sew across top to secure. Pin handle stops to upper sides of purse with top edges even with top of side gusset as shown in Figure 9. Sew around edges of handle stops to secure.

Step 17. Cut two strips lining fabric 1 1/2" x 11 1/4" for placket lining; sew a strip to the top edge of each purse lining piece. Complete lining as for bag eliminating zipper between placket pieces. Press under 1/4" on each placket edge. Insert lining in purse with wrong sides together; stitch lining to purse along edges of zipper to hold, easing ends as needed to finish. ❖

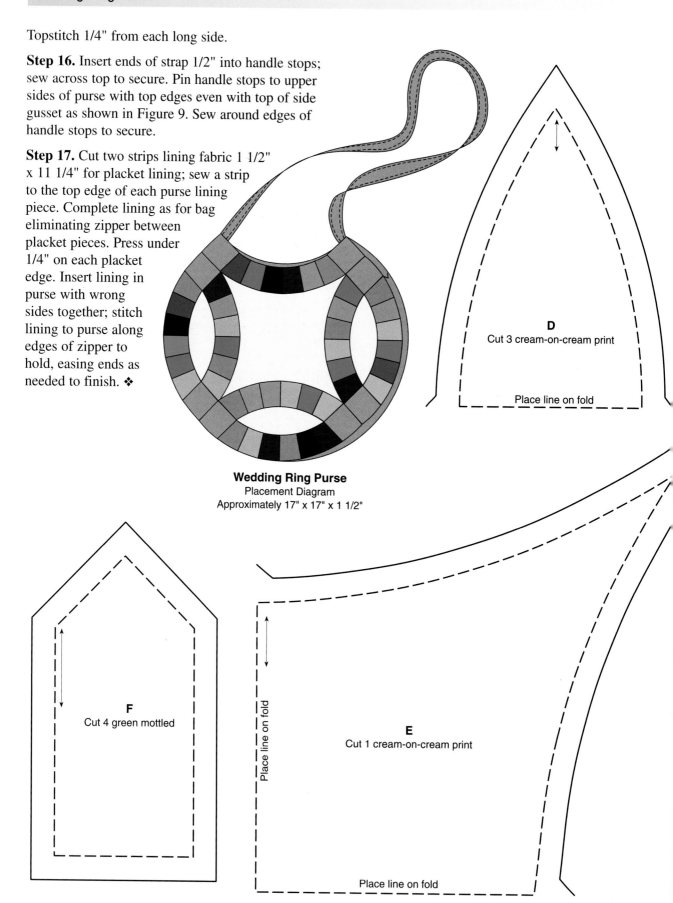

Wedding Ring Purse
Placement Diagram
Approximately 17" x 17" x 1 1/2"

D
Cut 3 cream-on-cream print

Place line on fold

F
Cut 4 green mottled

E
Cut 1 cream-on-cream print

Place line on fold

Place line on fold

Circle of Love

By Marian Shenk

Appliquéd hearts are centered in rings created with one-piece bands that make piecing easier in this table topper.

Project Specifications

Skill Level: Intermediate

Quilt Size: Approximately 26 3/8" x 26 3/8"

Materials

- 1/8 yard dark blue tone-on-tone
- 1/4 yard burgundy tone-on-tone
- 3/4 yard blue print
- 1 1/4 yards white-on-white print
- Backing 30" x 30"
- Batting 30" x 30"
- All-purpose thread to match fabrics
- White hand-quilting thread
- 3 yards 1"-wide dark blue bias binding
- Basic sewing tools and supplies

Instructions

Step 1. Prepare templates using pattern pieces given; cut as directed on each piece.

Step 2. To piece one melon unit, sew an A to B as shown in Figure 1. *Note: Start in the center, matching notches, and work to the outside when pinning pieces together before stitching; clip curves to allow pieces to lie flat after stitching.* Sew C to each end of another A and sew to the A-B unit referring to Figure 2; repeat for 24 melon units.

Step 3. Sew a melon unit to each side of D to complete 1 ring unit as shown in Figure 3; repeat for five ring units.

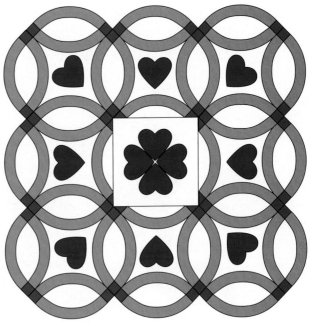

Circle of Love
Placement Diagram
Approximately 26 3/8" x 26 3/8"

Figure 3
Sew a melon unit to
each side of D to
complete 1 ring unit.

Figure 4
Sew a melon unit to D to
complete an edge unit.

Step 4. Sew a melon unit to one side of D to complete an edge unit as shown in Figure 4; repeat for four edge units.

Step 5. Join the pieced units as shown in Figure 5 to complete the pieced top; press.

Step 6. Cut one square white-on-white print 8" x 8"; turn under edges 1/4" all around and press.

Figure 5
Join the pieced units
as shown to complete
the pieced top.

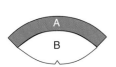

Figure 1
Sew A to B as shown.

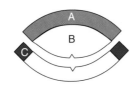

Figure 2
Sew C to each end of A
and sew to the A-B unit to
complete 1 melon unit.

Step 7. Prepare heart shapes for hand appliqué referring to the General Instructions. Arrange four heart shapes in the center of the 8" x 8" square referring to the Placement Diagram for positioning. Hand-appliqué in place.

Step 8. Place the appliquéd square over the center area of the pieced top with square corners extending over the C squares in the pieced units. Hand-appliqué in place. Trim pieced areas beneath square away to reduce bulk and prevent shadowing of underneath fabrics.

Step 9. Center a heart shape in each D piece referring to the Placement Diagram for positioning; hand-appliqué in place.

Step 10. Prepare quilt top for quilting and finish referring to the General Instructions. *Note: This quilt was hand-quilted around each heart shape and in the ditch of seams using white hand-quilting thread.*

Step 11. Trim batting and backing even with quilt top; bind edges with dark blue 1"-wide bias binding, turning entire binding piece to the wrong side and hand-stitching in place to finish. ❖

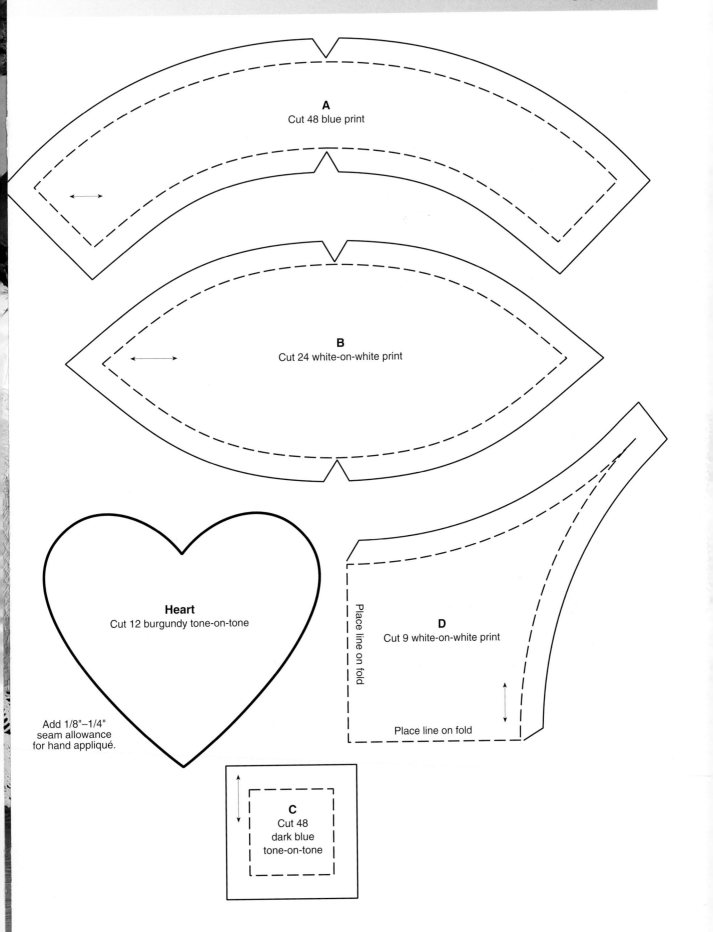

A
Cut 48 blue print

B
Cut 24 white-on-white print

Heart
Cut 12 burgundy tone-on-tone

Add 1/8"–1/4"
seam allowance
for hand appliqué.

Place line on fold

D
Cut 9 white-on-white print

Place line on fold

C
Cut 48
dark blue
tone-on-tone

Autumn Flight

By Sue Harvey

The colors of autumn make a beautiful statement in both trees and fabric.

Project Specifications

Skill Level: Intermediate

Quilt Size: 48" x 48"

Block Size: 6" x 6", 6" x 12" and 12" x 12"

Number of Blocks: 9, 12 and 4

Materials

• Fat quarter each 4 different green prints

• 1/2 yard gold mottled

• 3/4 yard total autumn-color prints

• 1 1/4 yards cream print

• 1 1/4 yards multicolored print

• Batting 52" x 52"

• Backing 52" x 52"

• All-purpose thread to match fabrics

• Cream and autumn-color variegated machine-quilting thread

• Basting spray

• Basic sewing tools and supplies, rotary cutter, mat and ruler

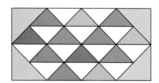

Geese in Flight
6" x 12" Block

Windblown Geese
6" x 6" Block

Pine Tree
12" x 12" Block

Instructions

Step 1. Prepare template for A using pattern piece given; cut as directed on pattern.

Step 2. Cut the following from each green print: one 2 3/4" x 2 3/4" square, cut on both diagonals to make B triangles; one 2 5/8" x 5 3/4" C rectangle; one 5 3/8" x 5 3/8" square, cut on one diagonal to make D triangles; and 16 squares 2 3/8" x 2 3/8", cut on one diagonal to make green F triangles.

Step 3. Cut one strip cream print 5 3/8" by fabric width; subcut into the following: four 5 3/8" x 5 3/8" squares, cut on one diagonal to make D triangles; two 3 7/8" x 3 7/8" squares, cut on one diagonal to make E triangles; and eight 2" x 2" G squares.

Step 4. Cut six strips cream print 2 3/8" by fabric width; subcut into 86 square segments 2 3/8" x 2 3/8". Cut each square on one diagonal to make 172 cream F triangles.

Step 5. Cut six strips cream print 3" by fabric width; subcut into 72 square segments 3" x 3". Cut each square on one diagonal to make 144 cream I triangles.

Step 6. Cut 36 squares autumn-color prints 2 3/8" x 2 3/8"; cut each square on one diagonal to make 72 autumn F triangles.

Step 7. Cut 72 squares autumn-color prints 3" x 3"; cut each square on one diagonal to make 144 autumn I triangles.

Step 8. Cut four strips gold mottled 3 7/8" by fabric width; subcut into 36 squares 3 7/8" x 3 7/8". Cut each square on one diagonal to make 72 gold H triangles.

Step 9. Cut two strips multicolored print 3 7/8" by fabric width; subcut into 3 7/8" square segments. Cut each square on one diagonal to make 36 multicolored H triangles.

Step 10. Cut one strip multicolored print 7 1/4" by fabric width; subcut into 7 1/4" square segments. Cut each square on both diagonals to make 12 J triangles.

Step 11. Cut one strip multicolored print 12 1/2" by fabric width; subcut into eight 3 1/2" x 12 1/2" segments for L and four 3 1/2" x 3 1/2" K squares.

Step 12. To piece one Windblown Geese block, sew a cream F to an autumn F as shown in Figure 1; repeat for four units.

Step 13. Sew a cream F to the autumn side and an autumn F to the cream side of each F unit as shown in Figure 2.

Figure 1
Sew a cream F to an autumn F.

Figure 2
Sew cream and autumn F triangles to the F unit.

Figure 3
Join the F units to make a square; add H to each side to complete 1 Windblown Geese block.

Step 14. Join the F units to make a square as shown in Figure 3; add a multicolored H to each side to complete one block, again referring to Figure 3. Repeat to make nine blocks.

Step 15. To piece one Geese in Flight block, sew a cream I to an autumn I as shown in Figure 4; repeat for 10 units.

Figure 4
Sew a cream I to an autumn I.

Step 16. Join I units with I triangles to make I strips as shown in Figure 5.

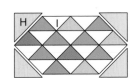

Figure 5
Join I units and triangles to make I strips.

Figure 6
Join the I strips to make an angled unit; add H to each angled side to complete 1 Geese in Flight block.

Step 17. Join the I strips to make an angled unit as shown in Figure 6; add a gold H to each angled side

to complete one block, again referring to Figure 6. Repeat to make 12 blocks.

Step 18. To piece one Pine Tree block, sew B to A and AR as shown in Figure 7.

Figure 7
Sew B to A and AR pieces.

Figure 8
Sew C between the A-B units; add D and E to complete the corner unit.

Step 19. Sew C between the A-B units as shown in Figure 8; add a green D and cream E to complete the corner unit, again referring to Figure 8.

Step 20. Sew a cream F to a green F as shown in Figure 1; repeat for 25 units.

Step 21. Join nine F units with

Figure 9
Join 9 F units with 3 green F triangles and 1 cream D triangle to make a side unit.

Autumn Flight
Placement Diagram
48" x 48"

Figure 10
Sew the side unit to
the corner unit.

Figure 11
Join 16 F units with 2 G squares,
3 green F triangles and 1 cream
D triangle to make a side unit.

three green F triangles and one cream D triangle to
make a side unit as shown in Figure 9; sew the side
unit to the corner unit as shown in Figure 10.

Step 22. Join the remaining
F units with two G squares,
three green F triangles and
one cream D triangle to make
a second side unit as shown
in Figure 11; sew the side
unit to the previously pieced
unit as shown in Figure 12 to
complete one block. Repeat
to make four blocks.

Figure 12
Sew the side unit to the
pieced unit to complete
1 Pine Tree block.

Step 23. Sew a gold H triangle to two adjacent sides of J
as shown in Figure 13; repeat
for 12 H-J units.

Figure 13
Sew a gold H to 2
adjacent sides of J.

Step 24. Join two Pine
Tree blocks with three Geese in Flight blocks
and two L segments to make a row as shown
in Figure 14; repeat for two rows.

A
Cut 8 cream print
(reverse half for AR)

Make 2

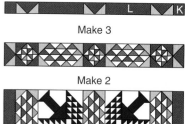

Make 3

Make 2

Figure 14
Join blocks with H-J units and K and L
segments to make rows as shown.

Step 25. Join two Geese in Flight blocks with three
Windblown Geese blocks and two H-J units to make a
row, again referring to Figure 14; repeat for three rows.

Step 26. Join three H-J units with two L segments and
two K squares to make a row, again referring to Figure
14; repeat for two rows.

Step 27. Join the rows to complete the pieced top as

Continued on page 123

Big House in the Woods

By Ruth Swasey

Fabrics in seasonal colors create the crazy-patch trees running diagonally on this large quilt. The house is shown with trees of all seasons.

Project Note

In the list of fabrics needed we refer to using 2 yards total of each seasonal color range. This means that you will need a total of 2 yards in tree colors for each season. For winter, blue and white; for spring, yellow and light green; for summer, darker green; and for fall, bright orange, gold and red. These fabrics are also used for the large fill-in blocks between the trees and for the house shape.

Project Specifications

Skill Level: Intermediate

Quilt Size: 92" x 104"

Block Size: 12" x 12" and 24" x 24"

Number of Blocks: 26 small; 1 large

Materials

- 1 strip yellow mottled 3" by fabric width and 1 rectangle 3" x 1 1/4"
- 2 strips light green solid 1 1/4" by fabric width and 1 rectangle 4" x 6 3/4"
- 14 1/2" x 24 1/2" rectangle blue print for house
- 1/4 yard total brown prints for tree trunks
- 1/3 yard brown print for roof
- 5/8 yard each yellow, blue and white prints for borders
- 2 yards total fabrics in each seasonal color range
- 2 yards total blue prints for sky
- Backing 96" x 108"
- Batting 96" x 108"
- 11 1/2 yards self-made or purchased binding
- All-purpose thread to match fabrics

- Machine-embroidery thread to match or contrast with tree fabrics
- Yellow machine-quilting thread
- 1/2 yard fusible transfer web
- 1/2 yard fabric stabilizer
- 1 roll freezer paper
- Black permanent pen
- Basic sewing tools and supplies

House
24" x 24" Block

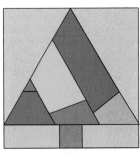

Tree
12" x 12" Block

Instructions

Step 1. Cut five fall, six spring, seven summer and eight winter fabric blocks 12 1/2" x 12 1/2"; set aside.

Step 2. Cut 26 squares brown print 2 1/2" x 2 1/2" for B. Cut 10 spring and 14 each summer, fall and winter fabric rectangles 2 1/2" x 5 1/2" for C, one 2 1/2" x 3 1/2" red/orange print rectangle for G and two 2 1/2" x 11" blue print rectangles for F; set aside.

Step 3. Prepare templates using pattern pieces given; cut as directed on each piece.

Step 4. Cut fabric scraps and press onto freezer-paper tree shape to cover paper shape.

Step 5. Using machine-embroidery thread and a decorative machine stitch, stitch over edges of fabrics through freezer paper, covering raw edges of pressed tree shapes. Trim excess fabric even with freezer-paper tree. Make five spring and seven each summer, fall and winter tree shapes.

Step 6. Sew A and AR to angled sides of trees.

Step 7. Sew B between two same-season C pieces and sew to the tree shapes to complete one Tree block as shown in Figure 1; repeat for all Tree blocks. Remove freezer paper.

Step 8. Sew the 3" yellow mottled strip between the two 1 1/4" light green solid strips with right sides together along length; press seams toward light green solid strips. Cut fusible transfer web strips to match pieced strip; fuse to wrong side of strip. Subcut strip set into nine 4 1/2" segments to make windows as shown in Figure 2; remove paper backing.

Figure 1
Sew B between 2 C pieces; sew to the tree shapes to complete 1 Tree block.

Figure 2
Subcut strip set into nine 4 1/2" segments to make windows.

Step 9. Arrange five window segments 2 1/2" down from one 24" edge of the blue print house piece referring to the block drawing; fuse in place. Arrange four window segments 1 1/2" below the first row of windows, again referring to the block drawing; fuse in place. Fuse transfer web to wrong side of the yellow mottled and light green solid rectangles; remove paper backing. Fuse the yellow mottled window piece to the light green solid door piece as shown in Figure 3. Place the door piece between the window pieces aligning bottom of door with bottom edge of house piece; fuse in place.

Figure 3
Fuse the 3" x 1 1/4" yellow mottled window piece to the 4" x 6 3/4" light green solid door piece.

Figure 4
Sew D and DR to E; sew to house section.

Step 10. Sew D and DR to E; sew to house section referring to Figure 4. Sew G between two F pieces and sew to top of the D-E unit to complete one House block as shown in Figure 5.

Step 11. Cut fabric stabilizer to fit behind window and door area; pin in place. Using thread to match fabric,

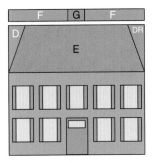

Figure 5
Sew G between 2 F pieces and sew to top of the D-E unit to complete 1 House block.

machine-appliqué around window and door pieces. Add lines in windows to make windowpanes as shown in Figure 6. Draw door handle on door piece using black permanent pen.

Step 12. Lay out the pieced Tree blocks with the 12 1/2" x 12 1/2" seasonal squares and House block in rows on a large flat surface referring to the Placement Diagram for positioning. *Note: The Tree blocks and seasonal squares will form diagonal rows from top right to bottom left of quilt.*

Figure 6
Add lines in windows to make windowpanes as shown.

Step 13. Join Tree blocks and squares in rows referring to Figure 7 for positioning of House block; press seams in one direction.

Figure 7
Join Tree blocks and squares with House block to make 1 row.

Step 14. Join rows to complete the pieced top; press seams in one direction.

Step 15. Cut border fabrics into 4 1/2" by fabric width strips. Join strips along short edges to make one long strip. Sew the strip to one long side of the pieced center; press seam toward strip and trim even with quilt top ends. Begin sewing the end just cut onto the bottom edge of the quilt top, trimming and cutting as before. Continue in this manner until entire quilt top is bordered referring to the Placement Diagram.

Step 16. Prepare the finished top for quilting and finish referring to the General Instructions. ***Note:*** *The quilt shown was machine-quilted in an allover pattern with yellow machine-quilting thread.* ❖

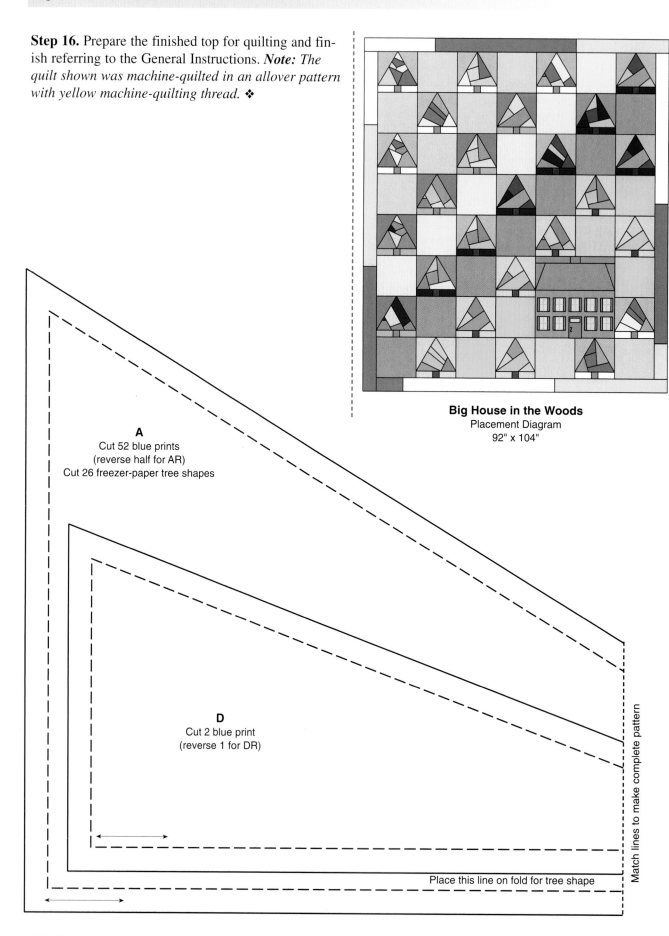

Big House in the Woods
Placement Diagram
92" x 104"

A
Cut 52 blue prints
(reverse half for AR)
Cut 26 freezer-paper tree shapes

D
Cut 2 blue print
(reverse 1 for DR)

Match lines to make complete pattern

Place this line on fold for tree shape

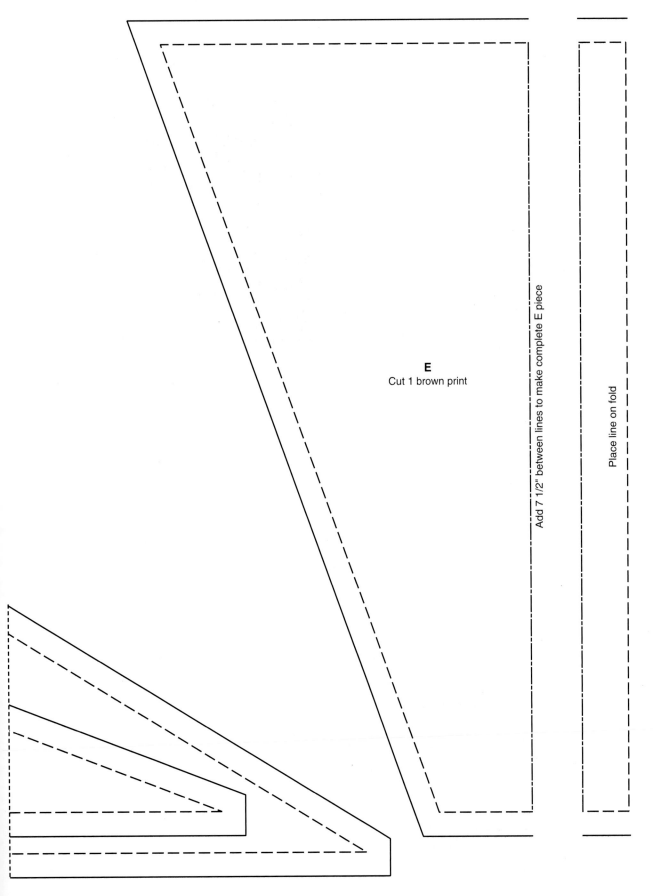

E
Cut 1 brown print

Add 7 1/2" between lines to make complete E piece

Place line on fold

Tall, Proud Pines

By Julie Weaver

Evergreen trees stay green all year round in nature or in fabric.

Project Specifications

Skill Level: Beginner

Quilt Size: 36" x 52"

Block Size: 8" x 12"

Number of Blocks: 9

Materials

- 1/8 yard brown print for tree trunks
- 1/6 yard nine different green prints for trees
- 1/6 yard nine different cream/white prints for backgrounds
- 1/6 yard tan print for corner squares
- 1/2 yard brown stripe for sashing and first border
- 2/3 yard green plaid for final border
- Backing 40" x 56"
- Batting 40" x 56"
- 5 yards self-made or purchased binding
- All-purpose thread to match fabrics
- Cream machine-quilting thread
- Basic sewing tools and supplies

Instructions

Step 1. To complete one block, cut one 4 1/2" x 8 1/2" rectangle and three 2 1/2" x 8 1/2" rectangles from one of the nine green print fabrics.

Step 2. Cut two 4 1/2" x 4 1/2" squares, six 2 1/2" x 2 1/2" squares and two 2 1/2" x 3 1/2" rectangles from one background print. Draw a diagonal line on both size squares.

Step 3. Cut one 2 1/2" x 2 1/2" square brown print.

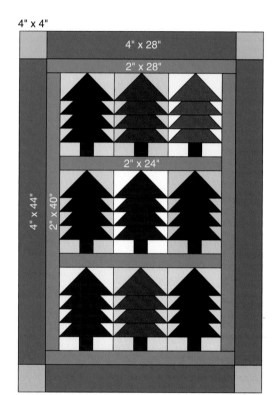

Tall, Proud Pines
Placement Diagram
36" x 52"

Tall, Proud Pine
8" x 12" Block

Step 4. Lay a 4 1/2" x 4 1/2" background square right sides together with the 4 1/2" x 8 1/2" green print rectangle as shown in Figure 1; stitch on marked line. Trim seam to 1/4"; press background triangle to the right side as shown

Figure 1
Lay a 4 1/2" x 4 1/2" background square right sides together with the 4 1/2" x 8 1/2" green print rectangle.

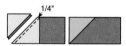

Figure 2
Stitch on marked line. Trim seam to 1/4"; press background triangle to the right side.

in Figure 2.

Step 5. Place another 4 1/2" x 4 1/2" background square on the stitched rectangle as shown in Figure 3; stitch, trim and press to complete the treetop unit as shown in Figure 4.

Figure 3
Place another 4 1/2" x 4 1/2" background square on the stitched rectangle as shown.

Step 6. Repeat steps 4 and 5 with the 2 1/2" x 2 1/2" background squares and the 2 1/2" x 8 1/2" green print rectangles to complete three branch units as shown in Figure 5.

Figure 4
Stitch, trim and press to complete the treetop unit.

Figure 5
Complete a branch unit as shown.

Step 7. Sew a 2 1/2" x 3 1/2" background rectangle to opposite sides of the brown print square to complete a trunk unit as shown in Figure 6.

Figure 6
Complete the tree trunk unit as shown.

Figure 7
Join the treetop unit with 3 branch units and the tree trunk unit to complete 1 block.

Step 8. Join the treetop unit with three branch units and the tree trunk unit to complete one Tall, Proud Pine block as shown in Figure 7; repeat for nine blocks.

Step 9. Cut two 2 1/2" x 24 1/2" strips brown stripe.

Step 10. Join three blocks to make a row; press seams in one direction. Repeat for three rows. Join the rows with the 2 1/2" x 24 1/2" strips brown stripe; press seams toward strips.

Step 11. Cut two strips each 2 1/2" x 28 1/2" and 2 1/2" x 40 1/2" brown stripe. Sew the longer strips to opposite long sides and shorter strips to the top and bottom of the pieced center; press seams toward strips.

Step 12. Cut four squares tan print 4 1/2" x 4 1/2". Cut (and piece) two strips each 4 1/2" x 28 1/2" and

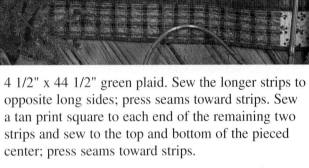

4 1/2" x 44 1/2" green plaid. Sew the longer strips to opposite long sides; press seams toward strips. Sew a tan print square to each end of the remaining two strips and sew to the top and bottom of the pieced center; press seams toward strips.

Step 13. Prepare quilt top for quilting and finish referring to the General Instructions. ***Note:*** *This quilt was machine-quilted in a meandering design in the background using cream machine-quilting thread and 1/4" from seams in an echo pattern using all-purpose thread to match fabrics in the green print areas.* ❖

Autumn Flight

continued from page 116

shown in Figure 15; press.

Step 28. Spray one side of the batting piece with basting spray; place wrong side of prepared backing on the sprayed side. Repeat on opposite side of batting with completed top.

Step 29. Hand- or machine-quilt as desired. ***Note:*** *The sample shown was machine-*

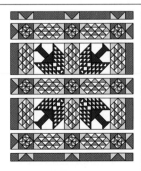

Figure 15
Join the rows to complete the pieced top.

quilted in a vine shape in the L segments and a meandering pattern in the cream print areas using cream and autumn-color variegated machine-quilting thread in the top of the machine and all-purpose thread in the bobbin.

Step 30. Trim batting and backing even with quilted top. Cut five strips multicolored print 2 1/4" by fabric width. Join strips on short ends to make a long strip. Fold strip in half with wrong sides together; press to make a binding strip. Bind edges of quilt to finish. ❖

Holiday Hot Mats

By Marian Shenk

These hot mats may be used at any time of the year, but are perfect accent pieces for the holiday when made using red and green fabrics.

Project Specifications

Skill Level: Intermediate

Mat Size: 9" x 9"

Block Size: 5 5/8" x 5 5/8"

Number of Blocks: 1 of each design

Materials

- 9" x 9" square cream-on-cream print
- Two 10" x 10" squares green leafy print
- Scraps white, dark green and beige prints
- Scraps burgundy, gold, teal, brown and yellow solids
- 2 backing squares 10" x 10"
- 2 batting squares 10" x 10"
- All-purpose thread to match fabrics
- White hand-quilting thread
- 2 1/2 yards teal 1"-wide bias tape
- Basic sewing tools and supplies and tracing paper

House Mat

Step 1. Transfer A–D paper-piecing patterns to tracing paper using pattern drawings given.

Step 2. Cut fabric patches 1/8"–1/4" larger than spaces on paper patterns in colors indicated in each piece. *Note: Shapes must extend beyond marked lines and may be trimmed to size after stitching making almost any scrap usable for most pieces.*

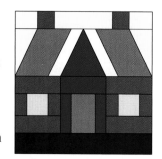

House
5 5/8" x 5 5/8" Block

Step 3. Beginning with paper-piecing pattern A for window section, pin piece 1 in place on the unmarked side of the paper; hold the paper pattern up to a light to check that piece 1 extends beyond the marked lines on the paper.

Step 4. Pin piece 2 right sides together with piece 1 extending at least 1/4" over the 1–2 stitching line; press flat and hold up to the light to be sure it covers the space for piece 2. Flip back down; stitch on the line on the marked side of the paper using a very close stitch length; trim seam and flip piece 2 to the right side and press referring to Figure 1.

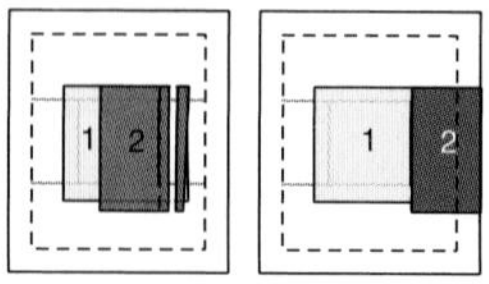

Figure 1
Trim seam and flip piece 2 to the right side and press.

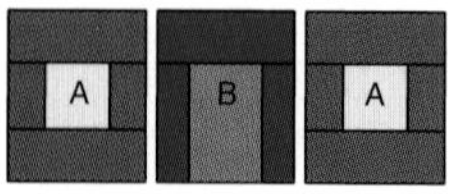

Figure 2
Sew the B unit between 2 A units

Step 5. Repeat the procedure in numerical order to paper-piece all sections as indicated with pattern for number to piece.

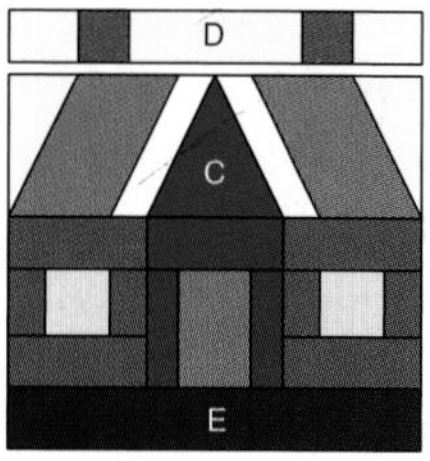

Step 6. Sew the B unit between two A units as shown in Figure 2; sew E to the bottom edge and the C unit to the top edge. Add the D chimney unit to the top edge to complete one House block as shown in Figure 3.

Figure 3
Add the D chimney unit to the top edge to complete 1 House block.

Step 7. Cut four strips each 1" x 7 1/8" gold solid. Sew a strip to each side of the pieced block, mitering corners; press seams toward strips. Turn under raw edges 1/4"; press.

Step 8. Prepare template for piece L; cut as directed on piece. Center the bordered House block on L; hand-stitch in place.

Step 9. Sandwich one batting square between completed top and prepared backing square; pin or baste to hold.

Step 10. Quilt as desired by hand or machine. *Note: The sample shown was hand-quilted in the ditch of seams using white hand-quilting thread.*

Step 11. Trim batting and backing even with piece L.

Bind edges with teal 1"-wide bias tape referring to the General Instructions to finish.

Tree Mat

Step 1. Transfer F and G paper-piecing patterns to tracing paper using pattern drawings given. Prepare templates for H–K using pattern pieces given; cut as directed on each piece.

Tree
5 5/8" x 5 5/8" Block

Step 2. Prepare the F and G units referring to Steps 2 –5 for House Mat.

Step 3. Sew a teal solid K to a dark green print K along the diagonal; repeat for 12 units. Join four units to complete one pinwheel unit as shown in Figure 4; repeat for three units.

Step 4. Sew H to a pinwheel unit; sew to the G unit as shown in Figure 5.

Figure 4
Join 4 units to complete
1 pinwheel unit.

Figure 5
Sew H to a pinwheel unit;
sew to the G unit.

Step 5. Join two pinwheel units with HR as shown in Figure 6.

Step 6. Join the pieced units as shown in Figure 7.

Sew the F unit to the G side of the pieced unit; add J to the pinwheel sides to complete the Tree block as shown in Figure 8.

Figure 6
Join 2 pinwheel units with HR.

Figure 7
Join the pieced units as shown.

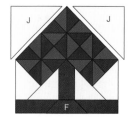

Figure 8
Add J to the pinwheel sides to
complete the Tree block.

Step 7. Cut four 1" x 7 1/8 strips burgundy solid. Sew a strip to each side of the pieced block, mitering corners; press seams toward strips. Turn under raw edges 1/4"; press.

Step 8. Complete the Tree Mat referring to Steps 8–11 for House Mat. ❖

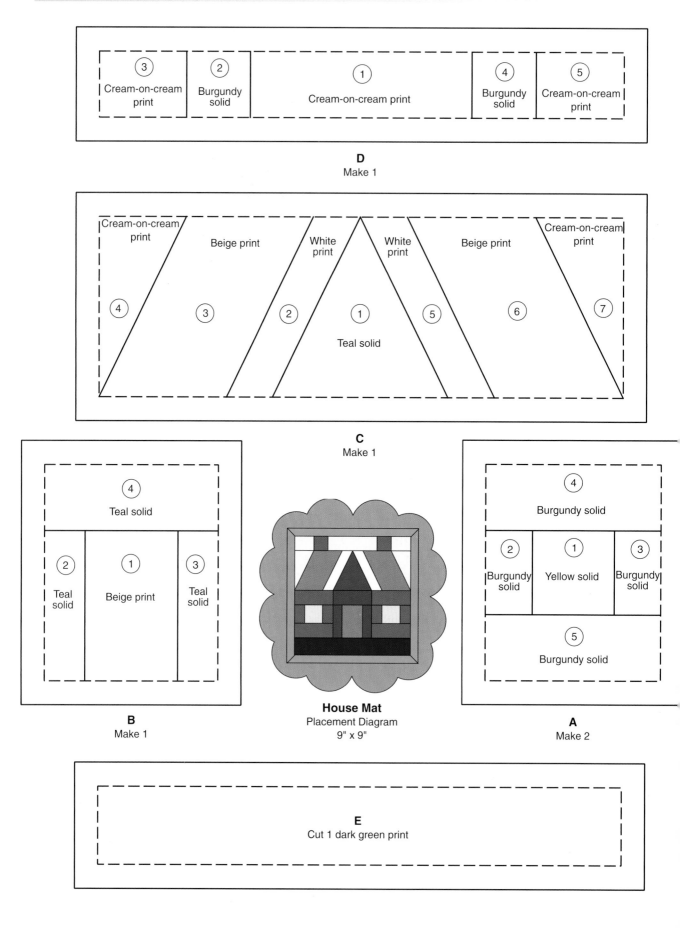

③ Cream-on-cream print ② Burgundy solid ① Cream-on-cream print ④ Burgundy solid ⑤ Cream-on-cream print

D
Make 1

Cream-on-cream print Beige print White print White print Beige print Cream-on-cream print
④ ③ ② ① ⑤ ⑥ ⑦
Teal solid

C
Make 1

④ Teal solid
② Teal solid ① Beige print ③ Teal solid

B
Make 1

House Mat
Placement Diagram
9" x 9"

④ Burgundy solid
② Burgundy solid ① Yellow solid ③ Burgundy solid
⑤ Burgundy solid

A
Make 2

E
Cut 1 dark green print

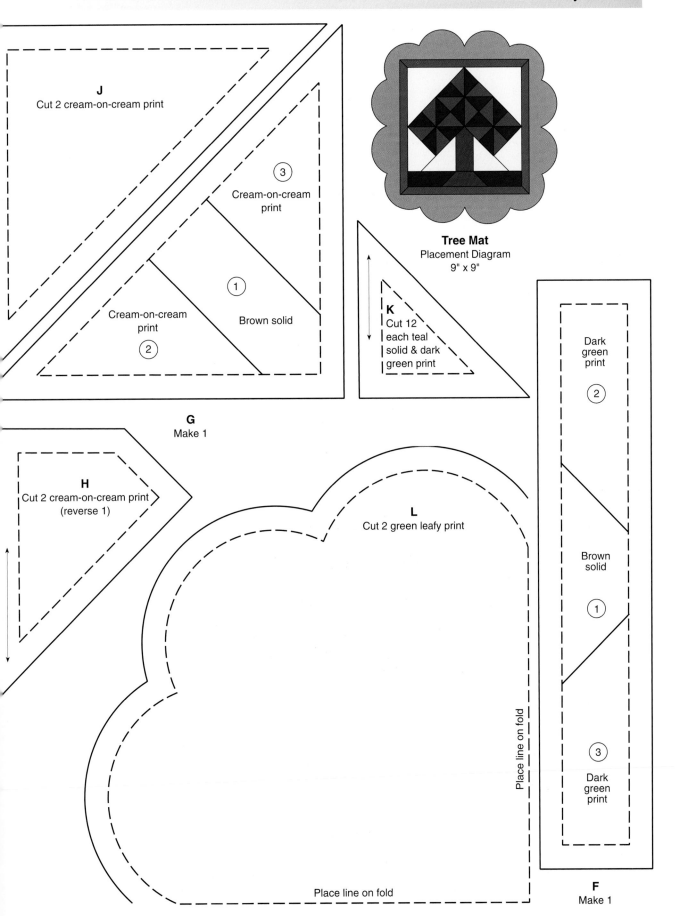

J
Cut 2 cream-on-cream print

③ Cream-on-cream print

① Brown solid

Cream-on-cream print ②

Tree Mat
Placement Diagram
9" x 9"

K
Cut 12 each teal solid & dark green print

G
Make 1

H
Cut 2 cream-on-cream print
(reverse 1)

L
Cut 2 green leafy print

Dark green print ②

Brown solid ①

Dark green print ③

Place line on fold

Place line on fold

F
Make 1

Sunbonnet Sue Quilts

Sue and Bill went up a hill
To quilt a comfy cover!

Sunbonnet Sue
Antique Quilt

❖

Sunbonnet Sue
Chair Pad

❖

Sue's Garden Wreath

❖

Sunday-Best Sue

❖

Sunbonnet Sue in
the Kitchen

❖

Twinkle, Twinkle
Little Star

Sunbonnet Sue Antique Quil

From the collection of Sandra L. Hatch

Sunbonnet Sue quilts were very popular in the 1930s. This old quilt is a perfect example of typical quilt made using lots of different dress fabrics with coordinating hats and shoes.

Project Notes

The batting or filling used in this old quilt is quite heavy. It could be a blanket, but I did not take it apart to check. I admire the quilter for making fairly good quilting stitches through such thick layers. Obviously, this quilt was made for warmth as well as a decorative bed cover. Pretty embroidery stitches adorn the hats and the hand-stitched button-hole stitches are very even.

Project Specifications

Skill Level: Intermediate

Quilt Size: 64" x 79"

Block Size: 11" x 11"

Number of Blocks: 20

Materials

- 20 assorted 7" x 7" pastel print squares to coordinate with solids
- 1/3 yard each pink, yellow, red, blue and green solids for hats, arms and shoes
- 5/8 yard pink print for sashing squares
- 2 yards pink solid for sashing
- 2 3/8 yards muslin for background
- Backing 68" x 83"
- Batting 68" x 83"
- 8 1/2 yards self-made or purchased pink binding
- White and pink all-purpose thread
- White hand-quilting thread
- 3 or 4 skeins black 6-strand embroidery floss
- Red, yellow, green, orange and pink 6-strand embroidery floss
- Basic sewing tools and supplies

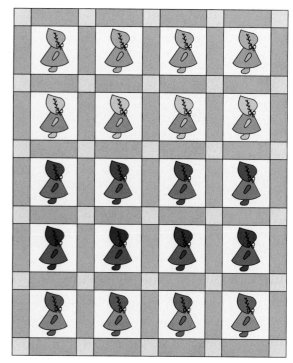

Sunbonnet Sue Antique Quilt
Placement Diagram
64" x 79"

Instructions

Step 1. Cut 20 squares muslin 11 1/2" x 11 1/2" for background; fold and crease to mark centers.

Step 2. Prepare templates for appliqué shapes using patterns given. Cut and prepare pieces for hand appliqué referring to the General Instructions. ***Note:*** *If you prefer to use machine methods, add 2 yards fusible transfer web, yards fabric stabilizer and black machine-embroider thread to the list of materials needed for quilt. Refer to the General Instructions to prepare pieces for fusible appliqué.*

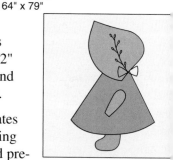

Sunbonnet Sue
11" x 11" Block

Step 3. Center one Sunbonnet Sue motif on one back ground square in numerical order using crease lines and center mark on pattern as a guide for positioning baste in place. Repeat for 20 blocks.

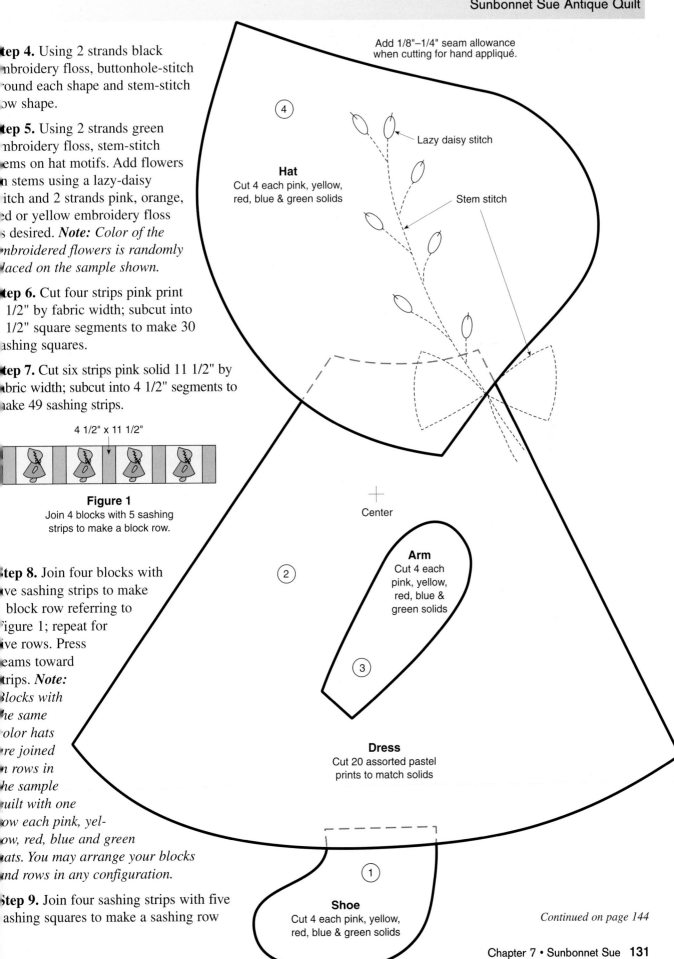

Add 1/8"–1/4" seam allowance when cutting for hand appliqué.

Step 4. Using 2 strands black embroidery floss, buttonhole-stitch around each shape and stem-stitch low shape.

Step 5. Using 2 strands green embroidery floss, stem-stitch stems on hat motifs. Add flowers on stems using a lazy-daisy stitch and 2 strands pink, orange, red or yellow embroidery floss as desired. *Note: Color of the embroidered flowers is randomly placed on the sample shown.*

Step 6. Cut four strips pink print 1 1/2" by fabric width; subcut into 1 1/2" square segments to make 30 sashing squares.

Step 7. Cut six strips pink solid 11 1/2" by fabric width; subcut into 4 1/2" segments to make 49 sashing strips.

4 1/2" x 11 1/2"

Figure 1
Join 4 blocks with 5 sashing strips to make a block row.

Step 8. Join four blocks with five sashing strips to make a block row referring to Figure 1; repeat for five rows. Press seams toward strips. *Note: Blocks with the same color hats are joined in rows in the sample quilt with one row each pink, yellow, red, blue and green hats. You may arrange your blocks and rows in any configuration.*

Step 9. Join four sashing strips with five sashing squares to make a sashing row

(4)

Lazy daisy stitch

Hat
Cut 4 each pink, yellow, red, blue & green solids

Stem stitch

Center

(2)

Arm
Cut 4 each pink, yellow, red, blue & green solids

(3)

Dress
Cut 20 assorted pastel prints to match solids

(1)

Shoe
Cut 4 each pink, yellow, red, blue & green solids

Continued on page 144

Sunbonnet Sue Chair Pad

By Chris Malone

Dress up your chairs and add color to a room with a pretty chair pad.

Project Specifications

Skill Level: Beginner

Quilt Size: 11" x 11"

Materials

- 8 1/2" x 8 1/2" square blue print
- 4 (2" x 8 1/2") strips dark blue floral
- 4 (2" x 2") squares medium blue floral
- Scraps red and yellow prints, white floral and black and rose solids
- Backing 13" x 13"
- High-loft batting 13" x 13"
- All-purpose thread to match fabrics
- Blue quilting thread
- Black 6-strand embroidery floss
- 1/8 yard fusible transfer web
- 4 (7/8") yellow buttons
- 4 yards 1"-wide blue grosgrain ribbon
- No-fray solution
- Basic sewing tools and supplies

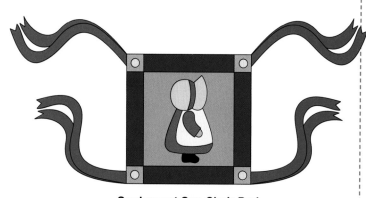

Sunbonnet Sue Chair Pad
Placement Diagram
11" x 11"

Instructions

Step 1. Prepare templates for appliqué shapes using patterns given. Prepare for fusible, machine appliqué referring to the General Instructions, and to patterns for color and number to cut.

Step 2. Arrange the appliqué motifs on the 8 1/2" x 8 1/2" square blue print referring to the Placement Diagram for positioning; fuse shapes in place in numerical order.

Step 3. Using 2 strands black embroidery floss and a buttonhole stitch, hand-stitch around each fused shape except hatband.

Step 4. Sew a 2" x 8 1/2" strip dark blue floral to opposite sides of the appliquéd center; press seams toward strips. Sew a 2" x 2" square medium blue floral to each end of the remaining two 2" x 8 1/2" dark blue floral strips; press seams toward squares. Sew these strips to the remaining sides of the appliquéd center; press seams toward strips.

Step 5. Cut ribbon into four 1-yard lengths. Fold one ribbon in half; place folded edge on raw edge of right side of one side border, a generous 1/4" down from top as shown in Figure 1; baste in place. Repeat with remaining three ribbon lengths so there are ribbons at the top and bottom of each side, again referring to Figure 1.

Step 6. Fold the ribbons in toward the center of the block; hold in place with straight or safety pins so ribbon ends will not get caught in seams.

Step 7. Place batting on a flat surface; lay backing piece right side up on top of batting. Place the appliquéd top right side down on backing; pin layers together. Trim batting and backing even with appliquéd top.

Figure 1
Place folded ribbon
1/4" from each corner.

Step 8. Stitch all around sides, leaving a 5" opening at the bottom center; clip corners. Turn right side out through opening; press. Hand-stitch opening closed.

Step 9. Using blue quilting thread, hand-quilt in the ditch of border seams and around appliquéd motif. Add another line of quilting 1/4" from edge of motif.

Step 10. Sew a yellow button in the center of each corner square. Trim ribbon ends in a V-cut; apply no-fray solution to ends to finish. ❖

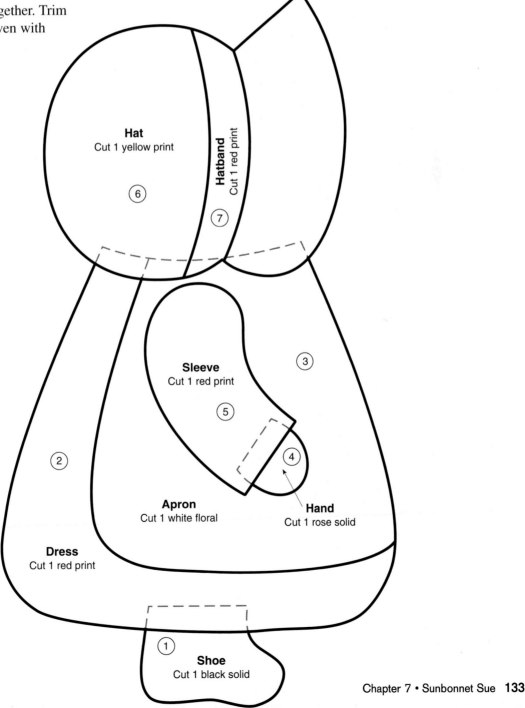

Hat
Cut 1 yellow print

6

Hatband
Cut 1 red print

7

Sleeve
Cut 1 red print

5

3

4

Apron
Cut 1 white floral

Hand
Cut 1 rose solid

2

Dress
Cut 1 red print

1

Shoe
Cut 1 black solid

Sue's Garden Wreath

By Pearl Louise Krush

Purchase reproduction prints or dig into your stash to dress Sue in colorful dresses and bonnets to match her garden flowers.

Project Notes

The sample quilt uses a total of 21 different fabric prints, all in five basic colors. For example, there are five different blue prints. We refer to these prints by color family. You may choose to use only one fabric in each color family or to make a scrappy version like the one shown. It is difficult to assign fabric names to so many different fabrics, so in the instructions we refer to the fabrics in their color family. Therefore, if we call for blue print, you may choose one blue print or several. Prints used with a white background are referred to as light prints. For example, a blue-on-white print is listed as a light blue print. The yardage is given as a total for each color. If four blue fabrics are used, divide the total yardage by four and purchase that amount of each fabric, or more of one and less of another. The border fabrics are given separately because you would need more of one fabric to create enough strips for borders.

Project Specifications

Skill Level: Intermediate

Quilt Size: 60" x 60"

Block Size: 11" and 23"

Number of Blocks: 8 Log Cabin;
   4 Sunbonnet Sue; 1 Wreath

Materials

- 6" x 6" scrap muslin
- 1/4 yard total each pink, yellow, blue, green and lavender prints
- 3/8 yard yellow print for second border
- 1/2 yard green print for first border
- 1/2 yard blue print for sashing
- 1/2 yard total each light pink, light blue, light green and light yellow prints
- 1 yard light pink print for sashing squares and outer border
- 1 1/4 yards white-with-pink print for background
- Backing 64" x 64"
- Batting 64" x 64"
- 7 1/8 yards self-made or purchased binding
- All-purpose thread to match fabrics
- Pink rayon thread
- 3/4 yard fusible transfer web
- 3/4 yard fabric stabilizer
- Basic sewing tools and supplies, rotary cutter, ruler and mat, and marking pencil

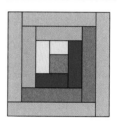

Log Cabin
11" x 11" Block

Sunbonnet Sue
11" x 11" Block

Wreath
23" x 23" Block

Instructions

Step 1. Prepare templates for appliqué shapes using patterns given. Prepare for fusible, machine appliqué referring to the General Instructions and to patterns for color and number to cut.

Step 2. Cut four 11 1/2" x 11 1/2" squares white-with-pink print for Sunbonnet Sue background.

Step 3. Arrange one Sunbonnet Sue appliqué motif on each background square in numerical order referring to the full-size pattern for positioning; fuse shapes in place in numerical order.

Step 4. Cut four 11" x 11" squares fabric stabilizer; place behind each fused square. Using pink rayon thread in the top of the machine and all-purpose thread in the bobbin and a machine buttonhole stitch, sew around each shape on each block in numerical order; remove stabilizer and set aside.

Step 5. Cut one strip 2 1/2" by fabric width pink print; subcut into 2 1/2" square segments for Log Cabin centers. You will need eight squares.

Step 6. Cut the following 2" by fabric width strips: two light yellow print; three light green print; four light pink print; five light blue print, three lavender print and two blue print.

Step 7. Sew the center square to the light yellow print strip as shown in Figure 1. Trim strip even with square as shown in Figure 2; press seam toward strip. Repeat with the same print strip; press and trim.

Figure 1
Sew the center square to the light yellow strip.

Trim

Figure 2
Trim strip even with square.

Step 8. Continue adding strips in this manner and referring to Figure 3 for color order until there are three logs on each side of the center. Repeat for eight blocks.

Step 9. Cut one 23 1/2" x 23 1/2" square white-with-pink print for center background. Fold and crease to mark center. Draw a 13" diameter circle in the center of the background as shown in Figure 4.

Figure 3
Continue adding strips in the order shown until there are 3 logs on each side of the center.

Figure 4
Draw a 13" diameter circle in the center of the background.

Step 10. Arrange prepared appliqué pieces on the circle using the full-size motif as a guide, repeating the motif five times on the circle. Fuse all leaves in place first, followed by the flowers.

Step 11. Machine-appliqué shapes in place as in Step 4.

Step 12. Prepare template for yo-yo; cut as directed on piece. Fold under edges of each yo-yo 1/8" all around. Hand-baste all around, knotting the end of the thread. Pull to gather as shown in Figure 5; tie a knot to hold. Repeat for all yo-yos.

Step 13. Arrange three yo-yos with gathered side up on the floral appliquéd wreath, overlapping as illustrated in the full-size motif; hand-stitch in place.

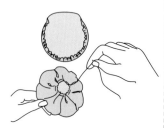

Figure 5
Make yo-yo as shown.

Step 14. Cut one 11 1/2" by fabric width strip blue print; subcut into 1 1/2" segments for sashing; you will need 20 sashing strips.

Step 15. Cut eight 1 1/2" x 1 1/2" squares light pink print for sashing squares.

Step 16. Join two Sunbonnet Sue and two Log Cabin blocks with three sashing strips to make a row as shown in Figure 6; repeat for two block rows. Press seams toward strips.

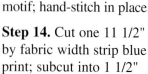

Figure 6
Join 2 Sunbonnet Sue and 2 Log Cabin blocks with 3 sashing strips to make a row.

Step 17. Join two Log Cabin blocks with one sashing strip as shown in Figure 7; repeat for two Log Cabin rows. Press seams toward strips.

Figure 7
Join 2 Log Cabin blocks with 1 sashing strip.

Figure 8
Join 2 sashing strips with 1 sashing square; sew to opposite sides of the Wreath block.

Step 18. Join two sashing strips with one sashing square; repeat. Sew to opposite sides of the Wreath block as shown in Figure 8; press seams toward strips.

Step 19. Sew the Log Cabin rows to opposite sides of the sashed Wreath block as shown in Figure 9; press seams toward sashing strips.

Step 20. Join four sashing strips with three sashing squares to make a sashing row as shown in Figure 10; repeat for two rows.

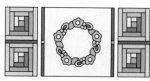

Figure 9
Sew the Log Cabin rows to opposite sides of the sashed Wreath block.

1 1/2" x 11 1/2"   1 1/2" x 1 1/2"

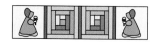

Figure 10
Join 4 sashing strips with 3 sashing squares to make a sashing row.

Step 21. Arrange the completed rows referring to the Placement Diagram; join rows to complete the quilt center. Press seams toward sashing rows.

Step 22. Cut and piece two strips each 2 1/2" x 47 1/2 and 2 1/2" x 51 1/2" green print. Sew the shorter strips to opposite sides and longer strips to the top and bottom of the quilt center; press seams toward strips.

Step 23. Cut and piece two strips each 1 1/2" x 51 1/2 and 1 1/2" x 53 1/2" yellow print. Sew the shorter strips to opposite sides and longer strips to the top and bottom of the quilt center; press seams toward strips.

Step 24. Cut and piece two strips each 4" x 53 1/2" and 4" x 60 1/2" light pink print. Sew the shorter strips to opposite sides and longer strips to the top and bottom of the quilt center; press seams toward strips.

Step 25. Prepare for quilting and finish referring to the General Instructions. ***Note:** The quilt shown was machine-quilted in a meandering design using pink rayon thread.* ❖

Hint

To avoid the shadow of the underneath fabric showing through when appliquéing a lighter fabric on top, apply a lightweight fusible interfacing to the lighter fabric before applying the fusible transfer web. This makes the fabric stiffer, but will help with the shadowing. If the top fabric is much lighter than the underneath fabric, it will help to trim away some of the underneath darker fabric before fusing using overlapping lines given on the full-size motifs as guides for trimming.

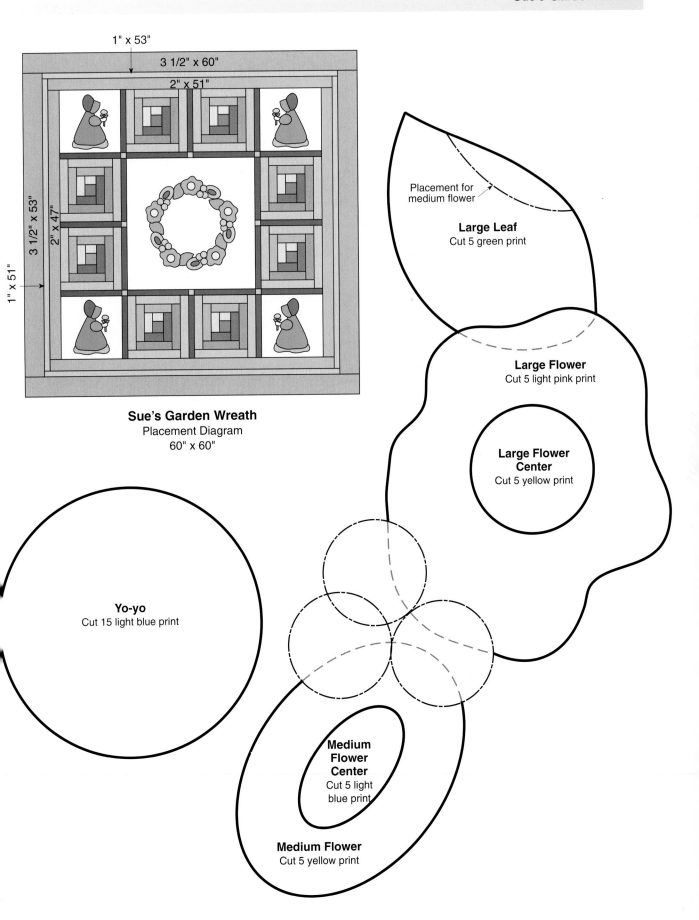

1" x 53"

3 1/2" x 60"

2" x 51"

3 1/2" x 53"

2" x 47"

1" x 51"

Sue's Garden Wreath
Placement Diagram
60" x 60"

Placement for
medium flower

Large Leaf
Cut 5 green print

Large Flower
Cut 5 light pink print

**Large Flower
Center**
Cut 5 yellow print

Yo-yo
Cut 15 light blue print

**Medium
Flower
Center**
Cut 5 light
blue print

Medium Flower
Cut 5 yellow print

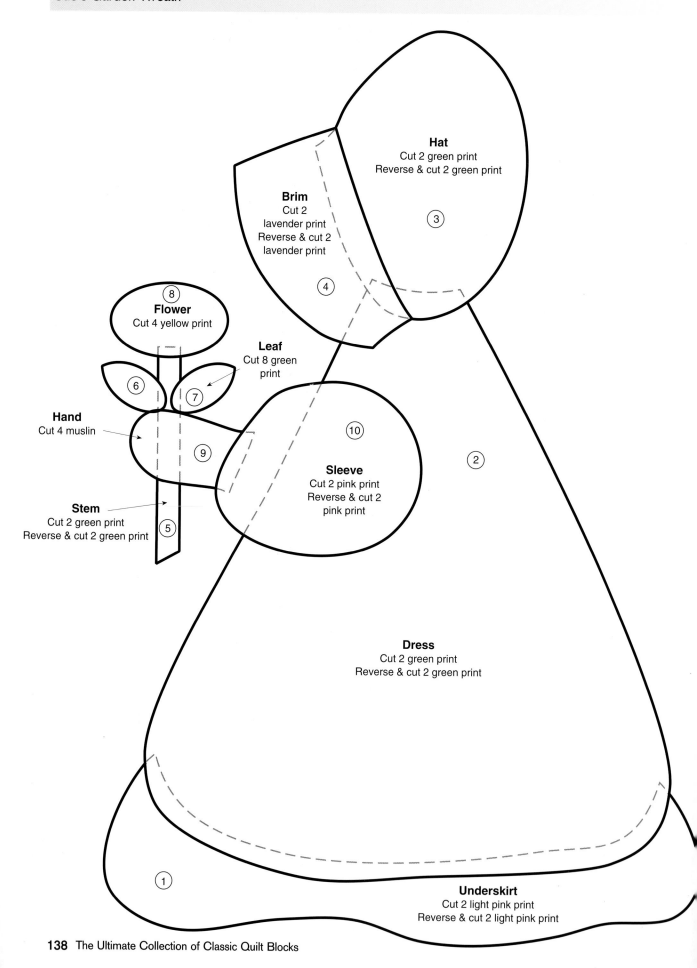

Hat
Cut 2 green print
Reverse & cut 2 green print

③

Brim
Cut 2
lavender print
Reverse & cut 2
lavender print

④

⑧
Flower
Cut 4 yellow print

Leaf
Cut 8 green
print

⑥

⑦

Hand
Cut 4 muslin

⑨

⑩

Sleeve
Cut 2 pink print
Reverse & cut 2
pink print

Stem
Cut 2 green print
Reverse & cut 2 green print

⑤

②

Dress
Cut 2 green print
Reverse & cut 2 green print

①

Underskirt
Cut 2 light pink print
Reverse & cut 2 light pink print

Sunday-Best Sue

By Marian Shenk

Sue is all decked out in her Sunday-best outfit, fit for a queen.

Project Specifications

Skill Level: Intermediate

Pillow Size: 16" x 16" without ruffle

Block Size: 16" x 16"

Number of Blocks: 1

Materials

- 6 different 9" x 9" squares coordinating floral prints
- 4" x 10" scrap burgundy tone-on-tone
- 3" x 3" scrap light rose solid
- 2" x 4" scrap muslin
- 1 yard cream-on-cream print
- Backing 16 1/2" x 16 1/2"
- Batting 16 1/2" x 16 1/2"
- Cream and pink all-purpose thread
- White hand-quilting thread
- Dark green 6-strand embroidery floss
- 3 pink/rose-tone ribbon flowers
- 3 pink/rose-tone ribbon flowers with leaves
- 1/2 yard 1/2"-wide white gathered lace
- 6 tiny crystal beads
- 2 yards 3/8"-wide cream ribbon braid
- 4 yards 1/2"-wide off-white flat lace
- 16" x 16" pillow form
- Basic sewing tools and supplies

Instructions

Step 1. Cut one 12 1/2" x 12 1/2" square cream-on-cream print for background; fold and crease to mark center.

Step 2. Prepare templates for appliqué pieces and prepare for hand appliqué referring to the General Instructions. For hand, place two pieces right sides together; stitch, leaving top edge open. Clip curves; turn right side out.

Sunday-Best Sue
Placement Diagram
16" x 16" without ruffle

Sunday Best
16" x 16" Block

Figure 1
Join 6 D pieces
to make skirt.

Step 3. Prepare templates for pieces A–D; cut as directed on each piece.

Step 4. Join six D pieces to make skirt for appliqué as shown in Figure 1; turn under outside edge seam allowance.

Step 5. Center and arrange the pieced D unit with the remaining appliqué shapes in numerical order on the background square. Hand-appliqué all pieces in place using all-purpose thread to match fabrics and referring to the General Instructions. Cut a 1" piece 1/2"-wide white gathered lace; turn ends under and stitch

Step 12. Join four A-A units with one A-B unit to complete a side strip as shown in Figure 2; repeat for four side strips.

Step 13. Sew a side strip to opposite sides of the appliquéd

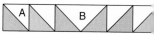

Figure 2
Join 4 A-A units with 1 A-B unit to complete a side strip.

center; press seams toward strips. Sew a C square to each end of the remaining two side strips; press seams toward squares. Sew these strips to the remaining sides of the appliquéd center; press seams toward strips to complete the block.

Step 14. Prepare completed pillow top for quilting and quilt referring to the General Instructions. *Note: The pillow shown was hand-quilted around the appliquéd motif, in the ditch of pieced seams and using a purchased quilting design in the background using white hand-quilting thread.*

Step 15. Pin the 3/8"-wide cream ribbon braid over seams between center background and pieced border strips. Machine-stitch in place.

between hand and sleeve after appliqué is complete.

Step 6. Cut a 14" piece 1/2"-wide white gathered lace; turn ends under and machine-stitch top edge of lace over bottom edges of D pieces to make ruffle at bottom of skirt edge.

Step 7. Transfer embroidery lines to appliquéd motif referring to pattern for placement. Hand-embroider stem using a stem stitch and leaves using a lazy-daisy stitch and 2 strands dark green embroidery floss.

Step 8. Sew a ribbon flower to the end of each stem. Sew three ribbon flowers with leaves in a cluster on the hatband referring to pattern for placement.

Step 9. Sew the crystal beads to the bodice area referring to pattern for positioning.

Step 10. Sew a cream-on-cream print A to a floral print A along the diagonal to make a triangle/square unit; repeat for 16 units.

Step 11. Sew a floral print A to the short sides of B to complete an A-B unit; repeat for four units.

Step 16. Cut three strips cream-on-cream print 2 1/2" by fabric width. Join strips on short ends to make a tube.

Step 17. Pin the 1/2"-wide off-white flat lace wrong side against wrong side of one raw edge of tube; stitch. Fold lace to the right side and topstitch in place. *Note: This may seem incorrect, but when the lace is turned to the right side, it provides a finished edge without a hem on the wrong side of the ruffle.*

Step 18. Stitch two lines of gathering stitches close to the remaining raw edge of the tube; mark four equal sections on the tube and pull threads to gather.

Step 19. Fit tube to the finished pillow top, matching marks with corners of pillow; pull threads to evenly distribute gathering. Pin right sides together with finished pillow top; stitch all around.

Step 20. Place backing piece right sides together with top piece; stitch all around, leaving a 10" opening on one side. Turn right side out; insert pillow form. Hand-stitch opening closed to finish. ❖

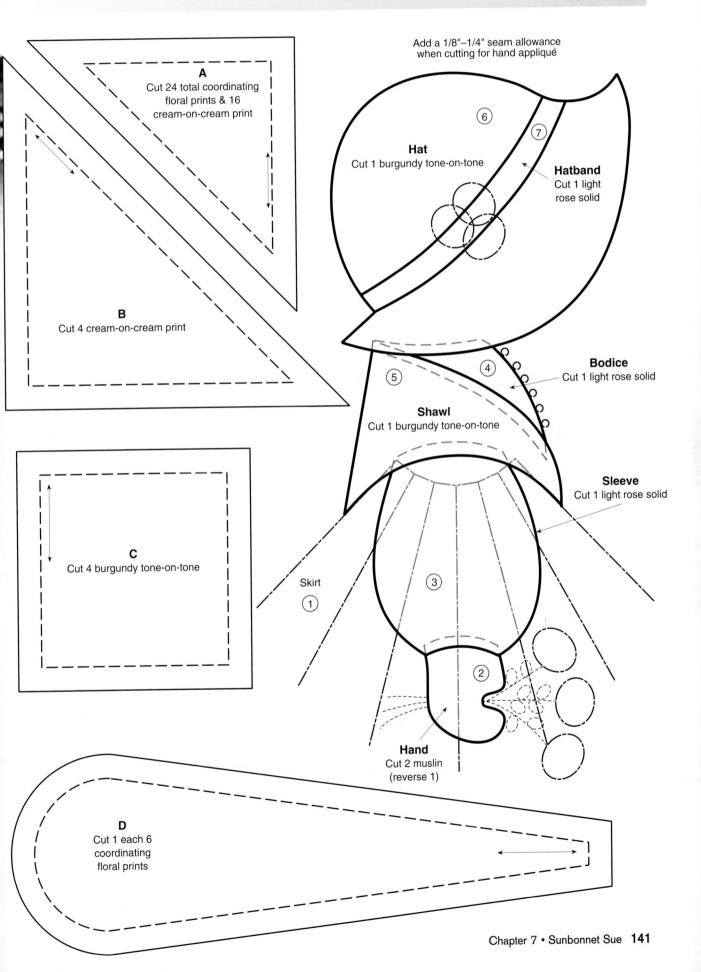

A
Cut 24 total coordinating
floral prints & 16
cream-on-cream print

B
Cut 4 cream-on-cream print

C
Cut 4 burgundy tone-on-tone

D
Cut 1 each 6
coordinating
floral prints

Add a 1/8"–1/4" seam allowance
when cutting for hand appliqué

⑥

⑦

Hat
Cut 1 burgundy tone-on-tone

Hatband
Cut 1 light
rose solid

④

⑤

Bodice
Cut 1 light rose solid

Shawl
Cut 1 burgundy tone-on-tone

Sleeve
Cut 1 light rose solid

Skirt
①

③

②

Hand
Cut 2 muslin
(reverse 1)

Sunbonnet Sue in the Kitchen

By Phyllis Dobbs

Sunbonnet Sue adds a fun decorative accent to any kitchen.

Project Specifications

Skill Level: Beginner

Project Size: 7 1/2" x 10 3/4"

Materials

- 2" x 3" scrap peach solid
- 1/4 yard yellow solid
- 1/4 yard floral print
- 16" x 16" batting
- All-purpose thread to match fabrics and buttons
- 3 (3/8") green buttons
- 1 (7/8") red heart button
- 24" (7/8") Cluny lace
- Small plastic ring for hanging
- Basic sewing tools and supplies

Instructions

Step 1. Prepare templates using pattern pieces given; cut as directed on each piece.

Step 2. Turn under 1/8" on the curved edges of the apron pieces, clipping into seam as necessary; stitch. Repeat on bottom edges. Stitch the Cluny lace along the bottom seam on one of the pieces.

Step 3. Pin each apron piece to a dress piece with top and side edges aligned; baste to hold.

Step 4. Pin the two hand pieces right sides together; lay on top of batting and stitch around curved edges. Trim seam and turn right side out.

Step 5. Layer sleeve pieces with batting, insert hand piece between the two fabric pieces as indicated on pattern. Stitch all around, leaving a 1" opening along one side. Trim seams; turn right side out. Hand-stitch opening closed.

Step 6. Sew the three green buttons across the bottom of the sleeve. Place the sleeve on the dress piece with lace. Stitch the red heart button through all layers,

referring to the X on the sleeve pattern for placement.

Step 7. Using 2 strands green all-purpose thread, quilt across the dress below the apron and across the sleeve above the green buttons.

Step 8. Stitch the basted apron/dress pieces along the side edges with right sides together, leaving top and bottom edges open; turn right side out and press. Repeat with remaining dress pieces for lining, leaving wrong side out.

Step 9. Stitch the side edges of the two dress batting pieces together; trim seams.

Step 10. Pin the stitched batting piece inside the apron/dress pieces; pin the lining pieces right sides

ether with the apron/dress unit. Stitch along bottom
ved edges. Turn lining to inside; press. Stitch Cluny
e on the outside at bottom edge, overlapping at
ginning and end.

p 11. Place bonnet pieces right sides together;
 two layers of batting on top. Stitch all
und, leaving a 2" opening on the bottom
k area as marked on pattern. Trim
ms, turn right side out and press,
ning under seam allowances on
en edges.

p 12. Place bonnet piece over
 edge of dress, inserting top
dress inside open seam in
nnet; hand-stitch layers
ether on both top and
k sides.

ep 13. Hand-stitch
 plastic ring to the
 backside of the
nnet to hang, if
sired, or use to
ver your dish
tergent. ❖

Sunbonnet Sue in the Kitchen
Placement Diagram
7 1/2" x 10 3/4"

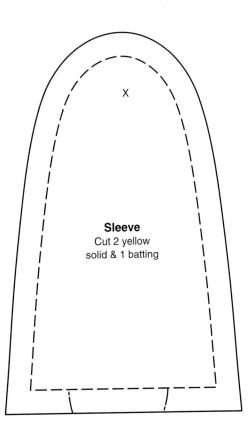

Place line on fold

Dress
Cut 4 yellow solid & 2 batting

X

Sleeve
Cut 2 yellow
solid & 1 batting

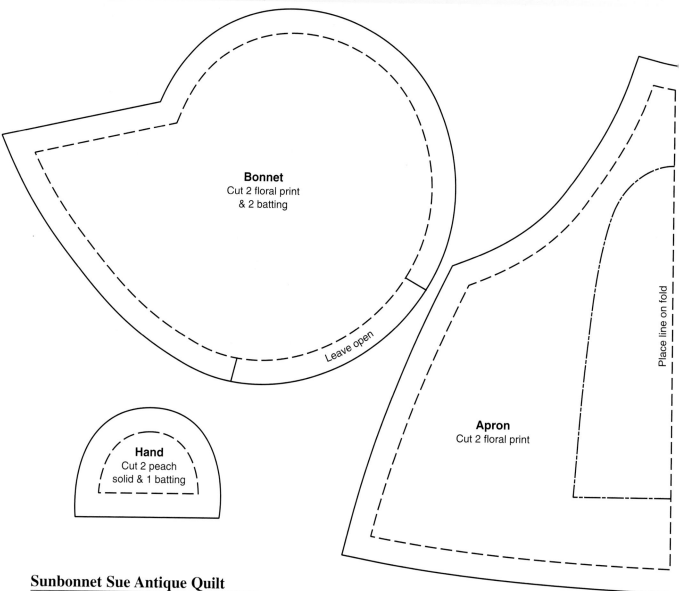

Bonnet
Cut 2 floral print
& 2 batting

Leave open

Place line on fold

Apron
Cut 2 floral print

Hand
Cut 2 peach
solid & 1 batting

Sunbonnet Sue Antique Quilt

Continued from page 131

referring to Figure 2; repeat for six sashing rows. Press seams toward sashing squares.

4 1/2" x 4 1/2"   4 1/2" x 11 1/2"

Figure 2
Join 4 sashing strips with 5 sashing squares to make a sashing row.

Step 10. Join the block rows with the sashing rows, beginning and ending with a sashing row. Press seams toward sashing rows.

Step 11. Prepare quilt top for quilting and finish using self-made or purchased pink binding referring to the General Instructions. ***Note:** The quilt shown was*

hand-quilted with white hand-quilting thread in a repeated curved design through all layers, including the appliqué designs. ❖

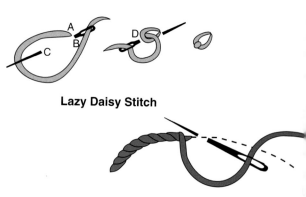

Lazy Daisy Stitch

Stem Stitch

Twinkle, Twinkle Little Star

By Mary Ayers

Sunbonnet Sue takes a ride on the moon in this pretty appliquéd wall quilt.

Project Specifications

Skill Level: Beginner

Quilt Size: 10" x 15"

Materials

- 10 1/2" x 10 1/2" square blue cloud print
- Two 3" x 10 1/2" rectangles light blue mottled
- 7" x 9" scrap yellow print
- Scraps white, light and dark pink, peach and blue tone-on-tone or mottleds
- Batting 12" x 17"
- Backing 12" x 17"
- All-purpose thread to match fabrics
- White and bright blue 6-strand embroidery floss
- 1 1/2 yards white jumbo rickrack
- 1/4 yard 1/4" dark blue satin ribbon
- 3 (7/16") flat white buttons
- 1 (1/2") flat yellow button
- 1/4 yard fusible transfer web
- Basic sewing tools and supplies, rotary cutter, mat and ruler

Instructions

Step 1. Prepare templates for appliqué shapes using patterns given. Prepare for fusible, machine appliqué referring to the General Instructions and to patterns for color and number to cut.

Step 2. Arrange the appliqué motifs on the 10 1/2" x 10 1/2" square blue cloud print referring to the Placement Diagram for positioning; fuse shapes in place in numerical order.

Step 3. Using 3 strands bright blue embroidery floss and a buttonhole stitch, hand-stitch around each fused shape.

Step 4. Transfer star rays to background referring to pattern for positioning. Straight-stitch ray lines using 3 strands bright blue embroidery floss.

Step 5. Center and transfer the word messages to the 3" x 10 1/2" rectangles. Using 3 strands white embroidery floss, make a French knot on the comma dot, wrapping floss around needle three times. Embroider comma line and letters using a stem stitch.

Step 6. Sew the "Twinkle, Twinkle" message to the top of the appliquéd square and the "Little Star" message to the bottom; press seams away from strips.

Step 7. Baste batting to wrong side of the appliquéd top; trim even. Sew the white jumbo rickrack around top edges 1/4" from edge, beginning and ending in a

Messages

bottom corner and sewing through the center of the rickrack.

Step 8. Place backing piece right sides together with appliquéd top; trim edges even. Stitch all around, leaving a 5" opening along bottom edges for turning. Trim corners; turn right side out. Hand-stitch opening closed.

Step 9. Tie the dark blue satin ribbon into a bow; trim ends even. Sew buttons and bow to wall quilt through all layers, using 3 strands blue embroidery floss; attach white buttons as dots for i letters, yellow button in center of star and bow to hat as indicated on pattern to finish. ❖

Twinkle, Twinkle Little Star
Placement Diagram
10" x 15"

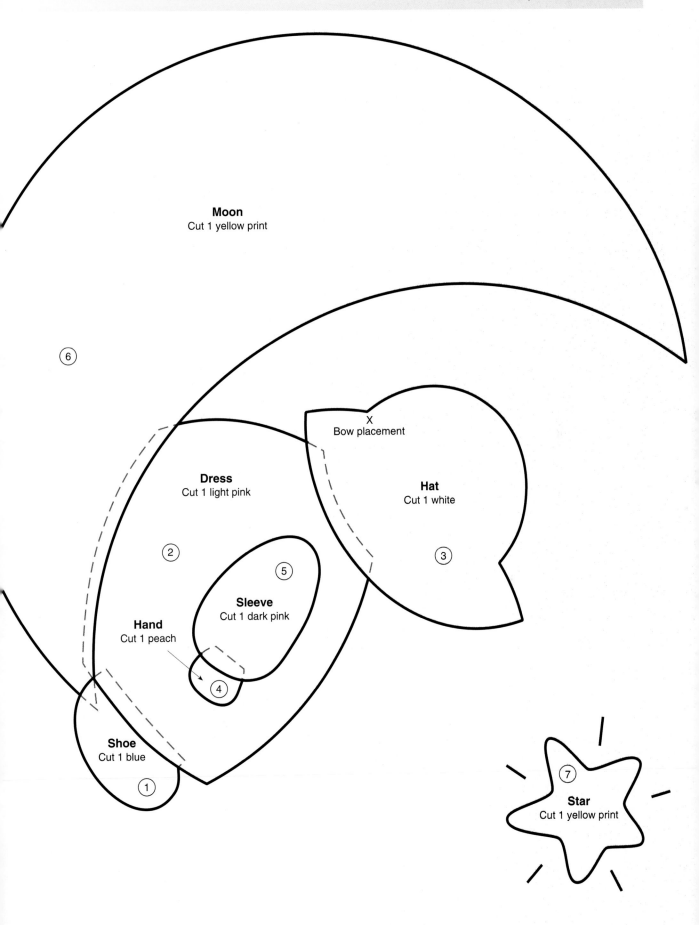

Moon
Cut 1 yellow print

⑥

X
Bow placement

Dress
Cut 1 light pink

Hat
Cut 1 white

②

③

⑤

Sleeve
Cut 1 dark pink

Hand
Cut 1 peach

④

Shoe
Cut 1 blue

①

⑦

Star
Cut 1 yellow print

Star Quilts

Star light, star bright,
Stars shine on my quilt
tonight!

Antique String Stars

From the collection of Sue Harvey

The maker of this turn-of-the-century quilt found a way to use her many scraps in the points of these eight-pointed stars. She saved the centers for the patriotic combination of red, white and blue fabrics.

Project Note

The antique quilt shown was pieced as one unit with large and small squares set in between the points of the stars. To simplify piecing, the stars were separated into individual blocks in these instructions.

Project Specifications

Skill Level: Advanced

Quilt Size: 69" x 83"

Block Size: 14" x 14"

Number of Blocks: 20

Materials

- 3/4 yard total each red and white scraps
- 3/4 yard red print
- 1 yard total navy scraps
- 2 yards muslin
- 3 yards total assorted scraps
- 3 3/4 yards green print
- Backing 73" x 86"
- Batting 73" x 86"
- All-purpose thread to match fabrics
- White quilting thread
- Basic sewing tools and supplies

Instructions

Step 1. Prepare templates for pattern pieces given; cut as directed on each piece for one block.

Step 2. Place an assorted scrap strip wrong side against one end of C as shown in Figure 1.

Step 3. Place another

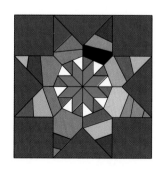
String Star
14" x 14" Block

assorted scrap strip right sides together with the first strip; stitch along the edge as shown in Figure 2. Trim the seam allowance to 1/4"; press the second strip open.

Figure 1
Place a scrap strip on 1 end of C.

Figure 2
Place a second scrap strip right sides together with the first strip; stitch along edge.

Step 4. Continue to add scrap strips in random widths and shapes to completely cover C; trim scrap edges even with C. Repeat to make four each crazy-pieced C and CR pieces.

Step 5. Sew a red scrap and a white scrap B to adjacent sides of A as shown in Figure 3; press seams toward B. Repeat for eight A-B units.

Step 6. Sew a crazy-pieced C to the B end of an A-B unit as shown in Figure 4; repeat for eight A-B-C units.

Figure 3
Sew a red and white B to adjacent sides of A.

Figure 4
Add a crazy-pieced C to A-B.

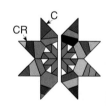

Figure 5
Join the A-B-C units.

Step 7. Join the A-B-C units as shown in Figure 5; set in the D and E pieces to complete one block as shown in Figure 6. Repeat to make 20 blocks.

Step 8. Join four blocks to make a row; repeat for five rows. Join the rows to complete the pieced center.

Step 9. Cut and piece two strips each 2 1/2" x 56 1/2" and 2 1/2"

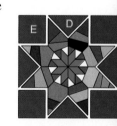

Figure 6
Set in D and E pieces to complete 1 block.

74 1/2" red print. Sew the shorter strips to the top
ad bottom of the pieced center and the longer strips
 opposite long sides; press seams toward strips.

ep 10. Cut and piece two strips each 5" x
 1/2" and 5" x 83 1/2" green print. Sew
e shorter strips to the top and bottom
f the pieced center and the longer
rips to opposite long sides; press
ams toward strips to com-
ete the top.

ep 11. Prepare top for
uilting and quilt
eferring to the
ontinued on
ge 158

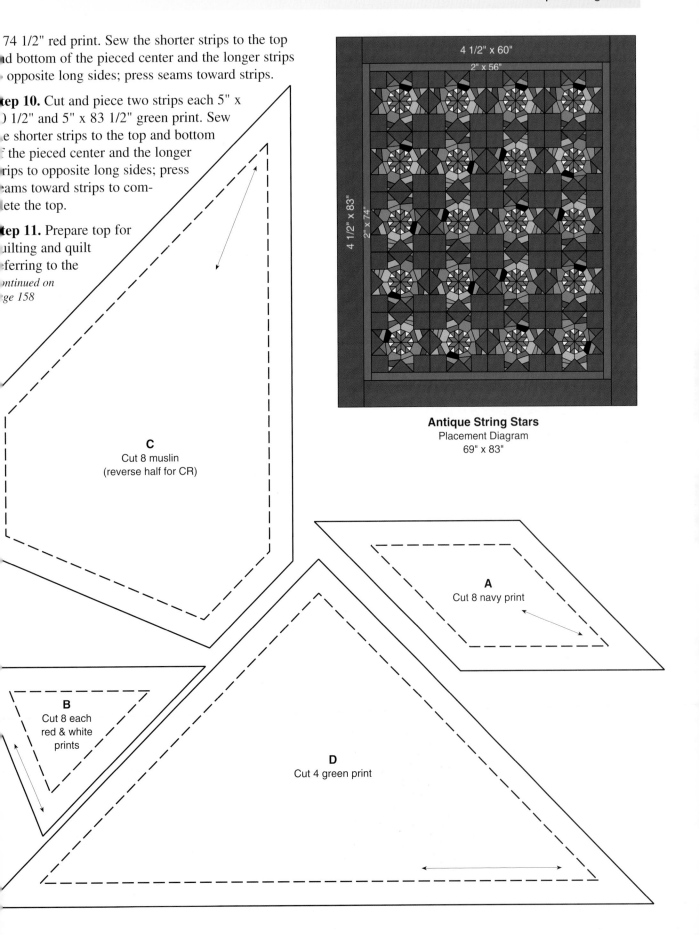

Antique String Stars
Placement Diagram
69" x 83"

C
Cut 8 muslin
(reverse half for CR)

A
Cut 8 navy print

B
Cut 8 each
red & white
prints

D
Cut 4 green print

Star Stages

By Sue Harvey

The traditional Sawtooth Star is shown in the three stages of its life cycle.

Project Specifications

Skill Level: Beginner

Quilt Size: 75 1/2" x 75 1/2"

Block Size: 18" x 18"

Number of Blocks: 9

Materials

- 5/8 yard gold print
- 1 1/4 yards floral print
- 1 5/8 yards stripe
- 2 yards each green mottled and burgundy print
- Batting 80" x 80"
- Backing 80" x 80"
- All-purpose thread to match fabrics
- Basic sewing tools and supplies, rotary cutter, mat and ruler

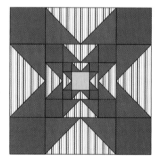

Star Stages A
18" x 18" Block
Make 5

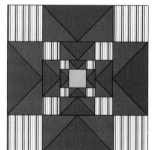

Star Stages B
18" x 18" Block
Make 4

Instructions

Step 1. Cut one strip gold print 2 3/4" by fabric width; subcut into 2 3/4" square segments for D. You will need nine D squares.

Step 2. Cut the following green mottled fabric-width strips: two 2", three 3 1/8" and six 5 3/8". Cut each strip into square segments and each square segment on one diagonal to make triangles as follows: 2" square segments to make 72 B triangles, 3 1/8" square segments to make 72 F triangles and 5 3/8" square

segments to make 72 I triangles.

Step 3. Cut the following stripe fabric-width strips: one 3 1/2", one 5 3/4" and two 10 1/4". Cut each strip into square segments and each square segment on both diagonals to make triangles as follows: 3 1/2" square segments to make 20 stripe A triangles, 5 3/4" square segments to make 20 stripe E triangles and 10 1/4" square segments to make 20 stripe H triangles.

Step 4. Cut the following stripe fabric-width strips: one 1 5/8", two 2 3/4" and two 5". Cut each strip into square segments as follows: 1 5/8" to make 16 stripe C squares, 2 3/4" to make 16 stripe G squares and 5" to make 16 stripe J squares.

Step 5. Cut the following burgundy print fabric-width strips: one 3 1/2", one 5 3/4" and one 10 1/4". Cut each strip into square segments and each square segment on both diagonals to make triangles as follows: 3 1/2" square segments to make 16 burgundy A triangles, 5 3/4" square segments to make 16 burgundy E triangles and 10 1/4" square segments to make 16 burgundy H triangles.

Step 6. Cut the following burgundy print fabric-width strips: one 1 5/8", two 2 3/4" and three 5". Cut each strip into square segments as follows: 1 5/8" to make 20 burgundy C squares, 2 3/4" to make 20 burgundy G squares and 5" to make 20 burgundy J squares.

Step 7. To piece one Star Stages A block, sew B to adjacent sides of a stripe A as shown in Figure 1; repeat for four A-B units.

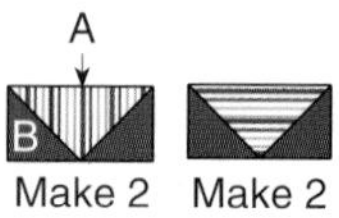

Make 2   Make 2

Figure 1
Sew B to adjacent sides of A.

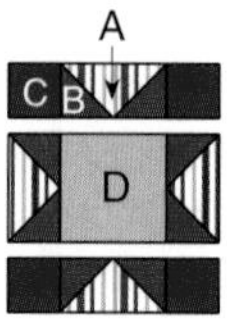

Figure 2
Sew C to each end of A-B; sew to the remaining sides of D.

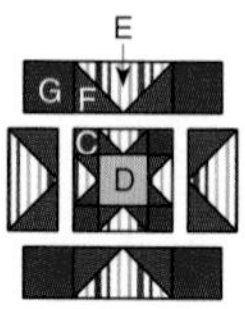

Figure 3
Sew E-F units and G squares to the pieced unit.

Step 8. Sew an A-B unit to opposite sides of D. Sew a burgundy C to each end of the remaining A-B units and sew to the remaining sides of D as shown in Figure 2.

Step 9. Sew F to adjacent sides of a stripe E; repeat for four E-F units. Sew E-F to opposite sides of the pieced unit; sew a burgundy G to each end of the remaining E-F units and sew to the remaining sides of the pieced unit as shown in Figure 3.

Step 10. Sew I to adjacent sides of a stripe H; repeat for four H-I units. Sew H-I to opposite sides of the pieced unit; sew a burgundy J to each end of the remaining H-I units and sew to the remaining sides of the pieced unit to complete one block as shown in

Figure 4. Repeat for five Star Stages A blocks.

Step 11. Repeat steps 7–10 to make four Star Stages B blocks using burgundy A, E and H triangles and stripe C, G and J squares as shown in Figure 5.

Step 12. Join two Star Stages A blocks with one Star Stages B block to make a row as shown in Figure 6; repeat.

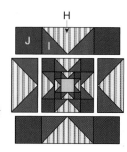

Figure 4
Sew H-I units and J squares to the pieced unit to complete 1 Star Stages A block.

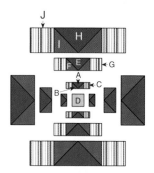

Figure 5
Complete 1 Star Stages B block as shown.

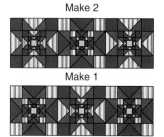

Make 2

Make 1

Figure 6
Join blocks to make rows as shown.

Step 13. Join two Star Stages B blocks with one Star Stages A block to make a row, again referring to Figure 6.

Step 14. Join the rows to complete the pieced center referring to the Placement Diagram for positioning of rows.

Step 15. Cut and piece two strips each 2 3/4" x 54 1/2" and 2 3/4" x 59" gold print. Sew the shorter strips to opposite sides of the pieced center and the longer strips to the remaining sides; press seams toward strips.

Step 16. Cut four strips each stripe and burgundy print 5" by fabric width. Join one strip each fabric along length to make a strip set; repeat for four strip sets. Cut each strip set into 5" segments as shown in Figure 7.

Figure 7
Cut strip sets into 5" segments.

Step 17. Join seven segments to make a border strip as shown in Figure 8; repeat for four border strips. Remove a burgundy square from one end of two border strips; sew the square to the stripe end of the remaining border strips as shown in Figure 9.

Figure 8
Join 7 segments to make a border strip.

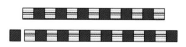

Figure 9
Remove a burgundy square from 1 end of 2 border strips; sew to the stripe end of the remaining strips.

Step 18. Sew the shorter border strips to opposite sides of the pieced center and the longer border strips to the remaining sides.

Step 19. Cut and piece two strips each large floral print 4 1/2" x 68" and 4 1/2" x 76". Sew the shorter strips to opposite sides of the bordered center and the longer strips to the remaining sides to complete the pieced top.

Step 20. Prepare quilt top for quilting referring to the General Instructions. *Note: The sample shown was professionally machine-quilted in an allover pattern.*

Step 21. Prepare 8 3/4 yards green mottled print binding and finish edges referring to the General Instructions.

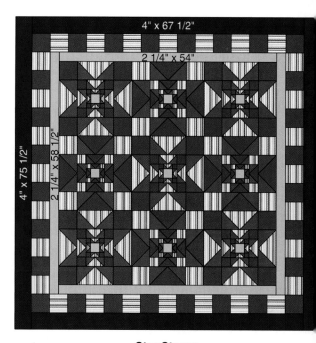

Star Stages
Placement Diagram
75 1/2" x 75 1/2"

Hands All Around Runner

By Ruth Swasey

If you like to fussy cut fabrics with a small motif, try centering a flower in the squares and triangles of the pieced blocks in this pretty table runner.

Project Specifications

Skill Level: Intermediate

Runner Size: 48" x 20"

Block Size: 12" x 12"

Number of Blocks: 3

Materials

- 1/4 yard purple print
- 1/2 yard green print
- 5/8 yard yellow print
- 3/4 yard red mottled stripe
- 1 yard white print
- Backing 52" x 24"
- Batting 52" x 24"
- 4 1/4 yards self-made or purchased binding
- All-purpose thread to match fabrics
- Yellow machine-quilting thread
- Basic sewing tools and supplies

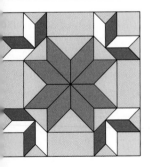

Hands All Around
12" x 12" Block

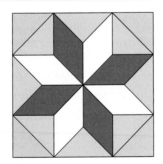

Eight-Pointed Star
12" x 12" Block

Instructions

Step 1. Prepare templates using pattern pieces given; cut as directed on each piece for one Eight-Pointed Star block, two Hands All Around blocks and 64 K triangles for borders.

Step 2. To piece one Eight-Pointed Star block, join two J pieces as shown in Figure 1; repeat for four J units. Join J units to complete star design.

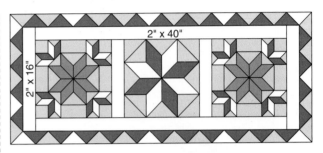

Hands All Around Runner
Placement Diagram
48" x 20"

Figure 1
Join 2 J pieces
as shown.

Figure 2
Join pieces to
complete a
corner unit.

Figure 3
Join pieces to
make a side unit.

Step 3. Sew a yellow print H to a green print H; repeat for four H units. Set L into side star points and an H unit into each corner to complete the Eight-Pointed Star block.

Step 4. To piece one Hands All Around block, sew C to CR; repeat. Join the two C units and set in B and A; add D to complete one corner unit as shown in Figure 2; repeat for four corner units.

Step 5. Sew G to GR; set in F and add E to complete one side unit as shown in Figure 3. Repeat for four side units. Join the side units and set in the corner units to complete one Hands All Around block; repeat for two blocks.

Step 6. Cut two strips 2 1/2" x 12 1/2" white print. Sew a strip to two opposite sides of the Eight-Pointed Star block; add a Hands All Around block to the strip sides of the block to complete the pieced center as shown in Figure 4; press seams toward strips.

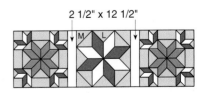

Figure 4
Join blocks with strips as shown.

Step 7. Cut two strips 2 1/2" x 40 1/2" white print; sew to opposite sides of the pieced center. Press seams toward strips.

Step 8. Cut two strips 2 1/2" x 16 1/2" white print; sew a strip to the two opposite short ends of the pieced center. Press seams toward strips.

Step 9. Join 11 red K triangles with white, yellow and green K triangles as shown in Figure 5; repeat for two strips, again referring to Figure 5. Sew a strip to opposite long sides of the pieced center; press seams away from K triangles.

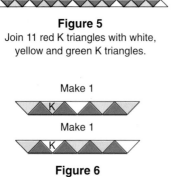

Figure 5
Join 11 red K triangles with white, yellow and green K triangles.

Make 1

Make 1

Figure 6
Join 4 red K triangles with white, yellow and green K triangles.

Step 10. Join four red K triangles with white, yellow and green K triangles as shown in Figure 6; repeat for two strips,

again referring to Figure 6. Sew a strip to opposite short ends of the pieced center; press seams away from K triangles.

Step 11. Prepare completed top for quilting and finish referring to the General Instructions. *Note: The quilt shown was machine-quilted in the ditch of seams on pieced blocks and 3/8" from seams in the white print border strips using yellow machine-quilting thread.* ❖

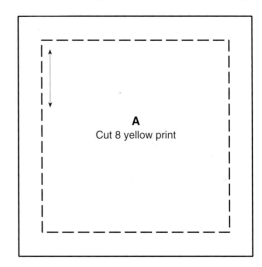

A
Cut 8 yellow print

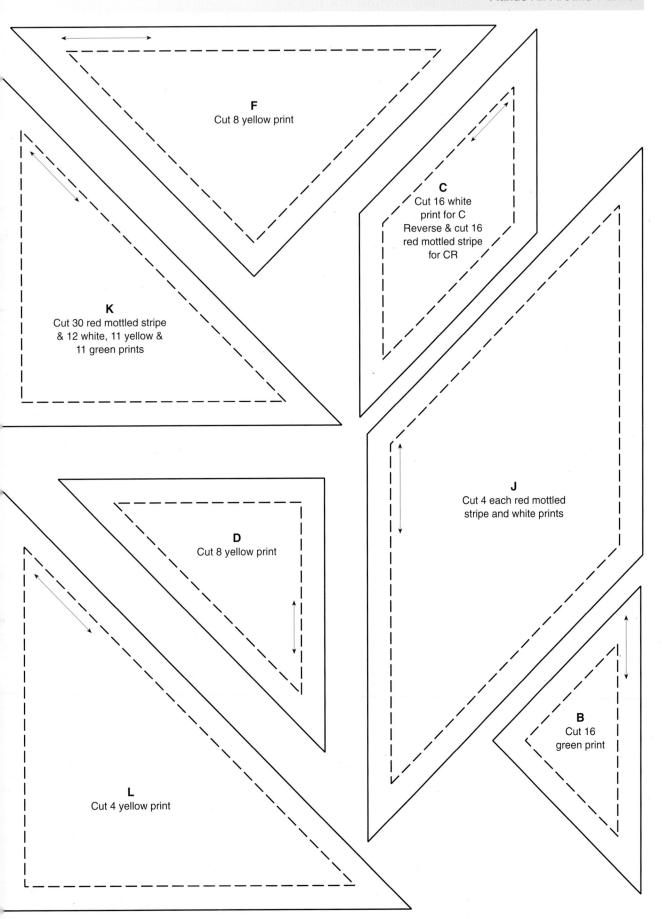

F
Cut 8 yellow print

C
Cut 16 white
print for C
Reverse & cut 16
red mottled stripe
for CR

K
Cut 30 red mottled stripe
& 12 white, 11 yellow &
11 green prints

J
Cut 4 each red mottled
stripe and white prints

D
Cut 8 yellow print

B
Cut 16
green print

L
Cut 4 yellow print

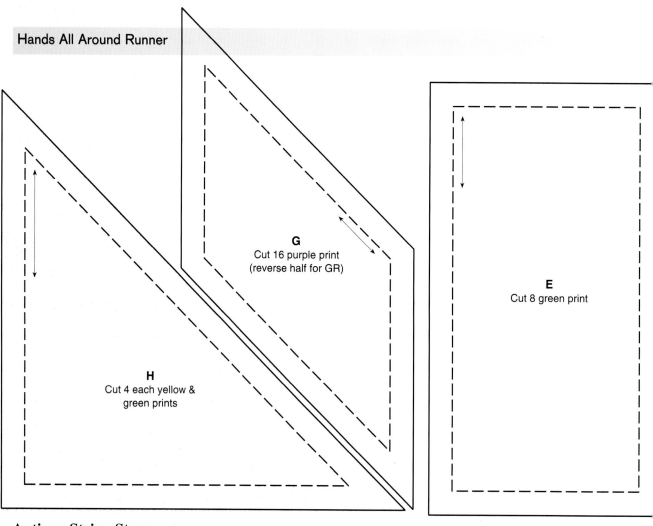

G
Cut 16 purple print
(reverse half for GR)

H
Cut 4 each yellow &
green prints

E
Cut 8 green print

Antique String Stars

Continued from page 151

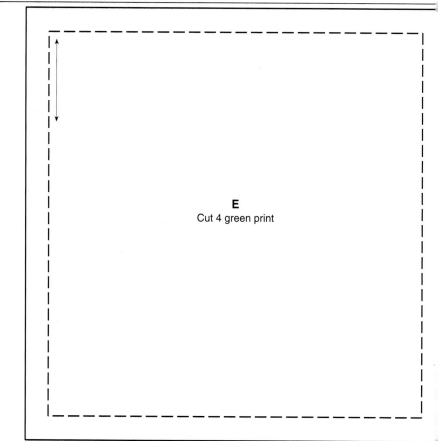

E
Cut 4 green print

General Instructions. **Note:** *The antique quilt shown was hand-quilted in a scallop pattern using white quilting thread.*

Step 12. Cut eight strips 2 1/4" by fabric width green print. Join strips to make 9 yards of binding; bind edges of quilt referring to the General Instructions. ❖

Hidden Stars

By Judith Sandstrom

Two pieced blocks combine to create a secondary design in this bed-size quilt.

Project Specifications

Skill Level: Beginner

Quilt Size: 81 1/2" x 96"

Block Size: 14 1/2" x 14 1/2"

Number of Blocks: 30

Materials

- 5/8 yard light green print
- 1 yard each rust and cream tone-on-tones
- 1 3/4 yards dark green tone-on-tone
- 1 3/8 yards green/rust print
- 1 7/8 yards black print
- 2 1/4 yards peach print
- Backing 86" x 100"
- Batting 86" x 100"
- All-purpose thread to match fabrics
- White hand-quilting thread
- Basic sewing tools and supplies, rotary cutter, ruler and mat

Hidden Stars
Placement Diagram
81 1/2" x 96"

Figure 1
Cut each square in half on both diagonals to make A triangles.

Figure 2
Cut each square in half on 1 diagonal to make B triangles.

Figure 3
Sew a light green B to each side of a C square.

Block A
14 1/2" x 14 1/2" Block

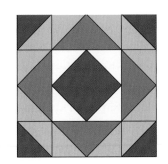

Block B
14 1/2" x 14 1/2" Block

Instructions

Step 1. Cut three 8 1/2" by fabric width strips each peach print and rust tone-on-tone; cut each strip into 8 1/2" square segments. Cut each square in half on both diagonals to make A triangles as shown in Figure 1; you will need 60 A triangles of each fabric.

Step 2. Cut four strips light green print, seven strips each dark green and cream tone-on-tones and black print and 10 strips peach print 4 1/2" by fabric width. Subcut each strip into 4 1/2" square segments for B; cut each square in half on one diagonal to make B triangles as shown in Figure 2. You will need 60 light green, 120 each black, cream and dark green and 180 peach B triangles.

Step 3. Cut five 5 5/8" by fabric width strips black print; subcut each strip into 5 5/8" square segments for C. You will need 30 C squares.

Step 4. To piece Block A, sew a light green B to each side of a C square referring to Figure 3; press seams away from C. Repeat for 15 B-C units.

Step 5. Sew a dark green B to two adjacent short sides of a peach A as shown in Figure 4; repeat for 60 A-B units.

Step 6. Sew a cream B to a black B to make a B unit as shown in Figure 5; repeat for 60 B units.

Figure 4
Sew a dark green B
to 2 adjacent short
sides of a peach A.

Figure 5
Sew a white B
to a black B to
make a B unit.

Step 7. Sew an A-B unit to opposite sides of a B-C unit as shown in Figure 6; sew a B unit to opposite ends of two A-B units and add to the pieced unit to complete one Block A, again referring to Figure 6. Repeat for 15 blocks.

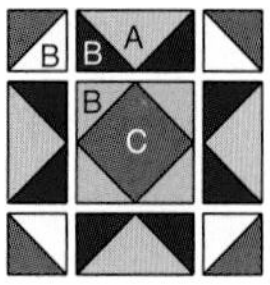

Figure 6
Join units as shown
to complete Block A.

Step 8. To piece Block B, sew a cream B to each side of a C square; press seams away from C. Repeat for 15 B-C units.

Step 9. Sew a peach B triangle to two adjacent short sides of a rust A; repeat for 60 A-B units.

Step 10. Sew a peach B to a black B to make a B unit; repeat for 60 B units.

Step 11. Sew an A-B unit to opposite sides of a B-C unit as shown in Figure 7; sew a B unit to opposite ends of two A-B units and add to the pieced unit to complete one Block B, again referring to Figure 7. Repeat for 15 blocks.

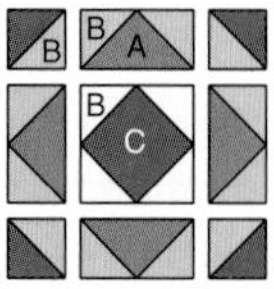

Figure 7
Join units as shown
to complete Block B.

Step 12. Join three A blocks with two B blocks to make a row; repeat for three rows. Join three B blocks with two A blocks to make a row; repeat for three rows. Press seams in one direction.

Step 13. Join the block rows, alternating rows, to complete the pieced center; press seams in one direction.

Step 14. Cut and piece two strips each 5" x 82" and 5" x 87 1/2" green/rust print. Sew the longer strips to opposite long sides and shorter strips to the top and bottom of the pieced center; press seams toward strips.

Step 15. Prepare quilt and finish referring to the General Instructions. *Note: The quilt shown was hand-quilted 1/4" from some seams and in the ditch of others using white hand-quilting thread.*

Step 16. Prepare 10 1/2 yards self-made dark green tone-on-tone binding and finish edges referring to the General Instructions. ❖

Harvest Sun Wall Quilt

By Christine Schultz

Combine paper piecing with appliqué to create this harvest wall quilt.

Project Specifications

Skill Level: Advanced

Quilt Size: 20 1/4" x 27"

Block Size: 15 3/4" diameter

Materials

- 5" x 5" square each green, dark mossy green and yellow mottleds, and red and gold prints
- Small scraps brown solid and green-on-green print
- 1/8 yard each light green and purple mottleds
- 1/4 yard each rust and green prints
- 1 1/8 yards tan-on-cream print
- Backing 24" x 31"
- Batting 24" x 31"
- All-purpose thread to match fabrics
- Cream hand-quilting thread
- Medium brown 6-strand embroidery floss
- 22" of 1/2"-diameter wooden dowel with 1" wooden ball glued to each end
- Basic sewing tools and supplies, tweezers, freezer paper, tracing paper and marking pencil

Instructions

Step 1. Transfer paper-piecing design to tracing paper using pattern given; the pattern has been reversed for paper piecing.

Step 2. Cut fabric patches 1/8"–1/4" larger than spaces on paper patterns in colors indicated in each piece. *Note: Shapes must extend beyond marked lines and may be trimmed to size after stitching, making almost any scrap usable for most pieces.*

Step 3. Pin piece 1 in place on the unmarked side of the paper; hold the paper pattern up to a light to check that piece 1 extends beyond the marked lines on the paper.

Harvest Sun Wall Quilt
Placement Diagram
20 1/4" x 27"

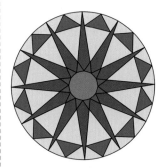

Mariner's Compass
15 3/4" Diameter Block

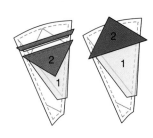

Figure 1
Trim and flip piece 2; press flat.

Step 4. Pin piece 2 right sides together with piece 1, extending over the 1–2 line; press flat and hold up to the light to be sure it covers the space for piece 2. Flip back down; stitch on the line on the marked side of the paper using a very close stitch length; trim seam, flip piece 2 to the right side and press referring to Figure 1.

Step 5. Continue to add fabrics in numerical order to complete the wedge unit; repeat for 12 wedge units. Trim fabric even with paper patterns.

Step 8. Prepare template for A; cut as directed on pattern piece. Iron the circle, shiny side to fabric on the wrong side of the gold print. Trim excess fabric 1/4" beyond paper circle.

Step 9. Mark the four equidistant points on the edge of the circle and line these points up with four equidistant points on the inner circle of the pieced compass design. Pin the circle to the compass design, matching marked points as shown in Figure 3.

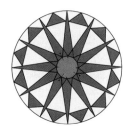

Figure 3
Pin the circle to the compass design, matching marked points.

Step 10. Hand-stitch the circle to the block center, turning under the seam allowance with the needle as you stitch; press, being careful not to stretch the circle design. Remove freezer paper circle.

Step 11. Cut a 21" x 28" piece tan-on-cream print for background; fold in half along length and press to crease.

Step 12. Cut an 18" x 18" square freezer paper; fold paper to find center and mark. Center and draw a 15 3/4" circle on the paper; cut out the circle, being careful not to damage the area outside the circle.

Step 13. Iron the freezer-paper circle with shiny side down to the wrong side of the fabric background piece with circle 3" from the bottom and 2 5/8" from each side edge and aligning fold in paper to crease on background piece. Carefully cut a circle of fabric from the center opening, leaving about a 3/16" seam allowance beyond the inner edge of the circle as shown in Figure 4. *Note: If you prefer, you may center the pieced block*

Step 6. Join wedge units in pairs as shown in Figure 2; do not remove paper until long side seams of segment pairs are stitched and then only remove paper from these seam lines. Press seam allowances open.

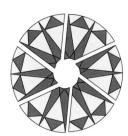

Figure 2
Join wedge units in pairs.

Step 7. Stitch three wedge pairs together to complete half of the Mariner's Compass block; repeat. Join the two halves; press carefully. Do not remove paper backing yet.

" from bottom edge with compass points in proper ·cation on fabric background and appliqué in place, ·rning under 1/4" seam allowance as you stitch. Trim ·bric behind block and remove paper pattern.

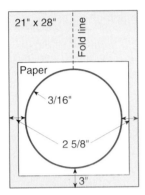

Figure 4
Carefully cut a circle of fabric from
the center opening, leaving about a
3/16" seam allowance beyond the
inner edge of the circle as shown.

·tep 14. Clip seam allowance around inner edge of ·ircle; turn under and press. Mark four equidistant ·oints around the circle, using fold marks on freezer ·aper as a guide.

·tep 15. Pin or hand-baste background in place on ·op of the pieced block, aligning four points of block ·vith marked points around circle as shown in Figure ·. Using beige thread, hand-stitch the background to ·he block. Press carefully when stitching is complete.

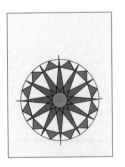 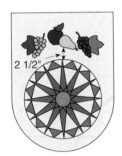

Figure 5
Align background on
top of pieced block.

Figure 6
Position appliqué
shapes as shown.

·tep 16. Gently remove all paper foundations and ·reezer paper.

·tep 17. Trace appliqué shapes onto the dull side of ·he freezer paper; iron the shapes onto the wrong ·ide of fabrics as directed on each piece for color. ·ut out shapes leaving a 1/8"–1/4" seam allowance ·vhen cutting.

Step 18. Arrange appliqué shapes 2 1/2" above the compass design using mark on pear as a guide for centering and referring to Figure 6 for approximate placement; pin in place, layering as necessary.

Step 19. Hand-appliqué shapes in place using matching all-purpose thread. Carefully cut slits in fabric behind appliqué shapes and remove freezer paper pieces with tweezers.

Step 20. Using 2 strands medium brown embroidery floss, stem-stitch tendrils at the top of each grape motif.

Step 21. Measure and mark 2 1/2" from the south, east and west points of the compass; connect marks to make a 2 1/2" circular shape around these points as shown in Figure 7; cut away background fabric.

Step 22. To mark for quilting, lay a ruler along one edge of a green point and extend the line of that side out to the edge of the background; repeat on all points.

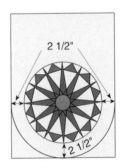

Figure 7
Measure and mark 2 1/2"
from the south, east and
west points of the compass
block; connect marks to
make a 2 1/2" circular
shape around these points.

Step 23. Prepare the completed top for quilting and quilt referring to the General Instructions. ***Note:*** *The sample shown was hand-quilted on marked lines, around appliqué motifs and in the ditch of block seams using cream hand-quilting thread.*

Step 24. Prepare 2 3/4 yards tan-on-cream print bias binding and bind edges referring to the General Instructions.

Step 25. Cut a 3" x 20" strip tan-on-cream print, prepare a sleeve and stitch to the top back of quilt referring to the General Instructions. ❖

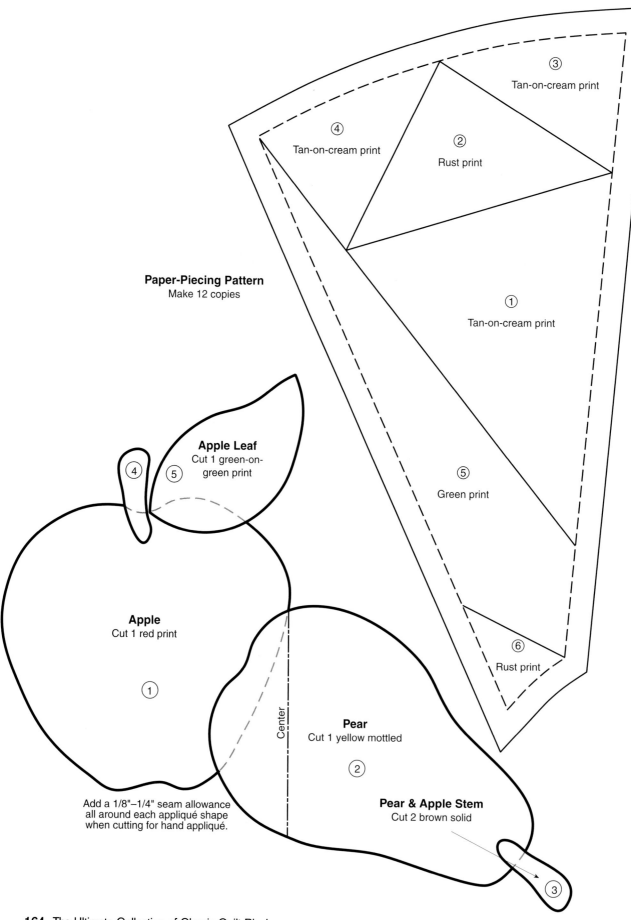

Paper-Piecing Pattern
Make 12 copies

③ Tan-on-cream print

④ Tan-on-cream print

② Rust print

① Tan-on-cream print

⑤ Green print

⑥ Rust print

Apple Leaf
Cut 1 green-on-green print

④ ⑤

Apple
Cut 1 red print

①

Center

Pear
Cut 1 yellow mottled

②

Pear & Apple Stem
Cut 2 brown solid

③

Add a 1/8"–1/4" seam allowance
all around each appliqué shape
when cutting for hand appliqué.

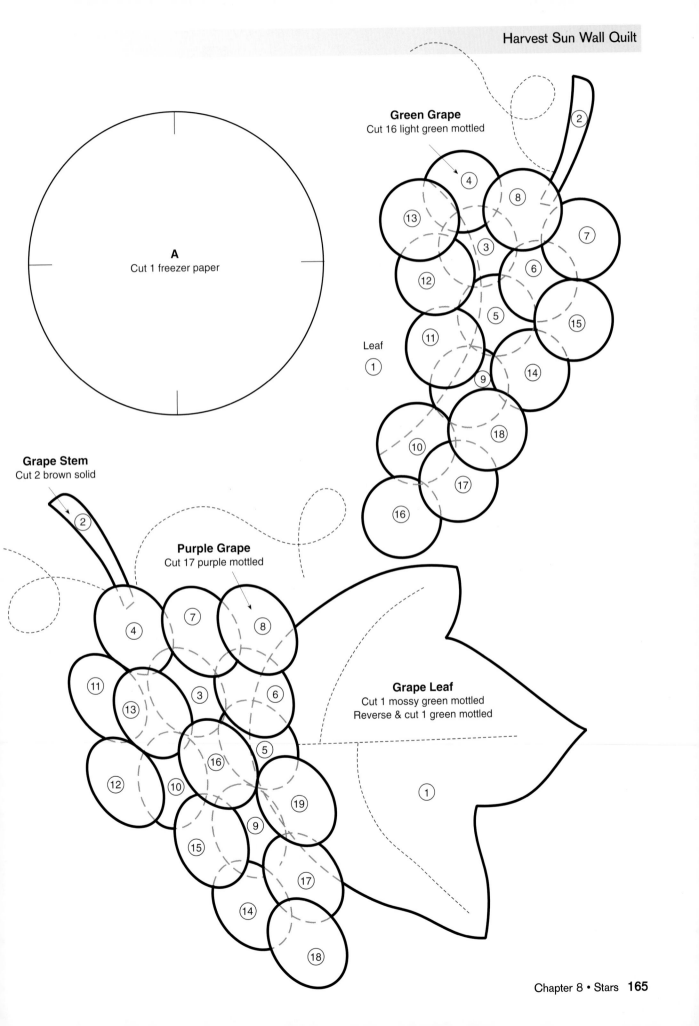

A
Cut 1 freezer paper

Green Grape
Cut 16 light green mottled

Leaf

Grape Stem
Cut 2 brown solid

Purple Grape
Cut 17 purple mottled

Grape Leaf
Cut 1 mossy green mottled
Reverse & cut 1 green mottled

Quiltmaking Basics

Materials & Supplies

Fabrics

Fabric Choices. Quilts and quilted projects combine fabrics of many types. Combine same-fiber-content fabrics when making quilted items, if possible.

Buying Fabrics. One hundred percent cotton fabrics are recommended for making quilts. Choose colors similar to those used in the quilts shown or colors of your own preference. Most quilt designs depend more on contrast of values than on the colors used to create the design.

Preparing the Fabric for Use. Fabrics may be prewashed or not. Whether you do or don't, be sure your fabrics are colorfast and won't run onto each other when washed after use.

Fabric Grain. Fabrics are woven with threads going in a crosswise and lengthwise direction. The threads cross at right angles—the more threads per inch, the stronger the fabric. The crosswise threads will stretch a little. The lengthwise threads will not stretch at all. Cutting fabric at a 45-degree angle to the crosswise and lengthwise threads creates a bias edge which stretches a great deal when pulled (Figure 1).

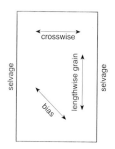

Figure 1
Drawing shows lengthwise, crosswise and bias threads.

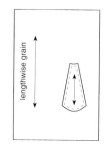

Figure 2
Place the template with marked arrow on the lengthwise grain of the fabric.

Pay careful attention to the marked grain lines on templates. Arrows indicate that the piece should be placed on the lengthwise grain with the arrow running on one thread. Although it is not necessary to examine the fabric and find a thread to match to, it is important to try to place the arrow with the lengthwise grain of the fabric (Figure 2).

Thread

For most piecing, good-quality cotton or cotton-covered polyester is the thread of choice. Inexpensive polyester threads are not recommended because they can cut the fibers of cotton fabrics.

Choose a color thread that will match or blend with the fabrics in your quilt. For projects pieced with dark and light color fabrics choose a neutral thread color, such as a medium gray, as a compromise between colors. Test by pulling at a stitched sample seam from the right side.

Batting

Batting is the material used to give a quilt loft or thickness. It also adds warmth.

Batting size is listed in inches for each pattern to reflect the size needed to complete the quilt according to the instructions. Purchase the size large enough to cut to the size you need for the quilt of your choice.

Some qualities to look for in batting are drapeability, resistance to fiber migration, loft and softness.

Tools & Equipment

There are few truly essential tools and little equipment required for quiltmaking. The basics include needles (hand sewing and quilting betweens), pins (long, thin sharp pins are best), sharp scissors or shears, a thimble, template materials (plastic or cardboard), marking tools (chalk marker, water-erasable pen and a No. 2 pencil are a few) and a quilting frame or hoop. For piecing and/or quilting by machine, add a sewing machine to the list.

Other necessary sewing basics are a seam ripper, pincushion, measuring tape and an iron. For choosing colors or quilting designs for your quilt, or for designing your own quilt, it is helpful to have graph paper, tracing paper, colored pencils or markers and a ruler on hand.

For making strip-pieced quilts, a rotary cutter, mat and specialty rulers are often used. We recommend an ergonomic rotary cutter, a large self-healing mat and several rulers. If you can choose only one size, a 6" x 24" marked in 1/8" or 1/4" increments is recommended.

Construction Methods

Templates

Traditional Templates. While many quilt instructions in this book use rotary-cut strips and quick-sewing methods, a few patterns require templates. Templates are like the pattern pieces used to sew a garment. They are used to cut the fabric pieces which make up the quilt top. There are two types—templates that include a 1/4" seam allowance and those that don't.

Choose the template material and the pattern. Transfer the pattern shapes to the template material with a sharp No. 2 lead pencil. Write the pattern name, piece letter or number, grain line and number to cut for one block or whole quilt on each piece as shown in Figure 3.

Figure 3
Mark each template with the pattern name and piece identification.

Some patterns require a reversed piece (Figure 4). These patterns are labeled with an R after the piece letter; for example, G and GR. To reverse a template, first cut it with the labeled side up and then with the labeled side down. Compare these to the right and left fronts of a blouse.

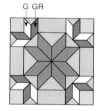

Figure 4
This pattern uses reversed pieces.

cutting one layer of fabric at a time, first trace the template onto the backside of the fabric with the marked side down; turn the template over with the marked side up to make reverse pieces.

Appliqué patterns given in this book do not include a seam allowance. Many designs are given in one drawing rather than individual pieces. To use the full-size design, trace on the background block to help with placement of the pieces later. Make templates for each shape using the drawing for exact size. Label each piece as for piecing templates.

For hand appliqué, add a seam allowance when cutting pieces from fabric. You may trace the template with label side up on the right side of the fabric if you are careful to mark lightly. The traced line is then the guide for turning the edges under when stitching.

If you prefer to mark on the wrong side of the fabric, turn the template over if you want your project motif to face the same way it does on the sample project.

For machine appliqué, a seam allowance is not necessary. Trace template onto the right side of the fabric with label facing up. Cut around shape on the traced line.

Piecing

Hand-Piecing Basics. When hand piecing, begin with templates which do not include the 1/4" seam allowance. Place the template on the wrong side of the fabric, lining up the marked grain line with lengthwise or crosswise fabric grain. If the piece does not have to be reversed, place with labeled side up. Trace around shape; move, leaving 1/2" between the shapes, and mark again.

When you have marked the appropriate number of pieces, cut out pieces, leaving 1/4" beyond marked line all around each piece.

To piece, refer to assembly drawings to piece units and blocks, if provided. To join two units, place the patches with right sides together. Stick a pin in at the beginning of the seam through both fabric patches, matching the beginning points (Figure 5); for hand-piecing, the seam begins on the traced line, not at the edge of the fabric (Figure 6).

Figure 5
Stick a pin through fabrics to match the beginning of the seam.

Figure 6
Begin hand-piecing at seam, not at the edge of the fabric. Continue stitching along seam line.

Thread a sharp needle; knot 1 strand of the thread at the end. Remove the pin and insert the needle in the hole; make a short stitch and then a backstitch right over the first stitch. Continue making short stitches with several stitches on the needle at one time. As you stitch, check the back piece often to assure accurate stitching on the seam line. Take a stitch at the end

Figure 7
Make a loop in a backstitch to make a knot.

of the seam; backstitch and pull thread through stitch loop to knot at the same time as shown in Figure 7.

Seams on hand-pieced fabric patches may be finger-pressed toward the darker fabric.

To sew units together, pin fabric patches together, matching seams. Sew as above except where seams meet; at these intersections, backstitch, go through seam to next piece and backstitch again to secure seam joint.

Not all pieced blocks can be stitched with straight seams or in rows. Some patterns require set-in pieces. To begin a set-in seam on a star pattern, pin one side of the square to the proper side of the star point with right sides together, matching corners. Start stitching at the seam line on the outside point; stitch on the marked seam line to the end of the seam line at the center referring to Figure 8.

Figure 8
To set a square into a star point, match seams and stitch from outside edge to center.

Figure 9
Continue stitching the adjacent side of the square to the next diamond shape in 1 seam from center to outside as shown.

Bring around the adjacent side and pin to the next star point, matching seams. Continue the stitching line from the adjacent seam through corners and to the outside edge of the square as shown in Figure 9.

Machine Piecing. If making templates, include the 1/4" seam allowance on the template for machine piecing. Place template on the wrong side of the fabric as for hand piecing except butt pieces against one another when tracing.

Set machine on 2.5 or 12–15 stitches per inch. Join pieces as for hand piecing for set-in seams; but for other straight seams, begin and end sewing at the end of the fabric piece sewn as shown in Figure 10. No backstitching is necessary when machine stitching.

Join units as for hand piecing referring to the piecing diagrams where needed. Chain piecing (Figure 11—sewing several like units before sewing other units) saves time by eliminating beginning and ending stitches.

When joining machine-pieced units, match seams against each other with seam allowances pressed in opposite directions to reduce bulk and make perfect matching of seams possible (Figure 12).

Figure 10
Begin machine-piecing at the end of the piece, not at the end of the seam.

Figure 11
Units may be chain-pieced to save time.

Figure 12
Sew machine-pieced units with seams pressed in opposite directions.

Tips & Techniques

Before machine piecing fabric patches together, test your sewing machine for positioning an accurate 1/4" seam allowance. There are several tools to help guarantee this. Some machine needles may be moved to allow the presser-foot edge to be a 1/4" guide.

A special foot may be purchased for your machine that will guarantee an accurate 1/4" seam. A piece of masking tape can be placed on the throat plate of your sewing machine to mark the 1/4" seam. A plastic stick-on ruler may be used instead of tape with the same results.

Cutting

Quick Cutting. Templates can be completely eliminated when using a rotary cutter with a plastic ruler and mat to cut fabric pieces.

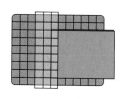

Figure 13
Fold fabric and straighten as shown.

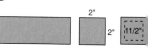

Figure 14
Wavy strips result if fabric is not straightened before cutting.

When rotary cutting strips, straighten raw edges of fabric by folding fabric in fourths across the width as shown in Figure 13. Press down flat; place ruler on fabric square with edge of fabric and make one cut from the folded edge to the outside edge. If strips are not straightened, a wavy strip will result as shown in Figure 14.

Always cut away from your body, holding the ruler firmly with the non-cutting hand. Keep fingers away from the edge of the ruler as it is easy for the rotary cutter to slip and jump over the edge of the ruler if cutting is not properly done.

For many strip-pieced blocks two strips are stitched together as shown in Figure 15. The strips are stitched, pressed and cut into segments as shown in Figure 16. The cut segments are arranged as shown in Figure 17 and stitched to complete, in this example, one Four-Patch block.

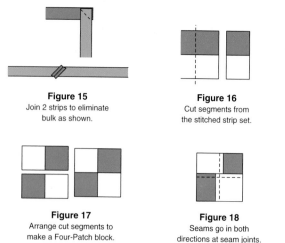

Figure 15
Join 2 strips to eliminate bulk as shown.

Figure 16
Cut segments from the stitched strip set.

Figure 17
Arrange cut segments to make a Four-Patch block.

Figure 18
Seams go in both directions at seam joints.

The direction to press seams in strip sets is important for accurate piecing later. The normal rule for pressing is to press seams toward the darker fabric to keep the colors

from showing through on lighter colors later. For joining segments from strip sets, this rule doesn't always apply.

It is best if seams on adjacent rows are pressed in opposite directions. When aligning segments to stitch rows together, if pressed properly, seam joints will have a seam going in both directions as shown in Figure 18.

If a square is required for the pattern, it can be sub-cut from a strip as shown in Figure 19.

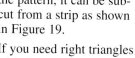

Figure 19
If cutting squares, cut proper-width strip into same-width segments. Here, a 2" strip is cut into 2" segments to create 2" squares. These squares finish at 1 1/2" when sewn.

If you need right triangles with the straight grain on the short sides, you can use the same method, but you need to figure out how wide to cut the strip. Measure the finished size of one short side of the triangle. Add 7/8" to this size for seam allowance. Cut fabric strips this width; cut the strips into the same increment to create squares. Cut the squares on the diagonal to produce triangles. For example, if you need a triangle with a 2" finished height, cut the strips 2 7/8" by the width of the fabric. Cut the strips into 2 7/8" squares. Cut each square on the diagonal to produce the correct-size triangle with the grain on the short sides (Figure 20).

Figure 20
Cut 2" (finished size triangles from 2 7/8" squares as shown.

Triangles sewn together to make squares are called half-square triangles or triangle/squares. When joined, the triangle/square unit has the straight of grain on all outside edges of the block.

Another method of making triangle/squares is shown in Figure 21. Layer two squares with right sides together; draw a diagonal line through the center. Stitch 1/4" on both sides of the line. Cut apart on the drawn line to reveal two stitched triangle/squares.

Figure 21
Mark a diagonal line on the square; stitch 1/4" on each side of the line. Cut on line to reveal stitched triangle/squares.

If you need triangles with the straight of grain on the diagonal, such as for fill-in triangles on the outside edges of a diagonal-set quilt, the procedure is a bit different.

To make these triangles, a square is cut on both diagonals; thus, the straight of grain is on the longest or diagonal side (Figure 22). To figure out the size to cut the square, add 1 1/4" to the needed

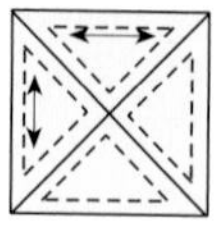

Figure 22
Add 1 1/4" to the finished size of the longest side of the triangle needed and cut on both diagonals to make a quarter-square triangle.

finished size of the longest side of the triangle. For example, if you need a triangle with a 12" finished diagonal, cut a 13 1/4" square.

If templates are given, use their measurements to cut fabric strips to correspond with that measurement. The template may be used on the strip to cut pieces quickly. Strip cutting works best for squares, triangles, rectangles and diamonds. Odd-shaped templates are difficult to cut in multiple layers using a rotary cutter.

Foundation Piecing

Foundation Piecing. Paper or fabric foundation pieces are used to make very accurate blocks, provide stability for weak fabrics, and add body and weight to the finished quilt.

Temporary foundation materials include paper, tracing paper, freezer paper and removable interfacing. Permanent foundations include utility fabrics, non-woven interfacing, flannel, fleece and batting.

Methods of marking foundations include basting lines, pencils or pens, needlepunching, tracing wheel, hot-iron transfers, copy machine, premarked, stamps or stencils. Copy patterns given here using a copy machine or trace each block individually. Measure the finished paper foundations to insure accuracy in copying.

There are two methods of foundation piecing—under piecing and top piecing. When under piecing, the pattern is reversed when tracing. We have not included any patterns for top piecing. **Note:** *All patterns for which we recommend paper piecing are already reversed in full-size drawings given.*

To under-piece, place a scrap of fabric larger than the lined space on the unlined side of the paper in the No. 1 position. Place piece 2 right sides together with piece 1; pin on seam line and fold back to check that the piece will cover space 2 before stitching.

Stitch along line on the lined side of the paper—fabric will not be visible. Sew several stitches beyond the beginning and ending of the line. Backstitching is not required as another fabric seam will cover this seam.

Remove pin; finger-press piece 2 flat. Continue adding all pieces in numerical order in the same manner until all pieces are stitched to paper. Trim excess to outside line (1/4" larger all around than finished size of the block).

Temporary foundation materials are removed when blocks are complete and stitched together.

Tips & Techniques

If you cannot see the lines on the backside of the paper when paper piecing, draw over lines with a small felt-tip marker. The lines should now be visible on the backside to help with placement of fabric pieces.

Appliqué

Appliqué. Appliqué is the process of applying one piece of fabric on top of another for decorative or functional purposes.

Making Templates. Most appliqué designs given here are shown as full-size drawings for the completed designs. The drawings show dotted lines to indicate where one piece overlaps another. Other marks indicate placement of embroidery stitches for decorative purposes such as eyes, lips, flowers, etc.

For hand appliqué, trace each template onto the right side of the fabric with template right side up. Cut around shape, adding a 1/8"–1/4" seam allowance.

Before the actual appliqué process begins, cut the background block and prepare it for stitching. Most appliqué designs are centered on the block. To find the center of the background square, fold it in half and in half again; crease with your fingers. Now unfold and fold diagonally and crease; repeat for other corners referring to Figure 23.

Figure 23
Fold background to mark centers as shown.

Center-line creases help position the design. If centering the appliqué design is important, an X has been placed on each drawing to mark the center of the design. Match the X with the creased center of the background block when placing pieces. If you have a full-size drawing of the design, as is given with most appliqué designs in this book, it might help you to draw on the background block to help with placement.

Transfer the design to a large piece of tracing paper. Place the paper on top of the design; use masking tape to hold in place. Trace design onto paper.

If you don't have a light box, tape the pattern on a window; center the background block on top and tape in place. Trace the design onto the background block with a water-erasable marker or light lead or chalk pencil. This drawing will mark exactly where the fabric pieces should be placed on the background block.

Hand Appliqué. Traditional hand appliqué uses a template made from the desired finished shape without seam allowance added.

After fabric is prepared, trace the desired shape onto the right side of the fabric with a water-erasable marker or light lead or chalk pencil. Leave at least 1/2" between design motifs when tracing to allow for the seam allowance when cutting out the shapes.

When the desired number of shapes needed has been drawn on the fabric pieces, cut out shapes leaving 1/8"–1/4" all around drawn line for turning under.

Turn the shape's edges over on the drawn or stitched line. When turning the edges under, make sharp corners sharp and smooth edges smooth. The fabric patch should retain the shape of the template used to cut it.

When turning in concave curves, clip to seams and baste the seam allowance over as shown in Figure 24.

Figure 24
Concave curves should be clipped before turning as shown.

During the actual appliqué process, you may be layering one shape on top of another. Where two fabrics overlap, the underneath piece does not have to be turned under or stitched down.

If possible, trim away the underneath fabric when the block is finished by carefully cutting away the background from underneath and then cutting away unnecessary layers to reduce bulk and avoid shadows from darker fabrics showing through on light fabrics.

For hand appliqué, position the fabric shapes on the background block and pin or baste them in place. Using a blind stitch or appliqué stitch, sew pieces in place with matching thread and small stitches. Start with background pieces first and work up to foreground pieces. Appliqué the pieces in place on the background in numerical order, if given, layering as necessary.

Machine Appliqué. There are several products available to help make the machine-appliqué process easier and faster.

Fusible transfer web is a commercial product similar to iron-on interfacing except it has two sticky sides. It is used to adhere appliqué shapes to the background with heat. Paper is adhered to one side of the web.

To use, reverse pattern and draw shapes onto the paper side of the web; cut, leaving a margin around each shape. Place on the wrong side of the chosen fabric; fuse in place referring to the manufacturer's instructions. Cut out shapes on the drawn line. Peel off the paper and fuse in place on the background fabric. Transfer any detail lines to the fabric shapes. This process adds a little bulk or stiffness to the appliquéd shape and makes hand-quilting through the layers difficult.

For successful machine appliqué a tear-off stabilizer is recommended. This product is placed under the background fabric while machine appliqué is being done. It is torn away when the work is finished. This kind of stabilizer keeps the background fabric from pulling during the machine-appliqué process.

During the actual machine-appliqué process, you will be layering one shape on top of another.

Thread the top of the machine with thread to match the fabric patches or with threads that coordinate or contrast with fabrics. Rayon thread is a good choice when a sheen is desired on the finished appliqué stitches. Do not use rayon thread in the bobbin; use all-purpose thread.

Set your machine to make a zigzag stitch and practice on scraps of similar weight to check the tension. If you can see the bobbin thread on the top of the appliqué, adjust your machine to make a balanced stitch. Different-width stitches are available; choose one that will not overpower the appliqué shapes. In some cases these appliqué stitches will be used as decorative stitches as well and you may want the thread to show.

If using a stabilizer, place this under the background fabric and pin or fuse in place. Place shapes as for hand-appliqué and stitch all around shapes by machine.

When all machine work is complete, remove stabilizer from the back referring to the manufacturer's instructions.

Putting It All Together

Finishing the Top

Settings. Most quilts are made by sewing individual blocks together in rows which, when joined, create a design. There are several other methods used to join blocks. Sometimes the setting choice is determined by the block's design. For example, a house block should be placed upright on a quilt, not sideways or upside down.

Plain blocks can be alternated with pieced or appliquéd blocks in a straight set. Making a quilt using plain blocks saves time; half the number of pieced or appliquéd blocks are needed to make the same-size quilt as shown in Figure 1.

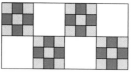

Figure 1
Alternate plain blocks with pieced blocks to save time.

Adding Borders. Borders are an integral part of the quilt and should complement the colors and designs used in the quilt center. Borders frame a quilt just like a mat and frame do a picture.

If fabric strips are added for borders, they may be mitered or butted at the corners as shown in Figures 2 and 3. To determine the size for butted border strips, measure across the center of the completed quilt top from one side raw edge to the other side raw edge. This measurement will include a 1/4" seam allowance.

Cut two border strips that length by the chosen width of the border. Sew these strips to the top and bottom of the pieced center referring to Figure 4. Press the seam allowance toward the border strips.

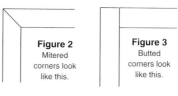

Figure 2
Mitered corners look like this.

Figure 3
Butted corners look like this.

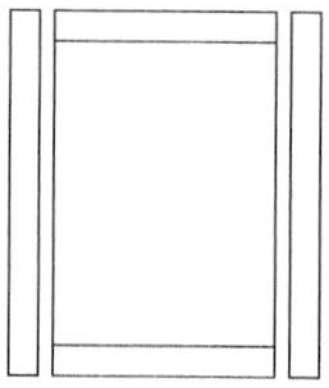

Figure 4
Sew border strips to opposite sides; sew remaining 2 strips to remaining sides to make butted corners.

Measure across the completed quilt top at the center, from top raw edge to bottom raw edge, including the two border strips already added. Cut two border strips that length by the chosen width of the border. Sew a strip to each of the two remaining sides as shown in Figure 4. Press the seams toward the border strips.

To make mitered corners, measure the quilt as before. To this add twice the width of the border and 1/2" for seam allowances to determine the length of the strips. Repeat for opposite sides. Center and sew on each strip, stopping stitching 1/4" from corner, leaving the remainder of the strip dangling.

Press corners at a 45-degree angle to form a crease. Stitch from the inside quilt corner to the outside on the creased line. Trim excess away after stitching and press mitered

...ams open (Figures 5–7).

...arefully press the entire ...ilt top. Avoid pulling and ...retching while pressing, ...hich would distort shapes.

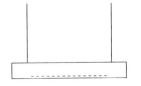

Figure 5
For mitered corner, stitch strip, stopping 1/4" from corner seam.

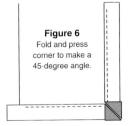

Figure 6
Fold and press corner to make a 45-degree angle.

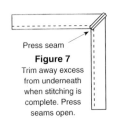

Press seam

Figure 7
Trim away excess from underneath when stitching is complete. Press seams open.

Getting Ready to Quilt

Choosing a Quilting Design. If you choose to hand- or machine-quilt your finished top, you will need to choose a design for quilting.

...here are several types of quilting designs, some of which ...ay not have to be marked. The easiest of the unmarked ...esigns is in-the-ditch quilting. Here the quilting stitches ...re placed in the valley created by the seams joining two ...ieces together or next to the edge of an appliqué design. ...here is no need to mark a top for in-the-ditch quilting. ...achine quilters choose this option because the stitches are ...ot as obvious on the finished quilt (Figure 8).

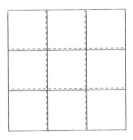

Figure 8
In-the-ditch quilting is done in the seam that joins 2 pieces.

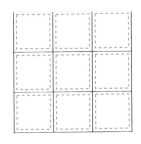

Figure 9
Outline-quilting 1/4" away from seam is a popular choice for quilting.

...utline-quilting 1/4" or more ...way from seams or appliqué ...hapes is another no-mark alterna- ...ive (Figure 9) which prevents ...aving to sew through the layers ...nade by seams, thus making ...titching easier.

...f you are not comfortable eye- ...alling the 1/4" (or other dis- ...ance), masking tape is available ...n different widths and is help- ...ul to place on straight-edge

Figure 10
Machine meander quilting fills in large spaces.

designs to mark the quilting line. If using masking tape, place the tape right up against the seam and quilt close to the other edge.

Meander or free-motion quilting by machine fills in open spaces and doesn't require marking. It is fun and easy to stitch as shown in Figure 10.

Marking the Top for Quilting or Tying. If you choose a fancy or allover design for quilting, you will need to transfer the design to your quilt top before layering with the backing and batting. You may use a sharp medium-lead or silver pencil on light background fabrics. Test the pencil marks to guarantee that they will wash out of your quilt top when quilting is complete; or be sure your quilting stitches cover the pencil marks. Mechanical pencils with very fine points may be used successfully to mark quilts.

Manufactured quilt-design templates are available in many designs and sizes, and are cut out of a durable plastic template material which is easy to use.

To make a permanent quilt-design template, choose a template material on which to transfer the design. See-through plastic is the best as it will let you place the design while allowing you to see where it is in relation to your quilt design without moving it. Place the design on the quilt top where you want it and trace around it with your marking tool. Pick up the quilting template and place again; repeat marking.

No matter what marking method you use, remember, the marked lines should never show on the finished quilt. When the top is marked, it is ready for layering.

Preparing the Quilt Backing. The quilt backing is a very important feature of your quilt. In most cases, the materials list for each quilt in this book gives the size requirements for the backing, not the yardage needed. Exceptions to this are when the backing fabric is also used on the quilt top and yardage is given for that fabric.

A backing is generally cut at least 4" larger than the quilt top or 2" larger on all sides. For a 64" x 78" finished quilt, the backing would need to be at least 68" x 82".

To avoid having the seam across the center of the quilt backing, cut or tear one of the right-length pieces in half and sew half to each side of the second piece as shown in Figure 11.

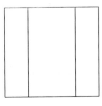

Figure 11
Center 1 backing piece with a piece on each side.

Figure 12
Horizontal seams may be used on backing pieces.

Quilts that need a backing more than 88" wide may be pieced in horizontal pieces as shown in Figure 12.

Layering the Quilt Sandwich. Layering the quilt top with the batting and backing is time-consuming. Open the batting several days before you need it and place over a bed or flat on the floor to help flatten the creases caused from its being folded up in the bag for so long.

Iron the backing piece, folding in half both vertically and horizontally and pressing to mark centers.

If you will not be quilting on a frame, place the backing right side down on a clean floor or table. Start in the center and push any wrinkles or bunches flat. Use masking tape to tape the edges to the floor or large clips to hold the backing to the edges of the table. The backing should be taut.

Place the batting on top of the backing, matching centers using fold lines as guides; flatten out any wrinkles. Trim the batting to the same size as the backing.

Fold the quilt top in half lengthwise and place on top of the batting, wrong side against the batting, matching centers. Unfold quilt and, working from the center to the outside edges, smooth out any wrinkles or lumps.

To hold the quilt layers together for quilting, baste by hand or use safety pins. If basting by hand, thread a long thin needle with a long piece of unknotted white or off-white thread. Starting in the center and leaving a long tail, make 4"–6" stitches toward the outside edge of the quilt top, smoothing as you baste. Start at the center again and work toward the outside as shown in Figure 13.

Figure 13
Baste from the center to the outside edges.

If quilting by machine, you may prefer to use safety pins for holding your quilt sandwich together. Start in the center of the quilt and pin to the outside, leaving pins open until all are placed. When you are satisfied that all layers are smooth, close the pins.

Quilting

Hand Quilting. Hand quilting is the process of placing stitches through the quilt top, batting and backing to hold them together. While it is a functional process, it also adds beauty and loft to the finished quilt.

Tips & Techniques

Use a thimble to prevent sore fingers when hand quilting. The finger that is under the quilt to feel the needle as it passes through the backing is the one that is most apt to get sore from the pin pricks. Some quilters purchase leather thimbles for this finger while others try home remedies. One simple aid is masking tape wrapped around the finger. With the tape you will still be able to feel the needle, but it will not prick your skin. Over time calluses build up and these fingers get toughened up, but with every vacation from quilting, they will become soft and the process begins again.

To begin, thread a sharp between needle with an 18" piece of quilting thread. Tie a small knot in the end of the thread. Position the needle about 1/2" to 1" away from the starting point on quilt top. Sink the needle through the top into the batting layer but not through the backing. Pull the needle up at the starting point of the quilting design. Pull the needle and thread until the knot sinks through the top into the batting (Figure 14).

Figure 14
Start the needle through the top layer of fabric 1/2"–1" away from quilting line with knot on top of fabric.

Some stitchers like to take a backstitch at the beginning while others prefer to begin the first stitch here. Take small, even running stitches along the marked quilting line (Figure 15). Keep one hand positioned underneath to feel the needle go all the way through to the backing.

Figure 15
Make small, even running stitches on marked quilting line.

Tips & Techniques

Knots should not show on the quilt top or back. Learn to sink the knot into the batting at the beginning and ending of the quilting thread for successful stitches.

When you have nearly run out of thread, wind the thread around the needle several times to make a small knot and pull it close to the fabric. Insert the needle into the fabric on the quilting line and come out with the needle 1/2" to 1" away, pulling the knot into the fabric layers the same as when you started. Pull and cut thread close to fabric. The end should disappear inside after cutting. Some quilters prefer to take a backstitch with a loop through it for a knot to end.

Making 12–18 stitches per inch is a nice goal, but a more realistic goal is seven to nine stitches per inch. If you cannot accomplish this right away, strive for even stitches—all the same size—that look as good on the back as on the front.

Machine Quilting. Successful machine quilting requires practice and a good relationship with your sewing machine.

Prepare the quilt for machine quilting in the same way as for hand quilting. Use safety pins to hold the layers together instead of basting with thread.

Presser-foot quilting is best used for straight-line quilting because the presser bar lever does not need to be continually lifted.

Set the machine on a longer stitch length (3 or eight to 10 stitches to the inch). Too tight a stitch causes puckering and fabric tucks, either on the quilt top or backing. An even-feed or walking foot helps to eliminate the tucks and puckering by feeding the upper and lower layers through the achine evenly. Before you begin, loosen the amount of ressure on the presser foot.

pecial machine-quilting needles work best to penetrate the aree layers in your quilt.

ecide on a design. Quilting in the ditch is not quite as visi-le, but if you quilt with the feed dogs engaged, it means urning the quilt frequently. It is not easy to fit a rolled-up uilt through the small opening on the sewing machine head.

Meander quilting is the easiest way to machine-quilt—and is fun. Meander quilting is done using an appliqué or arning foot with the feed dogs dropped. It is sort of like cribbling. Simply move the quilt top around under the foot nd make stitches in a random pattern to fill the space. The ame method may be used to outline a quilt design. The ick is the same as in hand quilting; you are striving for titches of uniform size. Your hands are in complete control f the design.

f machine quilting is of interest to you, there are several ery good books available at quilt shops that will help you ecome a successful machine quilter.

ied Quilts or Comforters. Would you rather tie your uilt layers together than quilt them? Tied quilts are often eferred to as comforters. The advantage of tying is that it akes so much less time and the required skills can be earned quickly.

f a top will be tied, choose a thick, bonded batting—one nat will not separate during washing. For tying, use pearl otton, embroidery floss or strong yarn in colors that match r coordinate with the fabrics in your quilt top.

ecide on a pattern for tying. Many quilts are tied at the orners and centers of the blocks and at sashing joints. Try o tie every 4"–6". Special designs can be used for tying, ut most quilts are tied in conventional ways. Begin tying n the center and work to the outside edges.

o make the tie, thread a large needle with a long thread yarn, floss or crochet cotton); do not knot. Push the needle hrough the quilt top to the back, leaving a 3"–4" length on op. Move the needle to the next position without cutting hread. Take another stitch through the layers; repeat until hread is almost used up.

ut thread between stitches, eaving an equal amount of hread on each stitch. Tie a knot with the two thread nds. Tie again to make a quare knot referring to igure 16. Trim thread ends o desired length.

Figure 16
Make a square knot as shown.

Finishing the Edges

After your quilt is tied or quilted, the edges need to be inished. Decide how you want the edges of your quilt fin-shed before layering the backing and batting with the uilt top.

Without Binding—Self-Finish. There is one way to elimi-ate adding an edge finish. This is done before quilting. lace the batting on a flat surface. Place the pieced top

right side up on the batting. Place the backing right sides together with the pieced top. Pin and/or baste the layers together to hold flat.

Begin stitching in the center of one side using a 1/4" seam allowance, reversing at the beginning and end of the seam. Continue stitching all around and back to the beginning side. Leave a 12" or larger opening. Clip corners to reduce excess. Turn right side out through the opening; slipstitch the opening closed by hand. The quilt may now be quilted by hand or machine.

The disadvantage to this method is that once the edges are sewn in, any creases or wrinkles that might form during the quilting process cannot be flattened out. Tying is the preferred method for finishing a quilt constructed using this method.

Bringing the backing fabric to the front is another way to finish the quilt's edge without binding. To accomplish this, complete the quilt as for hand or machine quilting. Trim the batting only even with the front. Trim the backing 1" larger than the completed top all around.

Turn the backing edge in 1/2" and then turn over to the front along edge of batting. The folded edge may be machine-stitched close to the edge through all layers, or blind-stitched in place to finish.

The front may be turned to the back. If using this method, a wider front border is needed. The backing and batting are trimmed 1" smaller than the top and the top edge is turned under 1/2" and then turned to the back and stitched in place.

One more method of self-finish may be used. The top and backing may be stitched together by hand at the edge. To accomplish this, all quilting must be stopped 1/2" from the quilt-top edge. The top and backing of the quilt are trimmed even and the batting is trimmed to 1/4"–1/2" smaller. The edges of the top and backing are turned in 1/4"–1/2" and blind-stitched together at the very edge.

These methods do not require the use of extra fabric and save time in preparation of binding strips; they are not as durable as an added binding.

Binding. The technique of adding extra fabric at the edges of the quilt is called binding. The binding encloses the edges and adds an extra layer of fabric for durability.

To prepare the quilt for the addition of the binding, trim the batting and backing layers flush with the top of the quilt using a rotary cutter and ruler or shears. Using a walking-foot attachment (sometimes called an even-feed foot attach-ment), machine-baste the three layers together all around approximately 1/8" from the cut edge.

The list of materials given with each quilt in this book often includes a number of yards of self-made or purchased bind-ing. Bias binding may be purchased in packages and in many colors. The advantage to self-made binding is that you can use fabrics from your quilt to coordinate colors.

Double-fold, straight-grain binding and double-fold, bias-grain binding are two of the most commonly used types of binding.

Double-fold, straight-grain binding is used on smaller projects with right-angle corners. Double-fold, bias-grain binding is best suited for bed-size quilts or quilts with rounded corners.

To make double-fold, straight-grain binding, cut 2 1/4"-wide strips of fabric across the width or down the length of the fabric totaling the perimeter of the quilt plus 10". Join strips as shown in Figure 17; press in half wrong sides together along the length using an iron on a cotton setting with no steam.

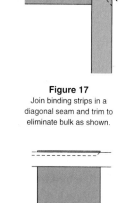

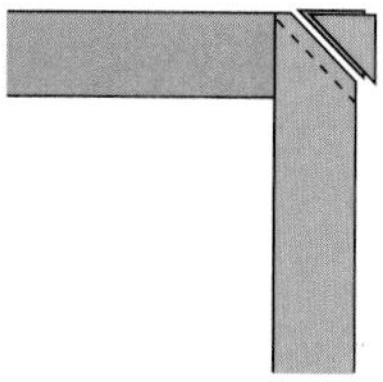

Figure 17
Join binding strips in a diagonal seam and trim to eliminate bulk as shown.

Lining up the raw edges, place the binding on the top of the quilt and begin sewing (again using the walking foot) approximately 6" from the beginning of the binding strip. Stop sewing 1/4" from the first corner, leave the needle in the quilt, turn and sew diagonally to the corner as shown in Figure 18.

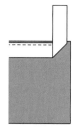

Figure 18
Sew to within 1/4" of corner; leave needle in quilt, turn and stitch diagonally off the corner of the quilt.

Fold the binding at a 45-degree angle up and away from the quilt as shown in Figure 19 and back down flush with the raw edges. Starting at the top raw edge of the quilt, begin sewing the next side as shown in Figure 20. Repeat at the next three corners.

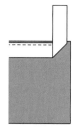

Figure 19
Fold binding at a 45-degree angle up and away from quilt.

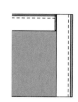

Figure 20
Fold the binding strips back down, flush with the raw edge, and begin sewing.

As you approach the beginning of the binding strip, stop stitching and overlap the binding 1/2" from the edge; trim. Join the two ends with a 1/4" seam allowance and press the seam open. Reposition the joined binding along the edge of the quilt and resume stitching to the beginning.

To finish, bring the folded edge of the binding over the raw edges and blind-stitch the binding in place over the machine-stitching line on the backside. Hand-miter the corners on the back as shown in Figure 21.

If you are making a quilt to be used on a bed, you will want

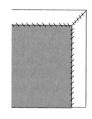

Figure 21
Miter and stitch the corners as shown.

to use double-fold, bias-grain bindings because the many threads that cross each other along the fold at the edge of the quilt make it a more durable binding.

Cut 2 1/4"-wide bias strips from a large square of fabric. Join the strips as illustrated in Figure 17 and press the seams open. Cut the beginning end of the bias strip at a 45 degree angle; fold the angled raw edge under 1/4" and press. Fold the joined strips in half along the length, wrong sides together, and press with no steam (Figure 22).

Figure 22
Fold end in and press strip in half.

Follow the same procedures as previously described for preparing the quilt top and sewing the binding to the quilt top. Treat the corners just as you treated them with straight grain binding.

Since you are using bias-grain binding, you do have the option to just eliminate the corners if this option doesn't interfere with the patchwork in the quilt. To round the corners, place a your dinner plates at the corner and rotary-cut the gentle curve (Figure 23).

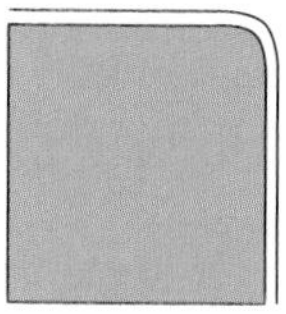

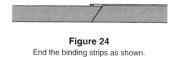

Figure 23
Round corners to eliminate square-corner finishes.

As you approach the beginning of the binding strip, stop stitching and lay the end across the beginning so it will sli inside the fold. Cut the end at a 45-degree angle so the raw edges are contained inside the beginning of the strip (Figur 24); resume stitching to the beginning. Bring the fold to th back of the quilt and hand-stitch as previously described.

Figure 24
End the binding strips as shown.

Overlapped corners are not quite as easy as rounded ones, but a bit easier than mitering. To make overlapped corners, sew binding strips to opposite sides of the quilt top. Stitch edges down to finish. Trim ends even.

Figure 25
Fold end of binding even with previous edge.

Figure 26
Enclose the previous bound edge in the seam.

Sew a strip to each remaining side, leaving 1 1/2"–2" excess at each end. Turn quilt over and fold end in even with previous finished edge as shown in Figure 25.

Fold binding in toward quilt and stitch down as before, enclosing the previous bound edge in the seam as shown in Figure 26. It may be necessary to trim the folded-down section to reduce bulk.

Making Continuous Bias Binding. Instead of cutting individual bias strips and sewing them together, you may make continuous bias binding.

Cut a square 21" x 21" from chosen binding fabric. Cut the square once on the diagonal to make two triangles as shown in Figure 27. With right sides together, join the two triangles with a 1/4" seam allowance as shown in Figure 28; press seam open to reduce bulk.

Figure 27
Cut 21" square on
the diagonal.

Figure 28
Sew the triangles together.

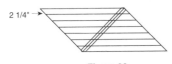

Figure 29
Mark lines 2 1/4" apart on wrong side.

Mark lines every 2 1/4" on the wrong side of the fabric as shown in Figure 29. Bring the short ends together, right sides together, offsetting one line as shown in Figure 30; stitch to make a tube. This will seam awkward.

Begin cutting at point A as shown in Figure 31; continue cutting along marked line to make one continuous strip. Fold strip in half along length with wrong sides together; press. Sew to quilt edges as instructed previously for bias binding.

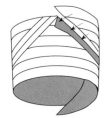

Figure 30
Sew short ends together,
offsetting lines to make a tube.

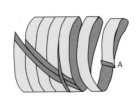

Figure 31
Cut along marked
lines, starting at A.

Final Touches

If your quilt will be hung on the wall, a hanging sleeve is required. Other options include purchased plastic rings or fabric tabs. The best choice is a fabric sleeve, which will evenly distribute the weight of the quilt across the top edge, rather than at selected spots where tabs or rings are stitched, and will keep the quilt hanging straight and not damage the batting.

To make a sleeve, measure across the top of the finished quilt. Cut an 8"-wide piece of muslin equal to that length—you may need to seam several muslin strips together to make the required length.

Fold in 1/4" on each end of the muslin strip and press. Fold again and stitch to hold. Fold the muslin strip lengthwise with right sides together; sew along the long side to make a tube. Turn the tube right side out; press with seam at bottom or centered on the back.

Hand-stitch the tube along the top of the quilt and the bottom of the tube to the quilt back making sure the quilt lies flat. Stitches should not go through to the front of the quilt and don't need to be too close together as shown in Figure 32.

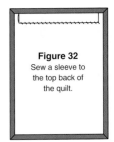

Figure 32
Sew a sleeve to
the top back of
the quilt.

Slip a wooden dowel or long curtain rod through the sleeve to hang.

When the quilt is finally complete, it should be signed and dated. Use a permanent pen on the back of the quilt. Other methods include cross-stitching your name and date on the front or back or making a permanent label which may be stitched to the back.

Fabrics & Supplies

Page 10: *Mama's Teacups*—Fabrics from the Wildflower Tea collection from Classic Cottons. Machine-quilted by Dianne Hodgkins.

Page 20: *Angel Table Runner & Stocking*—Hobbs Heirloom cotton batting, DMC thread and needles and Fiskars rotary-cutting tools.

Page 24: *Four-Patch Link*—Fabrics from the Rainforest collection from Classic Cottons. Machine-quilted by Sandy Boobar.

Page 37: *Log Cabin Tree Skirt*—Warm & Natural needled cotton batting from The Warm Co.

Page 41: *Courthouse Rounds*—Scarborough Faire fabric collection from Maywood Studios, Perfect Cotton Just Like Wool batting and Mettler Silk-Finish thread from American & Efird. Machine-pieced by Emma Jean Cook on a Brother Nouvelle PQ-1500 and machine-quilted by Sandy Boobar.

Page 43: *Home Sweet Home*—Warm & Natural needled cotton batting from The Warm Co.

Page 46: *Log Cabin Jacket*—Yours Truly Patchwork Jacket pattern 3737 by Jean Wells.

Page 64: *Cottage-Style Basket Pillows*—All cutting done using Master Piece Rulers.

Page 80: *Spanish Tile*—Hobbs Heirloom cotton batting, DMC quilting thread and needles and Fiskars rotary-cutting tools.

Page 99: *Nine-Patch Wedding Ring*—Hobbs Heirloom cotton batting, DMC quilting thread and needles and Fiskars rotary cutter, mat and ruler.

Page 114: *Autumn Flight*—Perfect Cotton Natural batting, Mettler Silk-Finish thread and Signature Machine-Quilting thread from American & Efird and 505 Spray and Fix basting spray.

Page 145: *Twinkle, Twinkle Little Star*—HeatnBond Ultrahold Iron-on Adhesive from Therm O Web and Warm & Natural needled cotton batting from The Warm Co.

Page 152: *Star Stages*—Aunt Nonnie Sun Porch fabric collection from Maywood Studios, Hobbs Heirloom Natural Cotton batting and Mettler Silk Finish thread from American & Efird. Machine-pieced by Emma Jean Cook on a Brother Nouvelle PQ-1500 and machine-quilted by Sandy Boobar.

Page 159: *Hidden Stars*—Hobbs Heirloom cotton batting, DMC quilting thread and needles and Fiskars rotary cutter, mat and ruler.

Special Thanks

We would like to thank the talented quilt designers whose work is featured in this collection.

Mary Ayres
Home Sweet Home, 43
Bear Pillow, 78
Twinkle, Twinkle Little Star, 145

Holly Daniels
Arctic Star, 13
Independence Square Picnic Quilt, 86
Wedding Ring Purse, 104

Phyllis Dobbs
Log Cabin Tree Skirt, 37
Sunbonnet Sue in the Kitchen, 142

Sue Harvey
Antique Log Cabin, 30
Courthouse Rounds, 41
Antique Flower Basket, 52
Goose Tracks, 72
Pine Tree, 112
Autumn Flight, 114
Antique String Stars, 150
Star Stages, 152

Sandra Hatch
Four-Patch Pinwheel, 8

Mama's Teacups, 10
Four-Patch Link, 24
Antique Double Wedding Ring, 94
Sunbonnet Sue Antique Quilt, 130

Connie Kauffman
Chicken Place Mat & Runner, 89

Pearl Louise Krush
Four-Patch Posy Lap Quilt, 17
Warm Neighbors, 34
Serendipity Table Runner, 54
Snowball Friends, 83
Sue's Garden Wreath, 134

Janice Loewenthal
Bunnies in the Clover, 75

Chris Malone
Sunbonnet Sue Chair Pad, 132

Jill Reber
Cottage-Style Basket Pillows, 64

Judith Sandstrom
Angel Table Runner & Stocking, 20
Spanish Tile, 80

Nine-Patch Wedding Ring, 99
Hidden Stars, 159

Christine Schultz
Harvest Sun Wall Quilt, 161

Marian Shenk
Welcome Basket, 66
Circle of Love, 107
Holiday Hot Mats, 124
Sunday-Best Sue, 139

Willow Ann Sirch
Log Cabin Jacket, 46

Ruth Swasey
Garden Basket Wall Quilt, 61
Big House in the Woods, 117
Hands All Around Runner, 155

Julie Weaver
Grandma's Baskets Quilt, 58
Tall, Proud Pines, 122

Johanna Wilson
Winter Wedding, 102